STRENGTH FOR THE STORM

STRENGTH
FOR THE STORM

FINDING GOD IN EVERY CRISIS

RICHARD EXLEY

THOMAS NELSON PUBLISHERS
Nashville

Published in Nashville, Tennessee, by Thomas Nelson, Inc.

Library of Congress Cataloging-in-Publication Data

Exley, Richard.
    Strength for the storm : finding God in every crisis / Richard Exley.
      p. cm.
    Includes bibliographical references.
    ISBN 0-7852-7113-9 (HC)
    1. Theodicy. 2. Faith. 3. Christian life. I. Title.
BT160.E965   1999
248.8'6—dc21

            98-53422
            CIP

Printed in the United States of America
1 2 3 4 5 6 BVG 04 03 02 01 00 99

To Jesus Christ, who promises to be with us
no matter how severe the storm.

All stories related in *Strength for the Storm* are true. I have, however, changed the names of nearly all of the participants as well as many of the insignificant details such as time and place in order to protect the participants' privacy.

CONTENTS

ACKNOWLEDGMENTS

Although the writing of a book is in many ways a solitary endeavor for the author it is nonetheless a team effort. This was especially true with the writing of *Strength for the Storm*. From the outset there were a number of distractions, hindrances really, that may only be described as a spiritual attack. Early on I solicited prayer support from family and friends. Those who prayed are too numerous to mention by name, but you know who you are and more important God knows. Thank you! I would like to express special thanks to my friend and pastor, Keith Butler, and his congregation for their faithful prayers. Equally beneficial was the moral support and prayers provided by the members of the Richard Exley Ministry Board: Bob Exley, Kurt Green, Jack Ingram, Keith Provance, Barry Tims, and Bill Tims. When I needed you most you were there.

Through the whole project no one was more supportive than Brenda Starr (my wife). Many years ago, when I first started writing, I asked her to listen to me read my "day's work" at the end of each day. Of course the first thing we had to do was set some ground rules. "Brenda Starr," I said, "I don't need for you to be an editor. I want you to be a cheerleader. The publisher has plenty of editors, but he doesn't have a single cheerleader." It goes without saying that Brenda is the best cheerleader an author could ever hope to have. Her encouragement made the long days of writing not only bearable, but blessed. Day after day when I went to the computer she went to her place of prayer. With a faithful intensity she interceded, not only for my writing, but also for every person who will read this work. The truth is her prayers seasoned every page I wrote.

The strength of this work is twofold: 1) the truth of the eternal Scriptures and, 2) the true life experiences of people just like you and me. Without their willingness to share their personal stories *Strength for the Storm* could not have been written. Although most of their names, and some of the insignificant details, have been changed, the truth of their experiences testify to God's sufficiency. Thank you for sharing your lives with me and ultimately with the reader. May God reward you for your courage and your transparency. This is your book as much as it is mine.

I am especially grateful to Bob Exley (my brother) who was part of the process from the beginning. He read the early drafts of the manuscript and made invaluable suggestions. His willingness to open his own life gives the last section of the book a vividness it would not have otherwise had. Thanks for being my brother and my friend.

As always John and Evelyn Looper kept the office running—scheduling speaking engagements, taking care of correspondence, shipping out books, and in general keeping my life in order. Your loyal support and faithful prayers are a constant source of strength.

A special word of thanks goes to Douglas and Leah Starr Baker (my daughter and her husband), who sacrificed their vacation at the cabin so I could have solitude to write, as did my sister and her family. I will make it up to you, I promise.

And finally a word to the reader: You have been the focus of my attention for months now. I have prayed for you, asking God to help me understand the storms you are facing that I might speak directly into your life. Having finished *Strength for the Storm* I now pray that my words may simply be containers that bring His Word to you. I pray that you will truly find God sufficient whatever storm you may be facing.

SURVIVING
THE STORM

Descending the stone steps leading to the waterfront of Sitka Sound, I waved a greeting to eighteen-year-old David, who was standing in the prow of a sixteen-foot rubber raft called a zodiac. Handing him the tackle box and fishing gear, Weldon and I climbed aboard. While he stowed the gear, I located the life vests and passed them out. Once we were situated, David started the outboard engine and nodded at his father, who pushed us away from the dock. Easing the zodiac around, David headed southwest toward the Gulf of Alaska. Our destination was a halibut hole near the tip of Viscary Island, about ten miles out.

Although the sun blazed brightly in the brilliant blue sky (a true rarity in southeast Alaska, which averages nearly one hundred inches of rainfall a year), it was none too warm. Turning up the collar of my jacket against the chilly wind, I gave myself to the moment. And what a moment it was. The sun had burned the last of the persistent mist away, revealing towering, snow-capped mountains that jutted thousands of feet into the sky. All around us were densely forested islands. There were no beaches, only rugged shorelines of jagged rocks where the ocean beat itself into a perpetual spray. Those islands—devoid of human habitation for the most part—were a small sprinkling of the more than one thousand that make up the Alexander Archipelago. Together with a narrow, mountainous strip of mainland, they constitute southeast Alaska, a dramatic contrast of mountains, glaciers, forests, and seas.

Drinking in this spectacular beauty I heard myself saying, "Good job, God, good job!"

Raising my arm, I waved a belated greeting to a fishing troller returning to Sitka after a morning of salmon fishing. On the horizon I counted the dark silhouettes of seven more still hard at it, their long outriggers trailing multiple lines with baited hooks.

Noticing my interest, Weldon said, "Fishing is a hard life. The season is short. The hours are long, and the chance of injury or death is much greater than you might think. Hardly a season passes without a major accident, sometimes several."

After about thirty minutes Viscary Island came into view, and we eased around the point to the windward side. As we were rigging our lines, I noticed a heavy bank of clouds rolling in, totally obscuring Sitka. It became noticeably colder, and the first huge raindrops were pitting the ocean's gray surface by the time we got our lines into the water. Neither Weldon nor David seemed concerned, so I pushed my growing uneasiness to the back of my mind.

Settling down to wait for a fish to strike, I reminisced about my good fortune. For the last fourteen days I had been privileged to see much of the forty-ninth state while preaching a conference for ministers and leading a men's retreat at a fishing camp on Admiralty Island. To get to the fishing camp we had to be ferried by floatplane from Juneau—a breathtaking experience affording us a truly exquisite view of Mount Juneau and the Mendenhall Glacier.

For five days we lived in a place cut off from the world, our only link to civilization being a shortwave radio. Each morning, while breakfast was being prepared, I brought a devotion and led the men in prayer. After eating our fill of bacon and sourdough flapjacks, we boarded the boats for a day of fishing. Every evening we dined on the day's catch: succulent salmon steaks grilled over a pit of white-hot coals, fresh halibut chunks dipped in beer batter and deep-fried to a golden brown, Alaskan King Crab, rich and sweet. Following these nightly feasts we settled down for a time of study and prayer to nourish our souls.

Alaska is the land of the midnight sun, and though our watches and our weary bodies told us it was bedtime, evening light lingered, giving the rugged terrain a softness it lacked when viewed in harsher light. Though human inhabitants were scarce there was an abundance of wildlife. Occasionally we saw brown bears come down to the stream to feed, and once we spotted several humpback whales. Always we saw the bald eagles—sometimes near, sometimes far.

My reminiscing was cut short by the abrupt roar of the outboard engine. David had reeled in his line and stowed his fishing rod in order to give his full attention to maneuvering the zodiac. The wind was up, and the waves were visibly larger now, making it a challenge to keep the raft positioned properly. I could not help noticing that there were no other fishermen in the vicinity. The two or three boats that were nearby when we arrived had apparently made a run for port, in hopes of beating the weather. Turning to Weldon I said, "It's getting pretty rough out here. Do you think we ought to call it a day and head in?"

He studied the sky for a minute before replying. "I think we will be OK. This time of the year these storms usually blow over in an hour or two. Besides, we need to let the fog lift so we can spot our landmarks to guide us back."

The wind continued to pick up, making it nearly impossible for David to keep the zodiac in position. Suddenly the sky seemed to crack open, dumping a deluge of icy rain, and cutting visibility to fifty feet or less. Though we were wearing slickers over our jackets, they were no match for the fury of the storm. In seconds we were drenched. When the storm showed no sign of abating after ten minutes, we belatedly decided to make a run for home. My fingers were stiff with cold as I struggled to crank in nearly three hundred feet of heavy line. Weldon was faring no better, but we eventually managed to get our gear stowed away.

David turned the zodiac toward home as Weldon hunkered down on the bench in the prow. It was his job to locate our landmarks and make sure we didn't run aground on one of the islands. Straining to see through the driving rain, he covered his eyes with one hand, peering through the tiny slit between his first and second fingers. His other hand gripped a safety strap that was fastened to the bench on which he sat. A good thing, too, for the waves were huge and we were taking a fearful pounding. I was seated on the second bench in the center of the raft, a safety strap firmly gripped in each hand; still I was being thrown around. In a matter of minutes my bottom was painfully bruised, and my shoulders felt like they had been jerked out of socket.

Everything was a blur—the rush of the wind, the roar of the engine, the punishing rain, the pounding waves, and the ever present cold. My teeth were chattering, but I wasn't sure whether it was from the cold or from the violent pounding we were taking. All I knew was that I had never, in all my life, been so miserable.

Finally, when I was sure that I could take no more, the rain began to ease a little. Weldon looked over his shoulder, smiled encouragingly, and gave me the thumbs-up sign. I managed to give him a forced smile in return. Then the engine coughed and almost died. Frantically, David worked the throttle, coaxing it to life once more. It responded with a roar, the prop biting into the frigid water, thrusting the zodiac into the teeth of the departing storm.

I heaved a sigh of relief. The possibility of spending a stormy night on an open raft in the Gulf of Alaska was more than a little unnerving. My relief was short-lived. Our engine troubles were not over. Now it sputtered and died.

I glanced a question David's way, but he just shrugged his shoulders noncommittally while working the starter. The engine turned over, but it would not fire. Finally he released the starter, lest he drain the battery, and an uneasy stillness settled over us.

The fury of the rain had passed, but a soundless drizzle, cold and merciless, continued to drip from the low-hanging gray clouds. Through the fog, I heard what sounded like surf pounding against the rocks. And a disconcerting sound it was, for without power we had no way of controlling the raft. If we drifted onto the rocks they would shred our rubber craft, plunging us into the frigid waters and pounding surf. Of course the alternative wasn't very comforting either. If we couldn't get the engine running the tide could carry us into the wide expanse of the Gulf of Alaska. I could only imagine how difficult it would be to locate our small raft in conditions like these.

Weldon joined David at the rear of the zodiac, where the two of them conferred in hushed tones. Though I was no mechanic, it was obvious to me that they were not either. After several minutes they concluded that the engine had gotten wet and was drowning out. Since it was raining steadily again, although nothing like it had been, they decided against lifting the cover to try and dry the spark plugs.

"What happens if we can't get it started?" I asked, trying not to sound alarmed.

"Don't worry," David replied. "We'll get it started."

Turning to Weldon I asked, "How far do you think it is to town?"

"It's hard to tell," he said. "We ran for the better part of two hours, but we weren't making much speed. Besides, visibility being what it was, I can't even be sure we were heading in the right direction."

"Do you have any idea where we are?" I asked, not bothering to hide my concern.

"Not really, but I'm sure it's nothing to be worried about. As soon as the clouds lift we'll be able to get our bearings."

For the first time I let my eyes roam over the zodiac, looking for survival gear. Nothing. No flare gun, no first aid kit, no radio, no packaged food, and no matches. Neither did I see a compass or a map.

"Maybe we could radio for help," I suggested hopefully, thinking that surely there must be a radio, although I hadn't spotted one.

Shaking his head, Weldon said, "Even if we had a radio, which we don't, it wouldn't be much help since I have no way of knowing our location."

"What about a compass," I asked, "or a map?"

"Nope."

Fear was like a cold knot in the pit of my stomach, and I couldn't help thinking how stupid we were to venture into the Gulf of Alaska so poorly prepared. The fog now lay like a damp shroud over the gray water, obscuring all but the most immediate objects. Even if we got the engine started we were still in trouble. Without a compass we had no way of determining if we were heading back to Sitka or out to sea.

While Weldon and I were talking, David had been in deep thought. Now he reached under the back bench and pulled out the gas tank. Lifting it up he gave it a good shake before pronouncing it empty. "Don't panic," he said. "There's another gas tank under here."

Working quickly he disconnected the fuel line from the empty tank and reconnected it to the second one. After giving the black bulb on the fuel line a half dozen firm squeezes, he hit the starter button. For a few seconds the engine turned over, but it didn't fire. Just when I was about to lose hope it roared to life.

Grinning, David gave his Dad a high five.

As Weldon made his way back to the prow, I gave the second gas tank a surreptitious shake. It couldn't be more than half full. Although I was thrilled to have the engine running again, we were not out of the woods yet. We had a limited amount of fuel. Visibility was still extremely poor, and without a compass we had no idea in which direction we were heading. If we had to spend the night on the water we could be in real trouble. Without survival gear hypothermia was going to be a problem as wet and cold as we were.

"It might be wise," I suggested, "to wait until visibility improves enough to allow us to determine if we are heading in the right direction, especially given our limited fuel supply."

"I think we will be all right," Weldon responded, motioning for David to put the engine in gear.

Glancing at my watch, I noted the time. It was nearly 5:00 P.M. and we had now been on the water more than four hours. Although it took only thirty minutes to reach Viscary Island on our way out, we were now battling the elements over two hours in our attempt to return. I was scheduled to preach at 7:00 P.M. at the Sitka Assembly of God where Weldon served as the senior pastor. If we were not back by that time our wives would know something was wrong. I took some comfort in that thought, but not much. I wasn't even sure we told them where we were going fishing.

As we plowed resolutely forward, through the damp gray mist, I couldn't help thinking how foolish we were. Alaska is still mostly wilderness and largely unforgiving. She does not suffer fools easily. No one should venture forth without proper survival gear. If we ran out of gas—a very real possibility if we were heading in the wrong direction—we might well have landed on some uninhabited island. An unnerving prospect when I remembered the jagged rocks and pounding surf along the shoreline of every island I'd seen. With an effort I pushed such thoughts from my mind and concentrated on conserving what little body heat I had left.

Eleven years have passed since that ill-fated fishing expedition. Eleven years in which I have had the time to ponder the lessons I learned from that near tragic trip. Most obvious are the lessons regarding my personal irresponsibility. I ventured forth without being prepared. I gave absolutely no thought to what we would do in the case of an emergency. Naively I assumed that Weldon or David had addressed these matters. Though I could not imagine anyone heading ten miles out into the Gulf of Alaska without a compass, a map, and a radio, not to mention survival gear, I did not ask. Nor did I give the possibility of a storm even remote consideration. Since the sun was shining brilliantly when we departed the dock, I assumed fair weather was in the offing. Not once did I check the weather forecast.

Those are important lessons to be sure, lessons that could save my life should I venture into the Gulf of Alaska in search of halibut at some future date. But as important as they are, they are hardly worth comparing with their spiritual counterparts—what I call life lessons.

Life Lesson #1: Storms are inevitable. No matter how well things are going right now you can be sure a storm is brewing. Jesus said, "In the world you will have tribulation [storms]; but be of good cheer, I have overcome the world" (John 16:33).

We cannot prevent the storms of life—accidents, disease, death, heartache, broken relationships, personal failures—but we can prepare for them.

Life Lesson #2: Be prepared. Make sure you have survival gear on hand before the storm strikes.

Recently I spoke with a pastor and his wife who were just emerging from a life storm of considerable magnitude. In a fifteen-month span, Julie had undergone two major surgeries. She had heart surgery, followed a few months later by the removal of one of her kidneys. The conditions that necessitated each surgery were life threatening, and Keith had been faced with the very real possibility of rearing three daughters alone.

"How," I asked them, "did you cope?"

Keith thought for a moment before replying. Finally he said, "Basic Christianity. The power of prayer, the comfort of Scripture, and the strength of friends."

Nodding in agreement Julie added, "The love and encouragement of our congregation was especially helpful to me. Every day we received a stack of cards in the mail. Each one contained notes that strengthened our faith. Just knowing we were not alone was enormously helpful."

Because Keith and Julie had practiced the disciplines of their faith—daily prayer, regular Bible study, worship, and fellowship—in the sunshine of their lives, they were prepared when trouble came, when the inevitable storm struck.

Life Lesson #3: Help is near even when we cannot see it. When the storm struck while we were fishing, visibility was instantly reduced to fifty feet or less. As far as we could tell we were totally alone. If the truth be known, it is quite likely that help was nearby. Only God knows how many fishing trawlers—equipped with global positioning systems, compasses, maps, radios, and all-weather gear—passed just out of our sight. Near but unseen.

So it is with life. When trouble comes, the storm is often so severe that it blinds us to the help that is at hand. It feels like we are totally alone, abandoned by both God and man, but we are not. "God is our refuge and strength, / A very present help in trouble" (Ps. 46:1).

Most of us, I'm convinced, can survive any storm if we can be assured of three things. First, we must know that God cares. Second, we must be certain that God is with us in the storm, that He will not abandon us. Finally, we must be convinced that God will redeem our situation; that He will bring some eternal good out of what looks, for all the world, like a senseless tragedy.

In Exodus 3:7–8, God told Moses, "I have surely *seen* the oppression of My people who are in Egypt, and have *heard* their cry because of their taskmasters, for I *know* their sorrows. So I have come down to *deliver* them out of the hand of the Egyptians" (emphasis mine).

In other words, God sees our situation. He hears our cry and knows our sorrows. Therefore, He comes to us; He meets us at the point of our need in order to deliver us out of the storm.

Life Lesson #4: The Lord always comes to us in the midst of the storm. He uses the very thing that is threatening to overwhelm us as a highway into our hearts and lives.

Following the miraculous feeding of the five thousand, Jesus told the twelve to get in a boat and go to the other side (see Mark 6: 47–51). After dismissing them, He found a solitary place on the mountain to pray. Almost immediately a storm blew up, and looking down from the mountainside He saw the disciples fighting a losing battling against the elements. No matter how hard they tried they could not make more than minimal progress. Still He continued in prayer, rather than going to their aid.

It was not cruelty that stayed His hand, but wisdom. Had the disciples sought God's help, Jesus likely would have intervened immediately. Unfortunately, like so many of us, they seemed incapable of recognizing their need until they had exhausted all of their resources. Only then did the Father allow Jesus to intervene. During the fourth watch of the night (some time between 3:00 and 6:00 A.M.) He went to them, walking on the water. By this time they had likely given up all hope of reaching the other side. Now they were simply battling the storm in a desperate attempt to survive.

Because we are so independent, so self-reliant, God sometimes allows us to reach the very end of our strength before He comes to our aid. Then, in the darkest hour, when it seems all hope is lost, He speaks to us out of the storm. He uses the very elements that are threatening our destruction as a pathway into our lives. He comes to us, "walking on the water." When He arrives, the storms often cease (see Mark 6:51), but even when they continue to rage His very presence brings us peace and we are no longer overwhelmed.

For more than an hour we maintained our course without spotting anything even vaguely familiar. To my untrained eye, every rocky shoreline and every heavily forested island appeared the same. Though the fog was lifting a little, I feared it was too late. It seemed to me that we were likely so far off the course that even if full visibility were restored we might not be able to locate our landmarks. Resolutely I began to steel myself to spend the night at sea. I was wet, cold, and hungry, but I was determined that I would survive. I had a wife and daughter to live for.

Belatedly I decided to pray. Bowing my head I cried, "Lord Jesus have mercy on us. Save us. Come and guide us safely back to Sitka."

Hardly had I finished praying before a fishing trawler emerged from a fog bank on a course that would intersect ours. Frantically we began waving to attract the captain's attention. Instantly the throb of the fishing boat's powerful engine fell off, and the captain brought her alongside our rubber raft. A crewman threw us a line, and we secured the raft.

"We got lost in the storm," Weldon told them. "We're trying to get back to Sitka. Could you tell us if we are heading in the right direction?"

The captain and the crewman exchanged a quick look. Though they were careful to maintain neutral expressions, I could imagine what they were thinking.

"So you're trying to get to Sitka, are you," the captain said in a gravelly voice. "Well, if you keep going the way you are heading you will eventually get there. Of course you will have to go completely around the world to do it."

Weldon had an embarrassed look on his face, while David pretended to ignore the conversation. With good reason, for if I understood the captain, we were exactly 180 degrees off the course that would take us safely home. Instead, we were heading directly away from Sitka and toward distant Seattle.

"On the other hand," the captain continued, "if you were to head in the opposite direction you could probably make it to Sitka in about thirty minutes."

Nodding toward the horizon where mountains draped in gray mist could now be seen against the sky, he added, "Just remember to keep those mountains to starboard, and you'll be all right."

Weldon threw the rope to the crewman, and we drifted away from the trawler. The throb of the boat's engine resumed its earlier cadence, and we watched as she pulled away. With a sheepish grin David reversed direction.

Thirty minutes later we were tying up at the dock. Once more, the sea was calm and the sun was shining brightly, painting the waterfront in golden hues. As peaceful as it now was, it hardly seemed possible that we were ever in any real danger, but I know we were. In fact, had it not been for God's faithfulness to answer prayer we might well be lost somewhere along the Inside Passage that links Sitka with the lower forty-eight states.

Some may scoff at the thought that the sudden appearance of that fishing trawler was an answer to prayer. More likely, they will suggest that it was a simple coincidence. I can appreciate their position. After all, the trawler was in position to intersect our path whether I prayed or not. Still, that doesn't change anything. God, who is beyond time, as we know it, has promised "that before [we] call, [He] will answer; / And while [we] are still speaking, [He] will hear" (Isa. 65:24).

Knowing where we would be at that precise moment, and knowing that I was going to pray for help, God had already arranged to have the fishing trawler in position. The Lord speaking to us in an audible voice, telling us to reverse our direction, would have been no greater an answer to prayer than that boat's sudden appearance.

These thoughts filled my mind as I climbed the stones steps toward the parking lot where our car awaited. In minutes I would be standing under the hot spray of the shower, scrubbing the cold from my aching body. In a couple of days all physical evidence of our ordeal would be gone, but in my heart the lessons I learned will remain. Lessons that will serve me well as I prepare for life's inevitable storms.

Strength for the Storms Life Brings

There are some who believe that God sends the storms in our lives, but I cannot conceive of our loving heavenly Father doing something like that. Perhaps He allows them to come. For certain, He redeems them—that is, He touches them with His Spirit, transforming them into instruments of grace that work for our eternal benefit. Of course this does not make the troubles we suffer painless, but it does give our pain purpose. Now instead of viewing pain as an enemy to be overcome, we see it as an ally. Instead of fighting it, we embrace it. Not masochistically, but in faith believing that what the evil one intended for our destruction God has redeemed and is now using for our eternal good.

That is what trusting God means—believing that no matter what happens He will redeem it. He will use it to fulfill His purpose in our lives (Ps. 138:7–8 NIV) thus disarming both personal failure and disaster, for what can overwhelm us if we believe God will turn it to our eternal good? He is the eternal craftsman, shaping our lives to the likeness of His

1

dear Son. Among the tools He uses are our life experiences, even the ones the enemy meant for our destruction. In truth, there is no experience He cannot use if we will surrender it to Him, no personal failure He cannot redeem and cause to contribute to our ultimate Christlikeness.

Chapter 1

WHY DO BAD
THINGS HAPPEN?

Why, you may be wondering, would anyone want to write a book about trouble? Surely there are more interesting and uplifting subjects. Without a doubt, but none cuts to the core of our human condition the way trouble does. It is the great equalizer. Sooner or later everyone experiences adversity. Try as we might, we cannot escape it. As the Bible says, "Yet man is born to trouble / as surely as sparks fly upward" (Job 5:7 NIV).

No one is immune. In one form or another trouble comes to every one of us. Do what you will, you cannot avoid it. You may minimize your risks, but there is no escaping it. Some people spend enormous amounts of time and energy, not to mention money, in a desperate attempt to keep it at bay, but in the end they discover that there is no avoiding it. It is inevitable—sooner or later trouble comes to us all.

The Trouble Life Brings

For some of us it is nothing more serious than a broken relationship, or a business deal that goes bad, or a stint of unemployment. Others experience trouble of a more grievous nature. A mother loses her children, or at least it seems that way to her: her firstborn, a son, ends up in prison, and her daughter is living with a lesbian lover. A wife discovers that her "Christian" husband is an abuser. Now she lives in terror, fearing for her safety and the safety of her children. A young husband and father learns that his wife has only a few weeks to live. As the doctor walks away, he is left reeling, wondering how he will cope. Something inside of him screams, "Why, God, why?"

Weeping, a young couple cling to each other while the tiny casket containing the body of their beloved child is lowered into the cold ground. Four days ago they had never heard of SIDS—Sudden Infant Death Syndrome; now it fills their minds like a dark fog. In the weeks and months ahead, grief will cause them to question the goodness of God. It will rend the fabric of their relationship and quite possibly destroy their marriage.

As you can readily see, the storms of life come to us all, each in our own turn. We may go for months, even years, relatively free from any significant difficulty or disappointment, then without warning tragedy strikes. That is how it happened in the small town of West Paducah, Kentucky.

Tragedy Strikes

It started like any other Monday morning. Parents got their children off to school before leaving for work themselves, never realizing that before the hour was out their lives would be forever altered. At Heath High School a group of students were meeting for prayer before heading for class. While they gathered, a fourteen-year-old classmate slipped into school carrying a satchel of stolen guns. Quickly he made his way to the site where several of his classmates had formed a circle and joined hands for prayer. Calmly he stuffed earplugs into his ears, drew a .22-caliber semiautomatic pistol from his backpack, and began firing. In seconds, eight students were down, their blood spreading over the tile floor.

As news of the shootings raced through that rural community located on the Ohio River, frantic parents converged on the high school, desperate to know if their sons and daughters were all right. For the parents of Nicole Hadley, Kayce Steger, and Jessica James the news could not have been worse—their children were dead; their lives snuffed out in a hail of .22-caliber bullets.

The alleged perpetrator of this obscene act was Michael Carneal, a bespectacled ninth-grader who played the saxophone in the high-school band.

His parents were among those who rushed to the school that fateful Monday morning, never imagining what would confront them when they arrived. Relief washed over them when they saw Kelly, their seventeen-year-old daughter, unharmed. But their relief was short-lived, giving way to a growing apprehension when they could not locate Michael. Now they imagined the worst. Perhaps he had been wounded or even killed. Maybe his body was even now lying in the hospital morgue waiting to be identified.

Finally someone directed them to the principal's office. Fearing the worst they hurried through the strangely silent halls wondering how they would cope if their beloved son was dead. Never, not in their wildest dreams, could they have envisioned what awaited them. Inside the office Michael was telling the principal how it happened. "It was kind of like I was in a dream," he said, "and then I woke up." While his parents watched in stunned disbelief, law enforcement officers arrived and placed their son under arrest. After putting him in handcuffs they led him away.

> Most of us mistakenly believe that we will be able to cope with personal tragedy if we can just make some sense of it.

According to news sources, Michael's father, a respected attorney and an elder in the Lutheran Church, told his pastor, "I'm numb. The worst thing that could happen in your life is for your child to shoot other children."

Where do the Carneals go from here? How do they get over a tragedy of this magnitude? In the weeks and months ahead they will repeatedly second-guess themselves. Where did they go wrong? What could they have done differently? How could they have failed their son so completely? How could they have missed the warning signs? Why didn't they notice something was troubling him? These and a host of similar questions will torment them for the rest of their lives.

And what about the parents whose children were gunned down? How will they cope? For them, the illusion of safety is forever shattered. If something like this could happen in West Paducah, Kentucky, of all places, then it can happen anywhere and at any time. If their children could be murdered while attending a prayer meeting at Heath High School, is anyone really safe?

How long will they grieve? For the rest of their lives, most likely, for it is nearly impossible to get over the death of a child, especially if she is the victim of a random act of violence. Only God knows how many nights they will toss fitfully, unable to sleep, wondering how their daughter felt in those last terrifying moments. Was she afraid? Did she suffer?

And the Heath High School tragedy is just one of many that marred 1997 and the early days of 1998. Early in 1997, comedian Bill Cosby's only son, Ennis, 27, was killed in an apparent robbery on an L.A. freeway. Thirty-nine members of a California cult committed mass suicide. Singer John Denver perished in the crash of his private plane. Michael Kennedy, 39, the son of the late Robert Kennedy, died in a skiing accident, as did congressman Sonny Bono. And perhaps most incomprehensible of all, Princess Diana was killed, at age 36, in a high-speed auto crash in a Paris tunnel.

Of course, this is just the tip of the iceberg, for it is only a small sampling of the tragedies making the headlines. Who can comprehend the pain and loss of the tens of thousands of survivors who grieve for loved ones who have been killed in wanton acts of genocide or in arbitrary acts of terrorism? And what of those personal tragedies that never make the news—a stillborn baby, a six-year-old who dies of leukemia, a child who runs away from home and is never heard of again, a young wife and mother who succumbs to breast cancer, a husband and father who suddenly drops dead of a heart attack?

Then there are the nonfatal tragedies. The twenty-five-year marriage that ends in the pain of betrayal. The loss of innocence for the child who is sexually molested, especially when the perpetrator is a beloved parent. A freak accident that leaves a robust young athlete a quadriplegic for life.

The "Why" Questions

Such pain and loss inevitably give birth to the why questions: Why do bad things happen to good people? Why did it happen to me? Why didn't God do something? Why didn't He answer my prayers?

I suppose the why questions are inevitable. Most of us mistakenly believe that we will be able to cope with personal tragedy if we can just make some sense of it. Unfortunately there often seems to be little or no explanation for many of the tragedies that befall us, making the why questions nothing more than an exercise in futility. Like a dog chasing his tail, we find ourselves going in circles.

Or if not going in circles, we find ourselves formulating conclusions that are only partially valid at best. For instance, some people conclude that the misfortunes that befall us are punishment for personal sin. While this may be the case in some instances (2 Sam. 12:13–23 and Acts 5:1–11) it is not a general rule. Jesus addressed this issue on at least two occasions, once when He and His disciples encountered a man who was blind from birth and again when discussing a fatal construction accident in Siloam. On both occasions He absolves the principles of personal responsibility.

In regard to the man born blind, the disciples apparently assumed he was in that condition because either he or his parents had sinned, though how a baby can sin in the womb is beyond me. Besides if blindness (sickness) is the direct result of personal sin we should all be blind (sick), for who among us hasn't sinned?

Jesus shed new light on this complex issue when He said, "Neither this man nor his parents sinned, but that the works of God should be revealed in him" (John 9:3). Rather than focusing on why it happened, Jesus turns our attention to what God is going to do about it—He is going to restore the man's sight, thus manifesting the works of God in him. God is going to bring good out of a tragic situation!

In the case of those who perished when the tower fell on them, He said: "Do you think that they were worse sinners

> When it comes to the storms of life, things are generally far more complicated than mere cause and effect.

than all other men who dwelt in Jerusalem? *I tell you, no*" (Luke 13:4–5, emphasis mine). Although Jesus does not tell us why these particular individuals died while others equally sinful were allowed to live, He does make it clear that the reason for their deaths was not because of a particular personal sin. In other words, when it comes to the storms of life things are generally far more complicated than mere cause and effect.

More often than not trouble comes our way simply because we are members of a fallen race living on a planet in rebellion. Until Jesus puts all enemies under His feet (1 Cor. 15:25–26) and fully redeems us (Rom. 8:21–23) we will have to contend with the vicissitudes of life like everyone else, even though we personally may be surrendered to Christ and living in the center of His will.

Others erroneously conclude that tragedies befall us because that is the will of God. In other words, God gets blamed for a lot of things that He has nothing to do with. It is not God's will that men sin, or that they suffer and die. Divorce is not God's will, nor is unemployment, or tragedy of any kind, yet sincere men and women continue to explain suffering and death as if they were gifts from God. Often they are careful to find a kind way of phrasing it, but in the end, there is no kind way to say an unkind thing.

Grieving parents are seldom comforted when they are told, "God must have loved your child especially much, to have removed her from this vale of tears so soon."

Such statements, while well intended, frequently do more harm than good. They tend to cause the bereaved parents to question the goodness of God. Not infrequently the grieving parents end up wishing God had loved their child a little less.

I've heard others explain suffering as the consequence of the sufferer's lack of faith. Or to phrase it another way, "If you have enough faith you will never be sick, you will never be in financial need, your marriage and family will never experience adversity." In short, "If you have enough faith you can live a trouble-free life."

I can't buy that, not totally. It's too simplistic, it ignores too many factors, including Scripture, not to mention that it places another burden on the already overburdened sufferer.

Don't misunderstand me, I am not minimizing the reality of faith. I have reaped its benefits in my own life and ministry. Yet faith is not a magic spell that wards off all disaster. Jesus made that clear when He said,

"In this world you will have trouble. But take heart! I have overcome the world." (John 16:33 NIV).

Life on a Stormy Planet

In Matthew 7, He gives us a picture of life on our storm tossed planet:

> Therefore everyone who hears these words of mine and puts them into practice is like a wise man who built his house on the rock. The rain came down, the streams rose, and the winds blew and beat against that house; *yet it did not fall, because it had its foundation on the rock.* But everyone who hears these words of mine and does not put them into practice is like a foolish man who built his house on sand. The rain came down, the streams rose, and the winds blew and beat against that house, and it fell with a great crash. (Matt. 7:24–27 NIV, emphasis mine)

Notice that Jesus used the same words to describe what happened to both houses. "The rain came down, the streams rose, and the winds blew and beat against that house" (Matt. 7:27 NIV). The only difference was the end result—one house survived the storm while the other did not.

Based on this passage, we can only conclude that believers are not immune to the storms of life no matter how strong their faith. In Christ we do, however, have faith to stand. The real difference then, between the believer and the unbeliever, is not that one is spared from life's inevitable storms while the other is not, but that in Christ the believer has resources to overcome the storm regardless of how severe it may be.

God's Eternal Craftsmanship

There are some who believe that God sends the storms, but I cannot conceive of our loving heavenly Father doing something like that. Perhaps He allows them to come. *For certain, He redeems them—that is, He touches them with His Spirit, transforming them into instruments of grace that work for our eternal benefit.* Of course this does not make the troubles we suffer painless, but it does give our pain purpose. Now instead of viewing pain as an enemy to be overcome, we see it as an ally. Instead of fighting it, we embrace it. Not masochistically, but in faith believing that what the evil one intended for our destruction God has redeemed and is now using for our eternal good.

You are undoubtedly familiar with the life and ministry of Joni Eareckson Tada. Perhaps more than any other person she exemplifies how God redeems the trouble that comes into our lives. At the age of seventeen she suffered a spinal cord injury as a result of a diving accident, leaving her a quadriplegic. In her autobiography[1] she graphically detailed her struggle to accept her condition. Her story is painfully real, honestly expressing her desperate battle with anger, despair, and thoughts of suicide.

Slowly her bitterness gave way to a tentative faith. At first she thought it necessary to intellectually comprehend how her accident fit into Romans 8:28. She wanted to understand how it was working "together for good" (Rom. 8:28). Was the "good" (Matt. 7:11) her heavenly Father wanted to give her the use of her hands, total healing, a loving Christian husband who was capable of coping with her handicap? As each of these expectations proved to be false she was forced more and more into an unconditional trust.

Once she was able to accept her condition and trust God with her situation, even though she couldn't intellectually explain how God was using it for good, she found freedom from bitterness and self-pity. Little by little God began to open doors for ministry until she found herself ministering to tens of thousands. Today Joni Eareckson Tada is an accomplished artist who draws by holding the pen with her teeth, a best-selling author, a radio personality, and a dynamic witness for Christ who fills auditoriums around the world. Some of the good God is working is now obvious, but much of it will remain hidden until eternity.

I do not believe God caused Joni's accident; perhaps He allowed it. For certain, He is redeeming it, using it to work for her "a far more exceeding and eternal weight of glory" (2 Cor. 4:17).

That is what trusting God means—believing that no matter what happens He will redeem it. He will use it to fulfill His purpose in our lives (Ps. 138:7–8 NIV) thus disarming both personal failure and disaster, for what can overwhelm us if we believe God will turn it to our eternal good? He is the eternal craftsman, shaping our lives to the likeness of His dear Son. Among the tools He uses are our life experiences, even the ones the enemy meant for our destruction. In truth, there is no experience He cannot use if we will surrender it to Him, no personal failure He cannot redeem and cause to contribute to our ultimate Christlikeness.

Consider Joseph, the long-awaited child born to Rachel, the beloved wife of Jacob. He was his father's favorite, and his brothers soon grew to hate him. Finally, nearly beside themselves with jealousy and resentment, they sold him into slavery. *But God was with Joseph in all his troubles* (Gen. 39:21) and exalted him to be the second most powerful man in Egypt. Years later, when Joseph confronted his brothers, he said, "You intended to harm me, but God intended it for good to accomplish what is now being done, the saving of many lives" (Gen. 50:20 NIV).

Like Joseph, the apostle Paul experienced many setbacks and spent the last years of his life as a prisoner in Rome. He was the church's foremost missionary, and his imprisonment brought his prolific church planting to a screeching halt. On the surface it seemed like a great victory for those who opposed him, but God had other ideas. While a prisoner, Paul was inspired to write much of the New Testament. At the time he probably had no idea that his prison letters would do far more for the

> There is no experience He cannot use if we will surrender it to Him, no personal failure He cannot redeem and cause to contribute to our ultimate Christlikeness.

kingdom than his missionary efforts, but no one doubts it now. Twenty centuries later the church continues to be strengthened and encouraged by his epistles. What the enemy intended as a deathblow for the young church, God turned into a divine opportunity. As Paul put it in his epistle to the Philippians: "The things which happened to me have actually turned out for the furtherance of the gospel" (Phil. 1:12).

Good News/Bad News

In reality, trouble is a "good news/bad news" scenario. The bad news is "Man born of woman / is of few days and full of trouble" (Job 14:1 NIV). The good news is "The righteous cry out, and the LORD hears them; / *he delivers them from all their troubles*" (Ps. 34:17 NIV, emphasis mine).

Therefore when trouble comes, as it surely will, we do not despair. We do not castigate ourselves for lack of faith, or berate ourselves for some imagined sin, nor do we blame God. Instead we simply recognize that as members of this human family—a family tainted by sin and death—we are subject to the inevitable storms of life. And because we know that "*in all things God works for the good* of those who love him" (Rom. 8:28 NIV, emphasis mine) we find strength in Christ, not only to endure trouble and hardship, but to overcome it.

In the coming chapters I will show you how people just like yourself overcame trouble of all kinds. I will identify the spiritual and emotional pitfalls that accompany adversity and show you how to survive them. From the Scriptures and real-life examples, you will learn what to do when tragedy strikes. Drawing upon my own experience as both a person and a pastor, I will help you understand what you are feeling and why. Using the story of my own parents' struggle to accept the death of Carolyn, my baby sister, I will show you how God eventually redeemed that tragedy, using it to uniquely prepare me for my life's work. No matter what form trouble takes—sickness or death, divorce or delinquency, adultery or homosexuality—I will help you find resources in Jesus Christ to overcome. In truth, "If God is for us, who can be against us?" (Rom. 8:31 NIV).

Chapter 2

In the Time
of Trouble

When our only child was just six years old she was stricken with strep throat and a severe congestion that clogged her head and chest. Her throat was swollen nearly closed, reducing her breathing to a ragged wheeze. In addition she was running a temperature of nearly 103 degrees and was in considerable pain. For two days and nights her mother nursed her before finally succumbing to physical exhaustion. Now it was my turn, and in the wee hours of the morning I found myself holding Leah's feverish body in my arms, while I tried to rock her to sleep.

A single kerosene lamp served as a night-light barely lighting the room, leaving dark shadows in the far corners. As I sat there listening to Leah fighting to breathe I was tempted with resentment. Silently I raged at God—why didn't He do something? Why didn't He heal Leah or at least ease her suffering? What kind of father would allow a child of his to suffer so when he had the power to do something about it?

Soon my resentment turned into melancholy, leaving me vulnerable to a menagerie of depressing thoughts. Just that week I had preached the funeral service of a child, and I suddenly found myself irrationally fearing for Leah's life. What if her illness wasn't just a strep infection? What if an undiagnosed virus was even now destroying her vital organs?

Through the years I had preached a number of funeral services, not a few of them for children, and now the memories of those little ones returned to haunt me. In my mind I saw again the tiny baby who had been killed in a auto accident, only it was Leah's face I saw in the casket and not hers. Then there was the little boy who accidentally shot and killed himself while playing with his father's gun. Once again my tormented mind superimposed Leah's features on his, and I saw her laid out for burial.

With an effort I pushed those gruesome thoughts from my mind, but I could not totally free myself from the fears they had birthed. Now I found myself wondering how I would survive if something really did happen to Leah. What would I do if she died? Being unable to rid myself of that thought I decided to go with it.

Alone in the middle of the night, holding Leah's feverish body in my arms, I allowed the possibility of her death to take shape in my mind. I tried to imagine my inconsolable grief, the gaping wound, the awful hole her absence would leave. I knew, as sure as I knew anything, that if Leah were to die, the laughter would go out of my life. It would be as if the sun were snuffed out, at least for a time, a long time.

Then a new thought took hold of my mind—what if something happened to Brenda? What if she died? What would I do then?

Once more I allowed my fear-infected imagination to run free. Although Brenda was in excellent health, I began to consider the possibility of her death. And a tragic thought it was, for without Brenda my life would be unbearably empty. Without her I would only be a part of a person.

Yet, even as I mulled over those morbid thoughts I sensed an undergirding presence. As unspeakable as I knew the loss of Leah and Brenda would be, I was suddenly possessed by an assurance that God would sustain me, that His abiding presence would give me the strength to go on. I realize my conclusions are purely speculative, still I must tell you that I was absolutely convinced that God would not fail me. Beneath were His everlasting arms (Deut. 33:27), and His love would never let me go (Ps. 103:17 NIV).

And then another thought leaped into my mind—out of the darkness, unbidden, uninvited, and unwelcome—a thought that I had never dared conceive until that very moment. Suddenly it completely filled my mind: What if something happened to God? What would I do if God died? How would I survive?

That is a preposterous thought, I know. God is eternal, He is omnipotent, He is the first and the last, nothing could ever happen to Him. Still, there in the middle of the night, that thought totally possessed my mind, and what a dreadful thought it was. If Leah died, God would be with me, His grace would sustain me. If something happened to Brenda, God would strengthen me and help me. He would uphold me with His right hand (Isa. 41:10). But if something happened to God, life would be impossible. Without God I simply could not go on living!

Why, you may be wondering, have I chosen to share such a bizarre incident? Because my experience, as both a pastor and a person, leads me to believe that these are the kinds of irrational reactions that many of us experience when we are blindsided by life. Let trouble suddenly cut us off at the knees, and we find ourselves tempted with thoughts and feelings we never imagined ourselves capable of having. And if we are not careful we may end up blaming God for the tragedies that befall us.

Trouble Tempts Us to Blame God

Consider the case of Franklin Pierce, the fourteenth president of the United States, and his wife Jane. Their first child, born in 1836, lived only three days. Franky, their second son, succumbed to typhus at the age of four in 1843. Then on January 6, 1853, just two months before his inauguration, the Pierces were in a train wreck that took the life of their third and last child, eleven-year-old Benjamin. After seeing her son crushed to death, Mrs. Pierce became a recluse, refusing to participate in public appearances. She blamed Franklin's political ambitions for Benny's death, claiming it was the price Providence had exacted for her husband's acceptance of the presidency. For his part, Franklin D. Pierce refused to place his hand upon the Bible when taking the oath of office because he no longer believed in the goodness of almighty God.[1]

Incidents like that test the strongest faith. The death of a single child is enough to try the faith of the most God-fearing parent, but to lose three children, as the Pierces did, would tempt almost anyone to blame God. Given the pain, the inexplicable agony of life's irrational catastrophes, we sometimes find ourselves questioning His character; or if not His character then His competence. "If God is a good God," we say, "how could He allow something like that to happen? How much can one family bear?"

Maybe you remember the bus accident near Carrollton, Kentucky, some years ago that claimed the lives of twenty-seven people. According to the AP report, the bus was carrying sixty-seven teenagers and adults from the First Assembly of God in Radcliff, Kentucky. They were returning home from an amusement park when a pickup traveling the wrong way on Interstate 71 crashed into the bus, turning it into a fiery death trap. In addition to the twenty-seven fatalities, between thirty and forty people were injured, many suffering from burns. The National Transportation Safety Board called it one of the worst bus accidents in United States history.

How do you suppose the pastor of that church felt? Was he tempted, for just a moment, to doubt the goodness of God? And what about the parents of those young people who died? Did they find themselves wondering why God hadn't intervened? Why He hadn't caused that pickup to throw a rod or blow a tire? Surely that would have been easy enough for God to do. Or why didn't He warn the bus driver? Couldn't He have spoken to him in a dream or a vision telling him to take a different route?

I cannot help but wonder how many of the faithful at First Assembly found themselves questioning God's goodness: What good is God's love if He lets senseless tragedies like this happen? From a purely human perspective it makes no sense. If God loves us, how can He allow us to suffer so?

I have to confess that similar questions tempted me while talking with my sister some years ago. She had telephoned to update me on the ongoing saga in their family. A few weeks earlier her father-in-law had been diagnosed with terminal cancer. According to the surgeon, both his liver and his pancreas were filled with malignant tumors. Cancer had also invaded his spine. There was nothing medical science could do, so they sent him home to die. After being home a few days his incision tore open in the middle of the night, creating a medical emergency. While the ambulance was transporting him to the hospital, he suffered an apparent stroke that left him unable to speak and with one side of his face paralyzed.

On top of everything else, my three-year-old niece fell, severely breaking her upper arm. While driving from the orthopedic surgeon's office to the hospital, my sister's car broke down. That was the last straw, and while she talked with me she wept in helplessness and frustration. "If God is a good God," she sobbed, "if He really cares about us, then you tell me why things like this happen."

It isn't really an explanation we seek when we rage at the Lord, but assurance. We know the Bible says God loves us (Ps. 103:8–18 NIV; Mal. 1:2; John 3:16; Rom. 5:8), but there are times when our tragic situations seem to make a mockery of the eternal Scriptures. There are times when we are tempted to conclude that the God who claims to love us is either lying or dead. In spite of the promises of Scripture we do not sense His presence or feel His love. Like the Israelites of Malachi's day we cry, "In what way have You loved us?" (Mal. 1:2). Or, to put it another way, "How can You say You love us, when there is such pain, such misery, in our lives?"

> It isn't really an explanation we seek when we rage at the Lord, but assurance.

More than once a desperately hurting person has looked me in the eye and said, "How can you say I'm God's child and that He loves me when He has allowed this to happen to me? I'm far from a perfect parent, but I would never treat my children the way God is treating me."

Others have flung the Scriptures in my face saying, "Didn't Jesus say, 'If you then, being evil, know how to give good gifts to your children, how much more will your Father who is in heaven give good things to those who ask Him!' [Matt. 7:11]? Well, I've asked until I'm hoarse. I've cried unto God until faith sticks like a bone in my throat. I've fasted. I've prayed. I've begged. I've believed. I've confessed. I've done everything anyone has ever told me to do, and look at the mess I'm in. How can you say God loves me?"

Perhaps you know what I'm talking about. In fact, you may be struggling with similar feelings right now. For all of your praying and pleading nothing has changed. As far as you can tell the heavens are brass. To your way of thinking the God of grace and mercy is dead. He died when you buried your six-year-old son. Now everything inside of you rages at the Almighty. Silently you scream, "How, in light of all of this, can I believe that God loves me?"

In times like that, we have a choice. We can blame God when trouble comes, or we can believe Him when He says, "I have loved you with an everlasting love" (Jer. 31:3). We can hug our hurts and make a shrine out of our sorrow, or we can offer them to God as a sacrifice of praise (Heb. 13:15). The choice is ours.

Be assured though, that what we choose in the time of trouble is terribly important, for it will determine our destiny. If we make a god out of our pain and anger, it will destroy us. But if we can resist the temptation to blame God, we will discover that He is very near to us, even when we were sure He was nowhere to be found. And in His own perfect time He will turn our mourning into dancing (Ps. 30:11) and restore the joy of our salvation (Ps. 51:12).

Trouble Tempts Us to Despair

When tragedy strikes we are not only tempted to blame God, but also to despair. Death is so final. There is nothing we can do to rescind it. When a loved one dies or is killed, there is absolutely nothing we can do to bring them back. We are utterly powerless to undo what is already done. If we are not careful, that sense of powerlessness will give way to a numbing hopelessness. Grief will tempt us to despair, to conclude that life will never be the same again, that we will never again experience the sweet comfort of companionship.

> We can hug our hurts and make a shrine out of our sorrow, or we can offer them to God as a sacrifice of praise. The choice is ours.

Not long ago I received a telephone call from a family friend who was dealing with those exact feelings. A little more than a year ago, her husband lost a two-year battle with cancer, leaving her a widow with three children to rear alone. For the most part she has held up amazingly well, but lately it seems to her that things are getting worse rather than better. Instead of subsiding, the storm seems to be intensifying.

She is still grieving the loss of her husband and will be for some time yet. Recovering from the death of a spouse often takes up to three years, sometimes longer. Added to her grief is the responsibility of being a single parent. For the first time in her life she is both breadwinner and home-maker. Now she has no one to help her with household chores or to share the mundane details involved in managing a family of four. Not only is she responsible for cooking, cleaning, laundry, and child-rearing, but she must also service the cars, take care of the yard, pay the bills, and recon-cile the checkbook. On top of all of that her job is extremely stressful.

"The thing I hate most," she said, confiding in me, "is that I am becoming such a negative person."

"What do you mean?" I asked.

"It's hard to put into words," she replied. "I guess I'm just really tired of living."

Without giving me a chance to say anything she plunged ahead. "I'm not suicidal. I could never do that to my children. I'm just tired of living. All the joy has gone out of my life. There's no color, no sunshine. Every-thing is a dirty gray. The things that once gave me pleasure—walking on the beach, tending my flower garden, reading to the children—no longer interest me at all. Now all I want to do is sleep, but no matter how much sleep I get I'm always tired."

"It takes a lot of energy to grieve," I offered.

"The worst part," she said, "is that I don't think it is ever going to end. If I were to be totally honest with myself I would have to say that I've lost all hope of ever being happy again. For me, the future is a black hole."

There were a lot of things I could have said to her, but I didn't. I could have reminded her of the great promises of Scripture:

Who shall separate us from the love of Christ? Shall trouble or hardship or persecution or famine or nakedness or danger or sword? . . . No, in all these things we are more than conquerors through him who loved us. For I am convinced that neither death nor life, neither angels nor demons, neither the present nor the future, nor any powers, neither height nor depth, nor anything else in all creation, will be able to separate us from the love of God that is in Christ Jesus our Lord. (Rom. 8:35, 37–39 NIV)

I could have shared those verses, but I didn't. Why? Because she already knows the Scriptures at least as well as I do, maybe better. What she needed was a safe place where she could honestly express her feelings, even the ones she doesn't think she should have. If we can provide that, she will be able to work through her hopeless feelings and rediscover her faith. In her heart of hearts she knows the plans God has for her—plans to prosper her and not to harm her, plans to give her hope and a future (Jer. 29:11).

No matter how severe the storm, we still have a choice. If we so choose we can abandon ship, we can give up the faith, but if we do we will surely perish. "Unless [we] stay with the ship, [we] cannot be saved" (Acts 27:31 NIV). Battered though our faith may be by the storm, it is the only ship still afloat. Therefore "I urge you to keep up your courage, because not one of you will be lost" (Acts 27:22 NIV). If we choose to trust God, even though both our emotions and our current circumstances suggest all hope is lost, He will see us through. The storm will finally pass.

Trouble Tempts Us to Think We Are Getting What We Deserve

Before I close this chapter I want to deal with one more temptation. When trouble comes we are not only tempted to blame God or to despair, but we are also tempted to blame ourselves, to think we are getting what we deserve. This is especially true if we have not been the kind of Christian we think we should be, or if there is hidden sin in our life.

If the truth be known, there is enough sin in the most saintly life to merit the worst trouble life could ever mete out. But God "Has not dealt with us according to our sins, / Nor punished us according to our iniquities. / For as the heavens are high above the earth, / So great is His mercy toward those who fear Him; / As far as the east is from the west, / So far has He removed our transgressions from us" (Ps. 103:10–12).

This does not mean that God ignores our sins or makes light of them. Rather as Max Lucado says, "God doesn't condone our sin, nor does he compromise his standard. He doesn't ignore our rebellion, nor does he relax his demands. Rather than dismiss our sin, he assumes our sin and, incredibly, incredibly sentences himself. God is still holy. Sin is still sin. And we are redeemed."[2]

Unfortunately there are many men and women who know nothing of this liberating truth. Instead they live out their lives under an ever-darkening cloud of condemnation. No matter what the Scriptures say they simply cannot believe God loves them. And if, perchance, He does love them it is only because they have pulled the wool over His eyes. They are absolutely convinced that if God knew them the way they really are, in their heart of hearts, He could not love them. Consequently when trouble comes they are only too ready to believe that it means God is out to get them.

James F. Stewart, the Scottish preacher, tells the story of the saintly Dr. John Duncan who taught Hebrew at Edinburgh College for many years. One day Dr. Duncan sat at a Communion in a highland church. When the elements came around he was feeling so unworthy that he allowed the bread and wine to pass without partaking. As he was sitting there, feeling absolutely miserable, he noticed a girl who also refused to partake of the bread and wine. Then she buried her face in her hands and burst into tears.

The sight of that girl weeping seemed to bring the old saint to a truth he had momentarily forgotten. In a caring whisper that could be heard in the whole church, he said, "Take it, lassie. Take it. It's meant for sinners."

That's what I'm trying to say in this chapter. God's love is for sinners. "As a father has compassion on his children, / so the LORD has compassion on those who fear him; / for he knows how we are formed, / he remembers that we are dust . . . / But from everlasting to everlasting / the LORD's love is with those who fear him, / and his righteousness with their children's children" (Ps. 103:13–14, 17 NIV).

When trouble comes, as inevitably it will, the enemy will likely remind you of your past failures in an effort to convince you that you are getting what you deserve. He will tell you that you are a lump of sin and God doesn't love you. You will face two dangers then. On the one hand, you will be tempted to defend yourself, to recount every godly thing you have ever done, in a misguided attempt to prove you are worthy of His love. On the other hand, you will be tempted to punish yourself with the memory of all your sinful failures. If you yield to either temptation you will soon despair, for each is an exercise in futility.

But there is a third possibility, and if you so choose you can embrace the truth of Scripture. The truth of the matter is, we are a lump of sin and the best among us deserves the worst kind of trouble. Yet for all of that we are loved. The Bible says, "God demonstrates His own love toward us, in that while we were still sinners, Christ died for us" (Rom. 5:8).

> There is no sorrow that He will not share; no darkness but what He will be our near companion.

If we will simply be still and listen we can, through the dark night of our trouble, hear Him say, "I have loved you with an everlasting love (Jer. 31:3), and I will not let you go."

"Oh, God," we cry, "how can you love us in our sinful brokenness?"

His voice again, nearer, more persistent. "I have loved you with an everlasting love, and I will not let you go."

"You don't love us," we protest. "You can't. We're sinful. We're unworthy of Your love."

Once more He says, "I have loved you with an everlasting love, and I will not let you go."

Finally we surrender, unable to resist His love any longer. Sinful? Yes, but loved. Troubled on every side? Yes, but loved.

Hear me. No matter how dark the night, no matter how miserable our failures, no matter how much we feel like a lump of sin, He still loves us. "For as high as the heavens are above the earth, / so great is his love for those who fear him" (Ps. 103:11 NIV).

When we are passing through great sorrow it can sometimes feel like God has forsaken us, but He hasn't. No matter how dark the night, however lonely the valley, He promised to be with us: "I will never leave you," He said, "nor forsake you." (Heb. 13:5).

There is no sorrow that He will not share; no darkness but what He will be our near companion. Therefore in the face of deepest despair we do not lose hope for we know that God loves us. It matters not how dark the night, nor how great the pain, nor how tragic the sorrow; we choose to believe that God loves us. In the face of the worst that the evil one can do, we affirm, "I am loved. I am loved. I am loved! And the lover of my soul is with me." Therefore we will not fear, for the Lord is our strength and a very present help in the time of trouble (Ps. 46:1).

Chapter 3

A STRATEGY FOR
OVERCOMING TROUBLE

Last summer I received a poignant letter from my dear friends Jim and Dolly Gilbert:

This letter was to have borne the most joyous tidings of our lives, that after years of praying, we were due to give birth to our first child this December. But on June 4th our gladness was suddenly silenced by a heart monitor that refused to beep the music of a tiny life. Mere seconds into that first exhilarating sonographic glimpse of our baby, the nurse said a gentle, but horrific, "I'm Sorry."

And then it was all over.

Dolly cried hard but quietly. I just stared at the small motionless, black-and-white image that only a minute ago had been heir to everything of value in our lives. It was too early—only our twelfth week—to call him Jim or her Holly. So we were making do with endearments like "precious" and "little treasure," until a future snapshot might let us in on Heaven's little secret.

Dolly's doctor had given us the good news at April's end, thus turning May into an exaggerated Spring ecstasy. Birds no longer flew; they soared. Flowers didn't bloom; they were born. And everything rhythmical, from jackhammers to washing machines, played a merry tune.

Since we were considered high risk, the doctor advised us to wait until the second trimester to announce the news to our friends. But he hadn't said anything about strangers, and I'd go crazy if I didn't tell somebody! So convenience store clerks from Tampa to Los Angeles shared—or pretended to share—my joy, if they so much as thanked me for buying a pack of gum.

A stack of books and videos were my nightly diet, while Dolly majored on juices and fruits and tried to cope with the world's only welcome nausea. We especially enjoyed the pregnancy week-by-week book that kept us informed on when tiny hearts start beating and little faces start forming. And the amazing full color photographs of A Child Is Born *were often the last images our eyes saw before we slept.*

On Mother's Day I had been out of town ministering, but coast-to-coast distance couldn't dent our happiness. I sent Dolly two cards and one big, heart-shaped bouquet of roses, with a note that said "I love you both." The flowers had cost a small fortune, but after all, you only have one first Mother's Day. And if you've been waiting for a very long time, why not give something that reflects the overwhelming joy of the occasion!

But then came June 4th.

I have put away the books and videos. Dolly kept two dried roses. And my Father's Day card remains unopened in a drawer upstairs.

So why should you be told such intimate sorrows? And why do I write with uncensored sadness? For two reasons dear friends:

(1) We want to say, in the face of Sorrow, that God is worthy to be praised at all times, even this time. It was easy to praise Him in May. But it is important to praise Him now. You are our witnesses.

(2) Our joy was even more profound than it was brief. It is worth enduring the heartache just to relive the wonder. We have been parents, and that can never be undone.

Please pray for us, but do not mourn beyond my signature.

Birds still soared today. There are more flowers to be born and bought and given. And my card will not stay sealed forever.

By the time I finished reading their letter I was struggling to make out the words through the mist that suddenly blurred my vision. Yet, even as I identified with their grief, I could not help thinking what an incredible tribute their letter was to the grace of God.

If you have never suffered a miscarriage, or been close to someone who has, you may be wondering what all the fuss is about. You may be thinking, *It was only a miscarriage* or *They can have another baby*. Honesty forces me to admit that I once felt the same way. Then I began providing pastoral care to young couples in my congregation who had suffered miscarriages. That experience soon changed my perspective.

One young woman, who experienced two miscarriages before giving birth to a baby daughter, said, "I grieved deeply the loss of my two babies. It was more than a passing depression brought on by hormonal changes or because I was questioning my ability to carry a baby to full term. I kept picturing what my babies would have looked like, what their personalities would have been. Make no mistake about it, when a woman miscarries it is her baby she mourns, not just the event."

"You can't really put into words the feelings that a miscarriage inflicts on you and your family," stated another woman who also lost a child through miscarriage. "The best words I can think of are 'extreme grief.' When you're talking about a miscarriage, you're talking about the loss of a child, and the more that child is wanted and hoped for, the greater the experience of loss."

Another couple talked about how isolated the father often feels. Everyone asks about the mother, but almost no one inquires about the father's well-being. "Finally," related one young wife, "my husband couldn't take it any more. One night he got off the phone and cried. 'Everyone asks how you feel. But nobody ever asks me. Doesn't anyone realize that I'm the father of this baby?'"

Undoubtedly Jim and Dolly struggled with similar feelings. To appreciate their grief you only have to catch a glimpse of the joy Dolly's pregnancy brought. "Birds no longer flew; they soared. Flowers didn't bloom; they were born. And everything rhythmical, from jackhammers to washing machines, played a merry tune." But on June fourth their "gladness was suddenly silenced by a heart monitor that refused to beep the music of a tiny life."

"[Jim] put away the books and videos. Dolly kept two dried roses. And [Jim's] Father's Day card remains unopened in a drawer upstairs."

Yet, in the midst of their pain, they found a way to go on. Jim closed their letter by saying, "Birds still soared today. There are more flowers to be born and bought and given. And my card will not stay sealed forever."

Ask for Help

After rereading Jim's letter I think there are several things he and Dolly can teach us about overcoming trouble. The most obvious is, *don't be afraid to ask for help*. Although Jim never comes right out and asks for anything other than prayer, the very fact that he discloses their sorrow suggests that he recognizes their need for support during this difficult time.

Contrary to what many of us think, asking for help when trouble comes is not a sign of weakness but wisdom. Consider the example of Jesus our Lord. On the night He was betrayed, "He took with Him Peter and the two sons of Zebedee, and He began to be sorrowful and deeply distressed. Then He said to them, '*My soul is exceedingly sorrowful, even to death. Stay here and watch with Me.*' He went a little farther and fell on His face, and prayed" (Matt. 26:37–39, emphasis mine).

If Jesus found it both prudent and necessary to seek the support of His friends in the time of trouble, shouldn't we also? If He dared not risk going it alone in His hour of distress, how dare we.

Sometimes we don't confide in our friends because we think there is nothing they can do. Apparently Jesus thought otherwise. To His way of thinking, His friends afforded Him at least two sources of encouragement—prayer and presence.

> If Jesus found it both prudent and necessary to seek the support of His friends in the time of trouble, shouldn't we also?

While in a foreign country, Professor John Killenger of Vanderbilt University had to undergo an operation, and the days immediately prior to the surgery were extremely painful ones. His mind and body were considerably worn by the ordeal. Of that experience he writes:

I felt terribly alone, entering a hospital in another land to be served by a physician who did not speak my language. On the morning of the day I was to enter the hospital, my wife attended church. She saw there a friend of ours who was a native of the country. "Tell John," he said to her, "that I am holding him in my prayers." I was standing at the bathroom sink when she told me, combing my hair. The impact of the words, in my nervous condition, was overpowering, and I burst into tears. I felt deliriously happy. To think he was praying for me. Somehow I was no longer alone.[1]

If you have ever had a similar experience, you know how enormously encouraging the presence and prayers of a compassionate friend can be. I don't understand all of the spiritual dynamics involved, but I know that something happens when we pray for each other. Our circumstances may not change immediately, but our burden is lighter. Somehow through the act of sharing our troubles and receiving the prayers of a special friend, God makes our heavy burden easier to bear.

We see this principle illustrated in the relationship between David and Jonathan. King Saul (Jonathan's father) had mounted an armed search for David, vowing to kill him. Although David was Saul's son-in-law and the most loyal of all his subjects (1 Sam. 22:14), the king believed otherwise. He was absolutely convinced that David was plotting a rebellion to seize his throne. Hear him as he screams in maniacal rage at his own son:

> You son of a perverse, rebellious woman! Do I not know that you have chosen the son of Jesse to your own shame and to the shame of your mother's nakedness? For as long as the son of Jesse lives on the earth, you shall not be established, nor your kingdom. Now therefore, send and bring him to me, for he shall surely die. (1 Sam. 20:30–31)

After months of running and hiding David was physically and emotionally exhausted. He had nowhere to go, no one to turn to. Each time he sought refuge he was turned away, lest the people incur the wrath of Saul. At long last Jonathan was able to slip away from his father and come to him in the wilderness of Ziph (1 Sam. 23:15–16). There, according to the Scriptures, Jonathan "helped him find strength in God" (1 Sam. 23:16 NIV).

Instead of delivering David into his father's hands, Jonathan strengthened him in the Lord: "Do not fear, for the hand of Saul my father shall not find you. You shall be king over Israel, and I shall be next to you. Even my father Saul knows that" (1 Sam. 23:17).

Amazing isn't it, how Jonathan was not at all like his paranoid father. While King Saul did everything in his power to destroy David, Jonathan risked his life to encourage him.

David never had an opportunity to return Jonathan's kindness, but he never forgot it either. So profound was Jonathan's ministry to David that day in the wilderness, that years later, after David became king, he still sought for a way to repay him.

> Then the king said, "Is there not still someone of the house of Saul, to whom I may show the kindness of God?" And Ziba said to the king, "There is still a son of Jonathan who is lame in his feet." . . .
>
> Then King David sent and brought him out of the house of Machir the son of Ammiel, from Lo Debar . . . So David said to him, "Do not fear, *for I will surely show you kindness for Jonathan your father's sake,* and will restore to you all the land of Saul your grandfather; and you shall eat bread at my table continually." (2 Sam. 9:3, 5, 7, emphasis mine)

Let a life-threatening crisis arise, and small kindnesses such as an encouraging word, the touch of a hand on the shoulder, or just the presence of another person suddenly take on a depth of significance heretofore unimagined. Even the bravest among us, the most self-reliant, experience an inner strengthening from such human contact. The circumstances may still be just as grim, but somehow they don't seem as dark or foreboding. Therefore when the storms of life come crashing in, the first thing we need to do is ask for help. Remember it is not weakness but wisdom that causes us to seek the help of others rather than trying to go it alone.

Don't Trust Your Emotions

In the midst of a crisis we must trust the infallible Word of God rather than our volatile emotions, or we will self-destruct. As you well know, it is easy to become temporarily disoriented when trouble strikes. Oftentimes our overwrought emotions are simply dazed by the cascade of events. Tragedy has concussed our emotions, and we no longer see things clearly.

It is sort of like what happened to me when I suffered a brain concussion while playing basketball as a teenage boy. One minute I was fine—driving hard for the basket. The next I was lying on the cold concrete of the playground, having been undercut by an overaggressive defender. Looking around in bewilderment I asked, "Where am I? What am I doing here?"

At first my teammates thought I was playacting, but they soon realized that my confusion was no act. Loading me into a car, they took me directly to the emergency room where my anxious parents awaited our arrival. In addition to my concussion, the doctor discovered I had also suffered a broken arm. Since I continued to be disoriented, he decided to keep me in the hospital for observation.

All night long I continued to ask, "Where am I? Why do I have this cast on my arm?" and other nonsensical questions. No matter how patiently mother explained the situation to me, my addled brain could not keep it straight. To this day I have absolutely no recall of that night. It has been completely erased from my memory—the basketball game, the trip to the emergency room, the stay in the hospital, everything. All of my memories of that night come from the accounts of others.

Now here is the frightening part. I did not feel confused. Had you asked me if I was in my right mind I would have answered in the affirmative. As far as I was concerned I was as capable as the next person of making sound decisions, but I wasn't. My bruised brain simply could not process information the way it should.

Thankfully my disorientation passed within twenty-four hours, but when trouble strikes it is often weeks, sometimes months, before we regain our spiritual and emotional equilibrium. During that time the counsel of a trusted spiritual friend can be invaluable. Not infrequently they protect us from ourselves. Their counsel can keep us from doing things that we will later regret.

Upon learning of his teenage daughter's illegitimate pregnancy, one godly father found himself considering an abortion. Although he knew abortion was morally wrong—the taking of an innocent human life—he now considered it a viable option. In his distraught state he found himself considering actions that he never would have considered under normal circumstances.

Thankfully he was brought to his senses by his own daughter. "Daddy," she said, "abortion is not an option. You have always taught us that two wrongs don't make a right, and I am not about to complicate my situation by having an abortion. I will not commit a second sin in order to cover my immorality or to protect your spiritual pride."

> Our only hope is to cling tenaciously to the truth of Scripture, even when it seems to make no sense. *Especially* when it seems to make no sense!

He was showing me pictures of his grandson (now nearly five years old) as he related that incident. His eyes blurred with tears as he said, "I don't know what got into me. I knew abortion was wrong, yet I was pressing my daughter to have one."

Pausing, he stared at the photos of his grandson. Finally he said, "Thank God my daughter stood her ground. This little guy has brought so much joy into all of our lives."

Now that the crisis has passed he is able to see how irrational his thinking was, but in the midst of that tragedy even wrong seemed right to him. In times like that we must not trust our emotions. Our only hope is to cling tenaciously to the truth of Scripture, even when it seems to make no sense. *Especially* when it seems to make no sense!

Go On Living

In Charles Dickens's classic novel *Great Expectations,* all the clocks at Satis House were stopped at 8:40 A.M. At that precise moment, life for Miss Havisham came to a screeching halt. Though she was to live to a ripe old age, her life "stopped" when the villainous Compeyson deserted her at the altar on their wedding day. The woman she once was died. She was put to death, according to Miss Havisham's thinking, by the treachery of the faithless groom. In her place there lived a bitter recluse.

Lest she forget her mistreatment at his hands, Miss Havisham insisted that everything in Satis House remain just the way it was that fateful day. In the far corner of the great hall, where the wedding was to be held, there sits an ancient wedding cake. After all these years, it is spotted with mold and draped with many tiers of dusty cobwebs. It is a pathetic reminder of what might have been, as is Miss Havisham herself. Attired in her original wedding gown, now yellow with age, she roams the decadent rooms of the once proud Satis House, infecting all who will listen with her bitterness.

Though Miss Havisham is a fictional character, her predicament is not. When we are in great pain there is often a temptation to isolate ourselves. We are tempted to withdraw from life, to stop seeing our friends. Church attendance becomes sporadic, telephone calls are not returned, invitations are not accepted. Life seems pointless, and we simply do not have the energy or inclination to make the effort. Not infrequently shame and self-pity leave us emotionally paralyzed as well.

Even when we force ourselves to get on with life it hardly seems worth the effort. Relationships and activities that once brought us so much pleasure now seem dull and uninteresting. The Scriptures, once a source of encouragement and wisdom, now leave us unmoved. Prayer often feels like a waste of time, and worship is empty at best, unfulfilling.

Such feelings are not a twentieth-century phenomenon, nor are they unique to you. In Psalm 11 David finds himself in the midst of trouble. Enemies surround him, and he is tempted to withdraw from life, to "flee as a bird" (Ps. 11:1). What else can he do?

That's the question, isn't it? "If the foundations are destroyed, / What can the righteous do?" (Ps. 11:3).

According to David, a man who was intimately acquainted with trouble, the righteous can do what they have always done—they can go on trusting the Lord. That's what he did. He said, "In the LORD I put my trust" (Ps. 11:1). "The LORD is in His holy temple, / The LORD's throne is in heaven" (Ps. 11:4).

That kind of trust is more than a feeling. It is a choice, a way of living and relating to life with all of its vicissitudes. Doubt if you must. Question if you will. But whatever you do, don't abandon the spiritual habits of a lifetime. Force yourself to go on living. Keep doing the things you know are right, no matter how artificial they may feel. Go through the motions if that is all you can do, for in time your motions will have meaning. Not all at once, but little by little, until one day you discover that you finally feel alive again.

Offer a Sacrifice of Praise

It isn't easy to worship in the time of trouble, but it is absolutely mandatory. It is the only thing that can put our sorrows into perspective. As my friend Jim wrote in his letter, "We want to say, in the face of sorrow, that God is worthy to be praised at all times, even this time. It was easy to praise Him in May. *But it is important to praise Him now.* You are our witnesses" (emphasis mine).

While doing a radio interview on grief, I focused on the importance of moving from grief to gratefulness. I told the audience that in the initial stages of grief, almost all of our thoughts are filled with loss. We cannot think of our departed loved one without remembering the depressing details of their death. No memory of them is free from pain. By and by those painful memories are replaced by earlier ones when we shared the joy of life, reminiscences of happier times when death seemed nothing more than a distant possibility.

Since this was a call-in program we soon began receiving telephone calls. One grief-stricken lady informed me that she had no good memories of her baby's short life, absolutely nothing for which to be grateful. Every moment of his brief life was filled with pain and suffering.

I was nearly undone by her naked anguish, and for a moment I could think of nothing to say. She was wise to ask for help, to look beyond her own resources, but I hardly seemed the one to help her. Then the Lord seemed to quicken my thoughts, and I heard myself gently suggesting that she could be grateful for the promise of eternal life. "Because your baby lived," I told her, "however brief and tragic his life may have been, you can now look forward to spending eternity together. In the hereafter the two of you will make nothing but happy memories."

It was obvious that she had never considered such a thought, and for a few seconds she didn't say a word. Finally she spoke, in a voice husky with emotion. "Thank you," she said. "For the first time I believe I can truly thank God for my son's life."

No matter how bad the situation, there is always something for which we can be thankful, something for which we can praise the Lord. If we focus on that, rather than on our loss, we will discover hope, even in the midst of the most despairing circumstances.

For Jim and Dolly it was the memory of their joy at being parents. Or as Jim writes, "Our joy was even more profound than it was brief. It is worth enduring the heartache just to relive the wonder. We have been parents, and that can never be undone."

Maxie Dunnam, writing in a similar vein in *The Communicator's Commentary Volume 8*, shares the story of his dear friend and fellow pastor, Doyle Masters, who was stricken with cancer at the age of forty-eight. After the doctor informed him that his cancer was inoperable, Doyle wrote an open letter to his congregation. In his letter he focused on what remained to him rather than what had been taken away. As a result his letter fairly sings with praise—a sacrifice of praise if you will. He wrote, in part,

> No matter how bad the situation, there is always something for which we can be thankful, something for which we can praise the Lord.

The options open to me medically are minimal and at best do not promise renewed energy nor longevity. The other option is to turn this over to God in faith for His healing and ultimate will. This we have been directed to do by God after much prayer and spiritual surrender. What the future holds we do not know, but we know God holds it . . .

These past few days have rolled over us like an avalanche, leaving in their wake some central certainties which make up my Thanksgiving list.

Out of the dark night of the soul has come the sunlight of God's love. I am thankful for God who is real and personal, for a Christ who is present in power, and for the Holy Spirit who is by our side in every struggle.

My gratitude overflows for a faith that is unwavering in the face of seemingly unsurmountable obstacles, and for the personal practice of prayer that brings all God's promises to bear in any situation . . .

My Thanksgiving list is made this year not from what I have but from who has me—a God who is able to do exceedingly abundantly above all I ask or think.[2]

The sacrifice of praise may not alter our painful circumstances, but it does put them into eternal perspective. Seen through the lens of our loss God seems small and far away—like looking at Him through the wrong end of a telescope. Praise turns the telescope around. It changes our focus. Now God is very near and greater than all our troubles!

> The sacrifice of praise may not alter our painful circumstances, but it does put them into eternal perspective.

The sacrifice of praise is a choice, it doesn't just happen, but when we choose it we are able to view our troubles from God's perspective.

> Therefore we do not lose heart. Though outwardly we are wasting away, yet inwardly we are being renewed day by day. For our light and momentary troubles are achieving for us an eternal glory that far outweighs them all. So we fix our eyes not on what is seen, but on what is unseen. For what is seen is temporary, but what is unseen is eternal. (2 Cor. 4:16–18 NIV)

As I close this chapter let me remind you of the things we have learned. In order to overcome the storms of life we must: 1) Ask for help; 2) Trust the truth of God's Word rather than our emotions; 3) Maintain the spiritual habits of a lifetime; and 4) Offer a sacrifice of praise. Do this and you will be an overcomer regardless of the trouble life may bring.

Chapter 4

FAITH FOR THE
HARD TIMES

Some years ago, while serving as the pastor of the Church of the Comforter in Craig, Colorado, I answered a frantic pounding on my door to find myself face-to-face with a grief-stricken man. Between sobs he said, "My son is dead. He was crushed when the tractor he was driving went off the road and turned over."

Although he was a total stranger my heart went out to him. Opening the door to the parsonage I invited him in. "No, thank you," he said. "I was really hoping you could talk with my wife. She is nearly hysterical."

Stepping outside, I followed him down the steps and across the yard toward the curb. Nearing his car I caught sight of his wife rocking back and forth, her face a suffering mask. "Lord," she shrieked, "in the name of Jesus I command you to raise Jimmy from the dead. Restore him to life right now!"

The awful weight of her grief struck me like a physical blow, momentarily stopping me in my tracks. Breathing a quick prayer I opened the car door and slid in beside her. Without a word I put my arm around her shoulders and took one of her tightly clenched fists in my hand. Seemingly oblivious to my presence, she continued to rave at God until her grief finally exhausted itself. At last her husband said, "Honey, this young man is the preacher. He is here to help us."

Although she was staring straight at me I had the distinct impression that she was looking right through me. Then her eyes seemed to focus, and a puzzled expression pinched her features as though she were wondering how I had suddenly appeared. Gripping my hand fiercely she hissed through clinched teeth, "Why did God do this to us?"

Desperately I tried to think of something to say, but words failed me. Finally I managed to mumble something to the effect that I was sure that God was not to blame. "In fact," I assured her, "when tragedy strikes, when a loved one dies, God's heart is the first of all hearts to break!"

Why Do Bad Things Happen?

Her terrible grief must have reopened some old wounds in me, for long after I had preached the funeral service, I found myself wrestling with issues I thought I had resolved. Once more I tried to reconcile the biblical image of God as a loving heavenly Father who gives good gifts to His children (Matt. 7:9–11) with the painfully reality of human suffering. Try as I might, I could not. In the end, I was left with a host of disturbing questions. Over and over I kept asking myself, "If God is a good God why do bad things happen to God's people? If He is the Good Shepherd watching over us why do we appear to be sheep without a shepherd?" I mean, who was watching over the little lambs in Auschwitz and Sarajevo, not to mention West Paducah, Kentucky?

I took some comfort in the fact that similar questions have plagued conscientious people since the dawn of human history. For instance, Job, the oldest book in the Bible, is devoted almost entirely to the problem of suffering. Philosophers and theologians have discussed and debated these very issues for centuries in an attempt to formulate a satisfactory explanation. Still the questions remain, as is evidenced by the immense popularity of Rabbi Harold Kushner's book *Why Do Bad Things Happen To Good People?*

My interest, however, was neither philosophical nor theological. Faced with the ongoing pain of personal loss, and the shared sufferings of my parishioners, I sought for a practical explanation. Why, I wanted to know, did my godly mother give birth to a baby daughter so severely disabled that she lived only three months? Why did a young woman of deep faith suffer three consecutive miscarriages? Why was a godly man of forty-two smitten with terminal cancer, leaving behind a widow and two small children? Why was a pastor's wife repeatedly raped by two armed assailants in her own home? Why, God, why?

For all my study and prayer I found no comprehensive explanation, at least none that fully satisfied my aching heart. Each time I attempted to comfort a grieving person I again found myself face-to-face with my own grief. Their questions were like an echo of my own. Beyond the simplistic explanation

> Suffering is not a riddle to be solved, but a mystery to be entrusted to the wisdom of God.

that suffering and death are a natural consequence of humanity's fallen state I had no answers. In the end, I concluded that suffering is not a riddle to be solved, but a mystery to be entrusted to the wisdom of God.

Carolyn Faye

My own pain was deeply rooted in the death of my baby sister Carolyn Faye. And not just her untimely death, but the fact that she was born hydrocephalic. At birth her head was larger than her entire body. Soon we discovered that she was also blind and deaf. My own recollection of those difficult days is a montage of memories. Distinctly I remember Mother placing Carolyn in my lap as I sat in the big green armchair. Carefully I fed her an ounce or two of formula while Mother watched with a painful love. Standing beside me, my brother Don tenderly stroked Carolyn's little cheek. Turning to Mom he said, "She won't ever be able to wear little bonnets, will she?" Biting her lip, Mother turned away lest we see her cry.

Family prayer had long been a regular part of each day at our house. Usually we gathered in the living room or around the kitchen table, but with increasing frequency we now prayed in the bedroom around Carolyn's bassinet. Dad always led us in prayer, his voice thick with barely suppressed emotion. "Lord," he would pray, "look down upon us and have mercy. Heal Carolyn Faye, and make her every bit whole. Do this we pray in the name of Your Son Jesus Christ."

With a pain that lingers still, I remember watching as Mother gave Carolyn her daily bath. Once she was bathed and clothed, Mother would carefully measure her head, hoping against hope that it might be smaller. It never was, and I remember wondering why God never answered my Daddy's prayers.

Silent tears ran down Mama's cheeks then as she folded the cloth tape measure and put it away. Next she wrapped Carolyn in a pretty pink blanket and hugged her to her breast. Mama's lips moved, but she made no sound. It didn't matter. I recognized her silent song. "Jesus loves the little children, all the children of the world. Red and yellow, black and white, they are precious in His sight. Jesus loves the little children of the world."

A miracle happened then—not the one we had prayed for, not a miracle of healing, but a miracle of love. As Mother wrapped Carolyn Faye in the folds of her love and hugged her to her breast, she was transformed. Somehow that grotesque baby was made lovely by her mother's love, at least to us.

Carolyn died in her sleep, at home, early one morning. Our family doctor and Aunt Elsie arrived at about the same time. He to make the official diagnosis, and Aunt Elsie to fix breakfast, which no one ate, and to look after my two brothers and me. A short time later, the mortician came and took Carolyn's tiny body away, and the gray December day passed in a maze of necessary activities.

The funeral service and trip to the cemetery have been completely blocked from my memory, leaving me without a single detail. I do, however, remember eating supper after the funeral. Grief rendered the food tasteless, but we ate anyway, mechanically, out of some misbegotten sense of obligation. We ate in the kitchen with one small lamp the only light. It left deep shadows around the table, shadows that matched the sorrow in our hearts. To this day I cannot remember a sadder meal.

Still, as I think about it now it is not the sadness that stands out in my mind, but the resilience my parents demonstrated. Their faith never wavered. Not once were they tempted to blame God or each other. Although studies suggest that upwards of 85 percent of couples who lose a child in death divorce,[1] my parents both insist that they never experienced any difficulties in that regard. In fact they contend that Carolyn's death brought them closer together.

That is not to say that they were not traumatized by the experience, for they were. Mom tells me it was the most painful experience of her life and, forty years later, Dad cannot talk about it without weeping. They seldom speak of it, for it only takes a few words to bring all the pain and sorrow rushing back.

To this day Dad cannot bear to see a baby with an enlarged head—it is simply too painful. I was reminded of this fact while talking with Dad and Mom a few days ago. We were discussing the material for this chapter, and as we talked Dad told me again of the time a coworker brought her infant daughter to the office where he worked. The baby's head was slightly enlarged and just a little pointed. In an instant he was reminded of Carolyn and a twenty-eight-year-old pain gnawed at his heart.

Another time he took the family to an amusement park where we visited a house of mirrors. All of us were having a great time racing from mirror to mirror, laughing at our distorted reflections. All of us that is, except Dad. Unbeknown to us he had slipped outside, fighting back tears. The images in the fun house mirrors had brought back memories too painful to bear. Memories of that fateful morning when he first learned that his baby daughter was suffering from hydrocephalus.

Although Mother is not as sensitive to sights that remind her of Carolyn, she has never gotten over her death either. Mom and Dad are not melancholy people, and you would never suspect that they still miss a baby girl who died long ago, but they do. There will always be an emptiness in their hearts, a place reserved for a little girl named Carolyn Faye. An emptiness, but no anger or bitterness.

Not "Why?" but "How?"

Talking with Dad and Mom over the years has helped me work through my own grief. Although the why questions remain unanswered, somehow they do not seem so important any more. And having made an uneasy peace with my grief, I have turned my attention to what I now considered a more worthwhile question: not "Why?," but "How?" How can we overcome the storms that life brings? How can we turn adversity into an opportunity for personal growth and development?

Once more I considered the example left me by my parents. Unlike so many believers today, they had no unrealistic expectations. They did not expect a trouble-free life, nor did they blame God when adversity befell them. Having lived through the Great Depression they were acquainted with trouble and not intimidated by it. The God they served would be with them, and He would sustain them no matter what trouble life might bring. Like the ancient psalmist they said, "God is our refuge and strength, / A very present help in trouble. / Therefore we will not fear, / Even though the earth be removed, / And though the mountains be carried into the midst of the sea" (Ps. 46:1–2).

Adversity was nothing new to them. As a young boy Dad watched his father writhe in the agonies of terminal cancer. By the time Dad was fourteen years old his father was dead. Growing up without a father, he learned to trust the Lord who is "A father of the fatherless" (Ps. 68:5).

Shortly after he and Mom married he went into the water well business with his brother-in-law. He was undercapitalized, his equipment was old and worn-out; consequently he was always on the edge of financial ruin. To make matters worse he suffered a debilitating wrist injury that forced him to be off work for several weeks. Of course this was before workers' compensation, so his income simply stopped. Though times were tough, Dad and Mom hung on. Mother went to work outside the home, and Dad left the water well business to find employment that would provide a regular income. Through it all they maintained a steadfast faith in the goodness of God. They were absolutely convinced that God was with them and that He would see them through.

These earlier hardships stood them in good stead when Carolyn was born. Having found God faithful in their previous difficulties, they were able to trust Him in the dark days following Carolyn's birth and her subsequent death. They knew that He who had sustained them through sickness and financial crisis would not fail them now, nor did He. As they walked through the valley of the shadow of death they were comforted by the Lord's abiding presence. And on those dark days when it seemed God was gone they encouraged one another. "It might seem God has forsaken us," they reminded each other, "but He has not."

These thoughts were on my mind this last time we talked, and I pressed them for details, insisting that they be more specific in regard to how they made it through that terrible time. In response to my probing they identified three or four foundational truths. First, as my father put it, they knew where Carolyn was. Picking up his well-worn Bible, Dad turned to 2 Corinthians 5 and began to read. When he came to verse 8 he paused to make sure I was listening, then he read "We are confident, yes, well pleased rather to be absent from the body and to be present with the Lord."

Looking me in the eye he said, "We were able to overcome our grief because we knew that Carolyn was not dead. She was in heaven with Jesus where there is no more pain or death, neither sorrow or crying."

"She suffered so much the short time she was with us," Mother added, trying hard not to cry. Composing herself she continued, "Knowing she would never suffer again was a great comfort."

Taking Mom's hand Dad said, "When I think of her now I don't see her the way she was. In heaven I know she is perfect—a beautiful child with soft brown curls and bright blue eyes."

As we talked I became aware of a second truth that sustained my parents. They draw enormous strength from the knowledge that they will see Carolyn again. They have no doubt that "the Lord Himself will descend from heaven with a shout, with the voice of an archangel, and with the trumpet of God. And the dead in Christ [including Carolyn] will rise first. Then we who are alive and remain shall be caught up together with them in the clouds to meet the Lord in the air. And thus we shall always be with the Lord" (1 Thess. 4:16–17).

"When tragedy strikes someone else," Dad mused, "you always think *I could never bear anything like that*. Then something unspeakable happens to you, and you discover a strength you never knew you had. Only it is not your own strength, but God's strength revealed in your hour of desperate need."

Nodding in agreement, Mother said, "For the most part I don't think we were aware of God's special strength except in retrospect. When we were going through the darkest hours of our grief, it mostly felt like we were alone. God had not forsaken us, but it often felt like He had. Only when our terrible pain began to ease a little did we become aware of the special ways in which God had sustained us."

By now it was late, and it was obvious that our conversation had worn Dad out, his health being poor, so I bid them good night. Sitting alone in the living room, after they went to bed, I reflected on the things they had said. Not once had they made light of their terrible grief or tried in any way to minimize the tragedy of Carolyn's condition nor the pain of her death. With disarming honesty they acknowledged their grief and the doubts it had birthed. Still their undergirding tone was one of faith.

Carolyn Faye was with Jesus, of this they were sure, and Jesus was with them. Even now, forty years after her death, they do not have a clue how God is going to use this tragedy for their eternal good, but that He will use it for good they have no doubt. And as they near the end of their lives they cling more closely to the promises of eternal life. They know it is only a matter of time until they are reunited with her, and when they meet again sickness and death will never intrude.

Thinking about it now I can only conclude that their faith gave them an eternal perspective that enabled them to live victoriously no matter what hardships came their way. It did not make their difficulties painless, but it did give them the strength to overcome.

Chapter 5

DIVINE
PUNCTUATION

"Good evening class," she said, to the amusement of nearly one hundred ladies attending the spring tea. "I'm Ms. Magilicuddy, and I'm here to give you a lesson in punctuation."

She looked like nothing so much as an old-maid schoolmarm. Her hair was pulled back in a tight bun, a pair of granny glasses perched primly on her nose. Walking to a dry erase board, which had been placed on an easel at the front of the room, she wrote: *Who knows. I thought? Maybe the child will live.*

Turning back to the ladies, whose amusement had been replaced by puzzled frowns, she asked, "Would someone like to tell us what these words mean?"

After some halfhearted discussion, in which nothing was resolved, she returned to the dry erase board where she rearranged the words and changed the punctuation. Now they read: *I thought, who knows? Maybe the child will live.*

Addressing the ladies once more she said, "Once we get the words arranged properly, with the correct punctuation, they begin to make sense. To fully understand them, however, we must put them into context. They are part of a conversation King David had with some of his servants following the death of his infant son. For seven days David had fasted and prayed, but in spite of his desperate prayers the child died. After David was informed of his son's death, he rose from the place of prayer, bathed and changed his clothes, then he went into the house of the Lord and worshiped. Finally he returned to his own house where he ate for the first time in a week.

"His servants were puzzled by his actions, having expected him to be more grief-stricken. 'Why are you acting this way?' they finally asked. 'While the child was alive, you fasted and wept, but now that the child is dead, you get up and eat' (2 Sam. 12:21 NIV).

"King David replied, 'While the child was still alive, I fasted and wept. *I thought, 'Who knows? The LORD may be gracious to me and let the child live.'* But now that he is dead, why should I fast? Can I bring him back again? I will go to him, but he will not return to me'" (2 Sam. 12:22–23 NIV, emphasis mine).

Pausing for effect, Ms. Magilicuddy said, "I believe our lives are a story. If we don't get the punctuation right, our story won't make any sense—not to us or to anyone else. There are three critical lessons to be learned from King David's story. Lessons that will serve us well as we try to make some sense out of the twists and turns our life stories sometimes take."

Ms. Magilicuddy is not her real name, nor is she a schoolmarm. In real life she is Barbra Russell, a wife of more than thirty years, the mother of a grown son, and a licensed counselor. Impressive credentials under any circumstances, but in her case doubly so. The punctuation lessons she shares in speaking engagements are truths she learned the hard way—by living them.

Lesson I: Don't Put a Period Where God Places a Comma

When we find ourselves in the midst of cruel sufferings—be they physical afflictions or adverse circumstances—most of us are tempted to give up too soon. Rather than persevere we are ready to throw in the towel, *to put a period where God has only placed a comma.* Don't! At least not yet. No matter how tough your situation is, God can turn it around.

Let David be your example. Although the prophet had decreed that the child would die as judgment for David's sin (see 2 Sam. 12:14), David refused to give up. He refused to put a period where there was only a comma. As long as his son breathed, he would hope for a miracle. "Who knows? The LORD may be gracious to me and let the child live" (2 Sam. 12:22 NIV). David's hope, his confidence, his

> When we find ourselves in the midst of cruel sufferings most of us are tempted to give up too soon.

boldness in prayer were not based on his own merit, but on what he knew about the character of God.

In David's case God did eventually put a period at this point in his life story—the child born of the illicit relationship between him and Bathsheba died. In many other cases, however, what at first appears to be a period is nothing more than a comma—a temporary setback—in the ongoing story of the outworking of God's grace in our lives.

Consider Barbra's story. For years she and her husband, Jerry, seemed to be living their own version of the American dream. They were not wealthy by any means, but they were comfortable. By the time they turned forty they had most of the things couples dream about—a son who stayed out of trouble, good jobs with a chance for advancement, two cars, and a contemporary home in a nice neighborhood, complete with solar heating and a hot tub. They were devoted Christians who loved the Lord deeply and served in leadership positions in their local church. Then things started to go wrong.

Awaking one morning in the summer of 1986, Barbra discovered that she had a painfully stiff neck. Over the next few days it grew progressively worse, but she continued to ignore it, believing it would eventually correct itself. Finally, she saw a doctor who prescribed muscle relaxers and anti-inflammatory medication. In addition, he suggested that she wear a soft cervical brace until her condition improved. Unfortunately nothing he prescribed helped, and as the time for the family's long awaited trip to the World's Fair in Seattle drew near, the pain was so intense that Barbra didn't see how she could make the trip.

Not wanting to disappoint her family, she decided to "tough it out" and go—a decision she would soon regret. The flight to Seattle was nearly unbearable. Sitting or standing put her in excruciating pain. She remembers little of Seattle or the World's Fair. Instead her memories are a nightmare of suffering—blinding headaches and a burning pain in her back like a cutting torch going down her spine. Try as she might she simply could not participate in the planned activities. Her only relief came when she was lying flat on her back.

The flight home was torturous, made bearable only by massive doses of prescription painkillers. As her condition worsened she found it impossible to lead a normal life. Soon she was confined to bed, her days and nights an endless odyssey of pain. Weeks turned into months, and she was no better. Her sick leave ran out, and her employer placed her on indefinite medical furlough. At home all of the household chores fell to her husband and son.

"Alone with my pain day after day," Barbra said, "I began seriously considering ways to end my life. In the wee hours of the morning, when pain made sleep impossible, suicide wooed me, tempted me with promises of a pain-free oblivion. Although I knew suicide was wrong, a mortal sin, I simply could not imagine living the rest of my life in this condition. With no end in sight, I felt like a burden to my husband, even to our friends. To my way of thinking suicide seemed the only answer. It would be better for everyone. I would be free from my unrelenting pain, and Jerry would be free from the burden of caring for me."

If you have never lived with a debilitating disease, or been close to someone who has, Barbra's reaction may seem extreme. In reality her response is not untypical. Given an apparently hopeless situation many people are tempted to despair. To use her words, "They are tempted to put a period in their life story, where God has only placed a comma." They are tempted to give up when God is just getting started.

Somehow Barbra found the inner strength to go on. For six long months she lived in her prison of pain. By now the doctors had diagnosed her condition as a degenerative cervical disc, but the prognosis was not good. "Since my ailment was not caused by an accident or injury," Barbra related, "they feared my condition would simply worsen with time."

But the doctors were wrong. Through rest, medical treatment, and prayer God healed her. It was a long process, fraught with much discouragement, and for many months she had to wear a hard plastic cervical collar. Even after she was able to return to work it served to remind her of how fragile life and health really are. Leaning toward me she said, "Never again will I take my health for granted. As far as I'm concerned, every day free from pain is a gift from God."

Once she was back on her feet, she determined to make the most of her life. Never again would she be content to simply "live the good life." Having been given a second chance she was determined to invest her life in others. With those thoughts in mind she decided to return to college at night and complete her degree. In the process she encountered more challenges.

After sixteen years with her company, the last ten as the administrative assistant to the director of the clinic, she was fired. Having just received an excellent performance evaluation, she was blindsided by the director's decision to dismiss her.

In the days and weeks immediately following her dismissal she ran the gamut of emotion. She was humiliated, embarrassed to face her friends. She was angry. How dare they treat her this way! Most of all she was overwhelmed with a feeling of powerlessness. Someone else was in control of her life, making decisions she was powerless to rescind.

Humiliation eventually gave way to a burning desire for justice. Not revenge, just justice. She had given the company sixteen years—more than one-third of her life—and they owed her. "They can't do this to me," she thought. "Surely there must be some way I can force them to right the terrible wrong they have done."

Lesson 2: Don't Put a Comma Where God Has Put a Period

"Through that humiliating ordeal," Barbra said, "I learned that the God who places commas in our life story is also God of the period. Sometimes He has to arbitrarily close one chapter of our life in order to write the next. By midlife most of us are inclined to choose financial security over the risk of starting a new career. I was no exception. Left to my own devices I would have most likely continued at the clinic until retirement, but God had other plans—better plans."

"When you say that God arbitrarily closes one chapter of our life," I asked, "are you suggesting that we have no choice in the matter?"

"Not at all. I could have refused to let it go. With the right attorney I might have been able to get my old job back, or at least some kind of settlement, but at what cost? And failing here I could have nursed my hurt until I became a bitter and vindictive person."

Pausing, she searched for the right words. "I guess what I'm trying to say is that there comes a point when we need to let go of the past and move on. In my field that is called 'closure.'"

As she talked my thoughts turned once more toward King David. As long as his son lived he pled with God for mercy. The affairs of state could wait, family responsibilities could be handled by others, his only concern was that little life that hung in the balances. But once his son died "David arose from the ground, washed and anointed himself, and changed his clothes; and he went into the house of the LORD and worshiped. Then he went to his own house; and when he requested, they set food before him, and he ate" (2 Sam. 12:20).

His behavior so defied custom that his servants were shocked, they didn't know what to make of it. He had inverted the usual order. While the child lived he mourned—he refused to eat, covered himself with sackcloth and ashes, and slept on the floor. As long as there was even a slender thread of hope David clung to it, but once the child died he accepted it and got on with his life.

Learning to turn loose of what we cannot change is not only one of life's most difficult lessons but one of its most important. Failing here we condemn ourselves to a life of regret. I can only imagine how tempting it must have been for David to give in to condemnation. Since his son's death was a result of his sin, who could blame him if he wallowed in his grief. Thankfully he did not. He refused to indulge in self-pity. Instead he accepted the

> Learning to turn loose of what we cannot change is not only one of life's most difficult lessons but one of its most important.

fact that matters were now out of his hands. As difficult as it must have been, he made a conscious choice to accept his son's death and move ahead with his life. A difficult choice? Yes, but a wise one.

At some point in life most of us will be faced with a similar choice. The form it takes will vary from person to person, but the consequences will ever be the same. The person who refuses to accept what he cannot change cuts himself off from the renewing power of the Holy Spirit. Conversely, the person who comes to terms with his past is now free to embrace the future.

I once counseled with a couple whose relationship had suffered a near fatal wound. The wife had committed a terrible sin against their marriage. Although her husband was willing to forgive her, she seemed unwilling to forgive herself. Of course her self-inflicted punishment made it impossible for her to accept her husband's forgiveness or to return his love. As terrible as her original sin was, it was no more damaging to the marriage than her continued self-absorption.

Well do I remember the day he confronted her. "You may need to punish yourself," he said, "but it's not fair to me or to our marriage. If you truly wish to atone for your sin then stop thinking about yourself—your sin, your failure, your guilt. Let it go. Let's get on with the business of rebuilding our lives. If you can't do it for yourself, then do it for me."

It wasn't easy, but she heeded his admonition. Instead of condemning herself, instead of indulging her need to be punished, she made a conscious effort to put the past behind her. Once she accepted the fact that the past could not be changed but only forgiven, she was able to allow God to write a new chapter in her life story—a chapter of love and mercy.

That's what David did. He could have punished himself by avoiding Bathsheba, but he didn't. Instead he "comforted Bathsheba his wife, and went in to her and lay with her. So she bore a son, and he called his name Solomon. Now the LORD loved him, and He sent word by the hand of Nathan the prophet: So he called his name Jedidiah, because of the LORD" (2 Sam. 12:24–25).

The birth of Solomon seemed to be God's way of assuring David that his sin was forgiven. And as amazing as it may seem to us, God chose Solomon to succeed David on the throne of Israel and to have a place in the lineage of Jesus: "David the king begot Solomon by her who had been the wife of Uriah" (Matt. 1:6). As great as David's sin was, God's grace was greater still!

Lesson 3: Don't Try to Replace a Period with a Question Mark

For Barbra, making peace with her past simply meant putting behind her everything that had happened at the clinic. Instead of seeking some kind of legal recourse, she put it in God's hands. Instead of trying to figure out why it had happened, she simply put her trust in the Lord. That particular wrong was never made right, but God did something better. He inspired Barbra to pursue her "impossible dream," and at the age of forty-eight she enrolled in Denver Seminary. Two years later she graduated with an M.A. in counseling. Today she is in private practice and also counsels part-time for the Minirth-Meier New Life Clinic in Pueblo, Colorado. Only God knows how many hurting people have found help and healing because she refused to put a question mark where God had placed a period.

Although that may sound easy, it's not. When trouble strikes the first thing most of us do is ask why: Why me? Why this? Why now? Our why questions are seldom answered. If we persist in demanding an explanation we will simply become more and more frustrated. But if we can find the faith to surrender our questions to God, to choose to believe in His goodness, He will give us something better than answers—unconditional trust. Although we may not be able to understand *why* this is happening to us or *how* it will work out for our

> If we can find the faith to surrender our questions to God, to choose to believe in His goodness, He will give us something better than answers—unconditional trust.

good, we can now leave it in God's hands. In the course of time He may reveal why, but even if He never does we are now at peace.

When Helen Roseveare arrived in the Belgian Congo (now Zaire), to serve as the only doctor to a half million people, she was dismayed to discover there were no adequate medical facilities. The first thing she did was learn to make bricks in order to build a hospital. One day she was called from the brick kiln to the temporary mud and thatch hospital to do an emergency surgery. Her hands were torn and bleeding from working in the kiln, and as she scrubbed them in preparation for surgery she found herself wondering why God didn't do something about her intolerable situation. Why, she wondered, was God allowing her to waste her medical skills doing construction work?

A few days later, local church elders told her that when she was "being a doctor" they were afraid of her. To their way of thinking she was the "white witch doctor." "But," they said, "when you are at the brick kiln, your hands as sore as ours, using our tribal language and making jokes that we all laugh at, then we are able to love you and trust you."

Bowing her head, Helen prayed silently, thanking God for helping her to understand the why of her situation. If making bricks enabled her to bond with the Africans and thus share the gospel, then she would gladly make bricks, her medical skills not withstanding. Still, as she goes on to say, God will surely lead us beyond the stage where we have to know the why before we can praise Him.

In her case God did just that. During the Simba uprising of the sixties, she was taken prisoner by the guerrillas. At their headquarters she was brutally beaten and raped. With the coming of day, her long night of terror finally ended, but her sufferings were just beginning. Alone in her cramped cell, she was tempted to believe that her ministry was over. She was tempted to turn her face to the wall and pray to die. But she didn't! With a fierce tenacity she chose to cling to her faith and little by little God began to show her how He was turning her terrible ordeal into material for ministry.

One morning, nine weeks into her incarceration, she was brusquely ordered from her cell. Praying desperately for courage, she stepped into the corridor, fearing the worst. Was she going to be executed, she wondered, or worse yet, abused again, as she was on the night she was taken prisoner? Thankfully, her fears proved groundless. Instead, her medical expertise was needed to treat about fifty Greek traders, with their wives and children. The day before they had suffered several hours of vicious brutality at the hands of the guerrillas, and now they were under arrest.

For twelve long years Helen had tried to minister to these same traders and their families, but to no avail. They simply had no interest in the gospel. Yet on this day, as she moved among them, tending the sick and wounded, they readily received the gospel she shared with them. When she prayed with them before being returned to her prison cell they were very responsive.

Why did they respond now and not before? Only God knows for sure, but I would like to suggest that the fact that Dr. Roseveare had also suffered horribly at the hands of the rebels had something to do with it. Knowing she had suffered the same cruelties just weeks before undoubtedly gave her witness a validity they could not deny. In desperation they looked to her and the God she served for help in their hour of need. Once more God enabled Helen to understand a little of the why.

Ten years went by, and she found herself speaking to a group of university students in the United States. At God's prompting she alluded to the fact that she had been raped by Simba guerrillas during the early days of the uprising. Rather than focus on the horrors of that traumatic experience she testified to the sufficiency of God's grace. "That very night," she said, "by the wonderful enabling of His Spirit I was able to thank God for trusting me with that experience. Although I had no idea why He would allow such a terrible thing to happen, I chose to praise Him."

At the close of the service, when all but two students had left the hall, one of them approached her and asked if she would speak to her teenage sister. "She was raped five weeks ago," the older girl explained, "and none of us can reach her. For five weeks she has not spoken to anyone."

Helen turned and looked at the younger girl, who slowly started toward her. Then she broke into a stumbling run and threw her arms around Helen's neck. For a long time they just stood there, as the young woman sobbed into Helen's shoulder. Finally she poured out her story, ending with a sob: "Nobody ever told me I could thank God for trusting me with such an experience, even if He never chooses to tell me why!"

It was a holy moment for both of them. For ten long years Helen had lived without a clue as to the why of that tragic experience. Then in a single encounter the why became obvious. Because she had suffered the trauma of rape she was uniquely prepared to help a terrified teenage girl who had also been raped. A testimony of divine deliverance could not have reached that shell-shocked child. It would have only reenforced her bitterness and distrust. Helen's experience, on the other hand, encouraged her to believe that God could redeem her devastating ordeal as well.[1]

If we were in Ms. Magilicuddy's class, she would probably tell us that those who overcome trouble and hardship do so because they have a good understanding of divine punctuation. They never put a period where God has only placed a comma—that is they never give up. By the same token, neither do they try to replace a divine period with a comma. When God says old things have passed away, they know it is time to move on. And most important of all they never try to insert a question mark where God has placed a period. As far as they are concerned the whys are the special providence of God. The overcomer has discovered something more important than understanding—unconditional trust.

And as Ms. Magilicuddy would say, "Class, you're dismissed."

Section 2

Strength for the Storms That Others Bring

There is no formula for overcoming trouble, no pat answer for surviving the storms of life. There are some helpful principles to be sure. Important things to remember: be prepared, ask for help, persevere, and focus on God, not your problems. Still if you put all of those principles together and shake them down you will end up with one undergirding truth: *Have faith in God!* As long as we have faith in God we can face anything. We can overcome any trouble. We can survive any storm.

Chapter 6

THE PAIN
OF BETRAYAL

The incessant ringing of the bedside extension jerked me from a deep sleep. Glancing at the clock on the nightstand as I reached for the telephone, I saw that it was just after 5:00 A.M. *Who*, I wondered, *would be calling me before daylight on Easter Sunday morning?*

After locating the receiver, I managed a "Hello" that sounded reasonably awake.

"Pastor Exley, I presume," said a professional-sounding voice.

"Yes," I replied. "May I ask who is calling?"

"I'm Officer Thompson of the police department. There has been a shooting—an apparent suicide. Mrs. Mathis asked me to call you. I think it would be best if you came right over."

Reaching for a pen, I jotted down the address and hung up the telephone. Hastily I dressed and hurried toward the car. In a matter of minutes I was speeding through the mostly deserted streets in the predawn darkness. As I drove I reviewed the little I could recall about Mr. and Mrs. Mathis. To the best of my knowledge they had only attended the Church of the Comforter once or twice. Although I had spoken to them, we were certainly not friends, hardly acquaintances. Still they apparently considered me their pastor, at least Mrs. Mathis did.

I arrived just as the emergency vehicle was leaving. There were no sirens or flashing lights, just an unnatural silence as it disappeared around the corner. Making my way toward the door, I couldn't help noticing the dark stains on the driveway. Apparently he had killed himself out there.

A policeman opened the front door before I could ring the bell. "I'm Officer Thompson," he said. "You must be Pastor Exley."

When I nodded he led me toward the back of the house. Gesturing toward a partially closed door, he said, "She's expecting you."

The room was mostly dark, the only light coming from a small bedside lamp. As my eyes adjusted I was able to make out the woman huddled in a corner. Though her eyes were dry and she made no sound, her anguish was obvious. Holding herself, she rocked back and forth.

Making my way across the room, I knelt beside her chair and placed my hand on her arm. The bedroom was warm, yet her skin felt cold to my touch. After a moment I asked, "Would you like to tell me what happened?"

She did not acknowledge my presence in any way. For the longest time she simply continued to rock back and forth, her mute torment an open wound.

At last, she began to talk, her voice sounding small and far away. "I hate him," she said. "I hate him. Now he has ruined everything."

When I only nodded she continued, her dark eyes glowing feverishly in her chalk white face. "Things weren't working out for us, and I asked him to move out. He wanted to know if there was someone else. When I told him there was, he seemed to fall apart. Crying, he begged me to let him stay. His whining disgusted me so I went out for a drink. I told him to have his stuff out of the house when I got back.

"When I returned he was still here. He said he wanted to have one last beer with me for old times' sake. When I refused, he walked over to the kitchen sink and poured his beer down the drain. Looking at me he said, 'That's how I feel. Like my life's going down the drain.'"

"When I didn't say anything he just shook his head and walked out the door. I was still sitting on the couch when I heard the gunshot. At first I thought he was trying to scare me, but when I didn't hear him start his pickup I decided to have a look. That's when I saw him. He was lying facedown on the driveway."

With stern self-control I managed to maintain my pastoral composure, but on the inside I was in a turmoil. A part of me wanted to comfort her, while on another level I was outraged at the nonchalant way she refused to accept any responsibility for her husband's suicide. He had killed himself not more than an hour ago, after learning that she was involved with someone else, and all she could think about was how it was going to complicate her new relationship.

Heart Wounds

Driving home, after comforting her as best I could, I found myself thinking about the pain of betrayal. It wounds in ways nothing else can. It inflicts a pain unlike any other because the hand that wields the dagger is the hand of a trusted friend rather than that of a known enemy. David described it well when he wrote:

> If an enemy were insulting me,
>   I could endure it;
> if a foe were raising himself against me,
>   I could hide from him.
> But it is you, a man like myself,
>   my companion, my close friend,
> with whom I once enjoyed sweet fellowship
>   as we walked with the throng at
>   the house of God. (Ps. 55:12–14 NIV)

> Even my close friend, whom I trusted,
>   he who shared my bread,
>   has lifted up his heel against me. (Ps. 41:9 NIV)

Let the betrayer be a beloved spouse, rather than just a trusted friend, and the impact of the betrayal is greater still. He who promised to forsake all others and cherish only you as long as he lived has now broken his holy vows. He has taken a lover, betrayed your trust, made a mockery of your life together. In absolute despair, you are tempted to conclude that if he cannot be trusted no one can.

Surviving Betrayal

Betrayal is a bitter blow regardless of the form it takes. Whether we are talking about an incestuous parent, a spouse who is unfaithful, a friend who turns on us, or a supervisor who steals our ideas and takes credit for the work we did, the emotional fallout is significant. No one is immune. At some point in life most of us will feel betrayed. How we respond to that experience will color the rest of our life; therefore, it is critically important that we learn how to survive betrayal.

Those who have already overcome betrayal can be a great help; still, the Scriptures provide the only infallible resource, the only fail-safe means of surmounting our loss. Though spiritual principles are important, the Bible's most critical lessons are usually communicated through the life experiences of others. According to the apostle Paul their stories are included in the Bible for our benefit. He

> How we respond to that experience will color the rest of our life; therefore, it is critically important that we learn how to survive betrayal.

wrote: "All these things happened to them as examples—as object lessons to us—they were written down so that we could read about them and learn from them" (1 Cor. 10:11 TLB).

For instance, the best way to learn how to overcome betrayal is to study the life of Joseph. He was betrayed, not once, but twice. Three times if we count what he initially suffered at the hands of Pharaoh's butler (Gen. 40:23). Yet he did not become a bitter or vindictive person. Instead, when it comes to spiritual character, he stands head and shoulders above almost any other biblical character. By studying his life we can learn how he overcame betrayal, and in the process we may even learn how to overcome our own.

Joseph's Story

When Joseph was seventeen years old, his father sent him to check on his older brothers who were tending the family flocks in Shechem. Spotting him while he was still some distance away, they plotted together to kill him (Gen. 37:18–20). Reuben, the oldest brother, suggested that, rather than kill Joseph outright, they throw him into a deep pit where he would die a slow death from dehydration and exposure; that is if some wild animal did not kill him first. This plan pleased his brothers, and when Joseph drew near they seized him, stripped him naked, and hurled him into a nearby pit.

Sitting down to eat, they entertained themselves at his expense. They may have taken turns parading about in his beautiful coat, or perhaps they allowed him to overhear their plans for duping their father. One said, "We will tell father, 'Some wild beast has devoured Joseph.'" Another suggested, "Let us slay a kid and dip Joseph's tunic in the blood. Then we can carry it to our father and say, 'We have found this. Do you know whether it is your son's tunic or not?'"

Given their envy and hatred (Gen. 37:4, 8, 11) it is not hard to imagine the sadistic pleasure they took in tormenting him. One after the other they may have gone to the edge of the pit and taunted him. "Let us see what will become of your dreams now."

Their sarcasm and cruelty was too much for Reuben, not to mention Joseph's pitiful pleas for mercy (see Gen. 42:21–22). Unable to bear any more he slipped away, intending to sneak back and rescue Joseph after they had gone (Gen. 37:21–22). Unfortunately, while he was away a merchant caravan passed by, and Judah persuaded his brothers to sell Joseph for twenty shekels of silver (Gen. 37:25–29). The Midianites then transported Joseph to Egypt where he was purchased by Potiphar, "an officer of Pharaoh and captain of the guard" (Gen. 37:36).

Although he was betrayed by his brothers and became an alien slave in a foreign land, Joseph did not allow his experience to devastate him. Instead of poisoning his spirit with futile plans for revenge, he determined to serve Potiphar to the best of his ability. Once more his exceptional character gained him favor (Gen. 39:3–4). In short order he was made the overseer of Potiphar's entire estate (Gen. 39:5).

There is an old adage that says lightning never strikes in the same place twice, but in Joseph's case it did.

And it came to pass after these things that his master's wife cast longing eyes on Joseph, and she said, "Lie with me."

But he refused and said to his master's wife, "Look, my master does not know what is with me in the house, and he has committed all that he has to my hand. There is no one greater in this house than I, nor has he kept back anything from me but you, because you are his wife. How then can I do this great wickedness, and sin against God?"

So it was, as she spoke to Joseph day by day, that he did not heed her, to lie with her or to be with her. (Gen. 39:7–10)

Unfortunately, she was not a woman to be denied. One morning she caught Joseph alone in the house. Grabbing his garment she demanded, "Lie with me now!"

Startled, Joseph pushed her away, ripping a seam in his robe in the process. As he turned toward the door, she seized his garment in both her hands, ripping it off of him as he fled. Outraged at being foiled yet again she began screaming, "Help! Help! This Hebrew is trying to rape me!"

Before he could flee the courtyard, several armed Egyptians surrounded him. Roughly they seized his arms and marched him to his quarters. After securing the room they posted a guard at the door.

So it was, when his master heard the words which his wife spoke to him, saying, "Your servant did to me after this manner," that his anger was aroused. Then Joseph's master took him and put him into the prison, a place where the king's prisoners were confined. (Gen. 39:19–20)

If ever a person had a right to be bitter, surely Joseph did. Twice he had been betrayed, first by his jealous brothers and now by Potiphar's unscrupulous wife. It was bad enough to be a slave in a foreign country, but he was now facing life in prison for something he did not do. On top of all of that there was his shame. An honorable man, he was ever mindful of his reputation. Though he was a slave he had gone out of his way to be absolutely aboveboard in all his dealings. Now his reputation was ruined. As far as his master was concerned he was a sexual predator. And there was not a thing he could do to clear his good name. Yet, for all of that Joseph did not despair.

The Secret of Joseph's Strength

A lesser man would have turned his face to the wall and prayed to die. He might have even cursed God, but Joseph did neither. For thirteen long years he remained faithful under the most adverse circumstances. As I study his life, in search of the source of his strength, four things stand out to me: (1) Joseph had an unusual awareness of God's presence; (2) He had an amazing ability to see things from God's perspective; (3) He had a genuine concern for others; (4) He was willing to forgive those who wronged him.

God Consciousness

It is easy to sense God's presence when everything is going well, as C. S. Lewis, the great Christian apologist, points out, but let the tide turn and it seems that God is gone.

> When you are happy, so happy that you have no sense of needing Him, so happy that you are tempted to feel His claims upon you as an interruption, if you remember yourself and turn to Him with gratitude and praise, you will be—or so it feels—welcomed with open arms. But go to Him when your need is desperate, when all other help is vain, and what do you find? A door slammed in your face, and a sound of bolting and double bolting on the inside. After that, silence. You may as well turn away. The longer you wait, the more emphatic the silence will become. There are no lights in the windows. It might be an empty house. Was it ever inhabited? It seemed so once. And that seeming was as strong as this. What can this mean? Why is He so present a commander in our time of prosperity and so very absent a help in time of trouble?[1]

Who hasn't struggled with those very thoughts and feelings at one time or another? Every betrayed person knows them well. The betrayed spouse weeps in the night, wondering aloud why God does not answer her prayer to restore her marriage. The abused child wonders if there even is a God. And if He does exist, why doesn't He protect her from her father's unnatural desires? Or at least He could comfort her as she lies alone in the darkness, trembling with fear and shame. To the betrayed it seems that God does not care, or if He cares then He must be powerless to do anything on their behalf. In either case they feel abandoned by God when they need Him most, and a horrible feeling it is.

While Joseph surely struggled with such feelings there is no indication that he entertained them for long. Instead the Scriptures seem to indicate that the deeper his trouble, the darker the night in which he found himself, the more real God became to him. Whether he was a slave in Potiphar's house (Gen. 39:2) or a prisoner in the king's prison (Gen. 39:21) he knew God was with him. Acts 7:9–10a declares, "But God was with [Joseph] and delivered him out of all his troubles." And if God was with him, Joseph knew that all was well whatever his circumstances.

Of course being conscious of God's presence in the time of trouble doesn't just happen, even though it may seem that it does. Rather it is the result of daily practicing the presence of God. When we live with a disciplined awareness of His nearness we reap the benefits in the time of trouble. It is kind of like having a compass in our soul. Although the fierceness of the storm may temporarily blind us to the reality of His presence, our past experience guides us into the safe harbor of His abiding nearness with unfailing accuracy. However, if you fail to practice the presence of God during the trouble-free days of your life you will be hard-pressed to sense His nearness at the height of the storm.

> If you fail to practice the presence of God during the trouble-free days of your life you will be hard-pressed to sense His nearness at the height of the storm.

Take the experience of Elaine St. Johns for instance. She experienced God's supernatural presence and the peace it brings following a serious automobile accident. Of that experience she writes,

It does not take long for a car to go over a cliff. One instant the convertible in which I was a passenger was right side up on the night-black, mountainous Topanga Canyon Road between the bright lights of the

San Fernando Valley and the beach houses on the Pacific Ocean. The next instant it was upside down in a tangle of scrub and brush far below. And I was pinned under the car, fully conscious, paralyzed from the neck down.

It should have been one of the darkest moments of my life.

But it wasn't.

For between that one instant and the next, I had actually felt God's presence. It came as an inner voice repeating three times the beautiful promise, "Lo, I am with you always" [Matt. 28:20]. Simultaneously I entered into a timeless moment where the love of God was a substance—comforting, warm, light-bright, peace-filled, enveloping.

The moment passed, but the peace, His peace, remained.

Subsequent events unfolded rapidly. I smelled gas fumes. I called to my driver-companion—he had been thrown clear and was confused, but unhurt—to turn off the ignition. All at once, although I had no medical competence, I knew my neck was "broken." I asked my companion to pull me out from under the wreckage firmly, steadily, holding both feet. As he did so, the spinal cord was released from pressure. Feeling returned. (Later we were told how dangerous this procedure was, to be attempted only in surgery after a series of X-rays, and then not always successful.)

A car came along the lonely road, stopped, two men carried me carefully up the cliff, drove me to a hospital, and disappeared. (Again, a most dangerous procedure, yet it could have been hours before we were discovered, and, since we were in a no-man's-land which was in controversy between ambulances from the Valley and the coast—more hours before help arrived.)

At the hospital the doctors waited for me to go into shock. I never did. Nor did I lose my calm during the medical crises and emergencies of the ensuing weeks.

All this, the hospital staff decided, was a series of minor miracles. I knew it wasn't. It was the result of one great miracle, that moment in which I experienced God's love.

I had labored long, sometimes very discouraged, in an effort to receive Christ's work "in an honest and good heart, and bring forth fruit with patience" (Luke 8:15). Too often it seemed that patience itself was to be the chief fruitage. Then, in a moment of extremity, when I could do nothing of myself, when I had no time to labor, or pray, or even think, the fruitage appeared as instant grace—"Lo, I am with you always."

And He was.[2]

In one sense the peace of God that Elaine St. Johns experienced was the result of His sovereign grace. Suddenly, instantly, she possessed it, or more likely it possessed her. She didn't do anything to generate it. It was just there! Yet in a deeper and more profound sense it was the consequence of her spiritual disciplines. For some time she had been preparing for this moment or one like it. Daily she hid the Word in her heart, tuned her ear for His voice. "Then," to use her words, "in a moment of extremity, when I could do nothing of myself, when I had no time to labor, or pray, or even think, the fruitage appeared as instant grace—'Lo, I am with you always.'"[3]

You may be struggling with an overwhelming situation right now, or perhaps you know and love someone who is. Yet you don't have the peace of God; fear and anxiety have invaded your life leaving you feeling tormented and alone. What, you may be wondering, can you do to find His peace?

First, change your focus. When you are in the midst of a difficult situation, it is easy to become preoccupied with your troubles, to become problem-centered, as it were, rather than God-centered. The problem-centered person seems to be looking at God through the wrong end of a telescope—He looks small and far away. As a result, his life is dominated by seemingly insurmountable problems, and he is driven to despair.

> God-centered thinking does not deny the reality of our present situation, but it does put our troubles into perspective.

The God-centered person, on the other hand, focuses on God's sufficiency, on His love and His presence, and like the apostle Paul concludes,

"If God is for us, who can be against us?" (Rom. 8:31). Such thinking does not deny the reality of our present situation, but it does put our troubles into perspective.

Divine Perspective

As a young man Joseph received two special dreams that enabled him to view his life from God's perspective. In the first dream (Gen. 37:5–8) he and his brothers were binding sheaves in a field. Suddenly his sheaf stood upright and his brother's sheaves bowed down before it. In the second dream (Gen. 37:9–11) the sun and moon and eleven stars made obeisance to him. Probably Joseph should have kept his dreams to himself, seeing how jealous and angry his brothers became after hearing about them. Be that as it may, those dreams stood him in good stead when life caved in around him—not once, but twice.

No matter how tough things got, no matter how dark the night, no matter how harsh the storm, *Joseph refused to allow his present circumstances to determine his future destiny.* When he was tempted to despair, to believe he would spend the rest of his life languishing in an Egyptian prison, he remembered his dreams (Gen. 42:9). His brothers could sell him into slavery, Potiphar's wife could lie about him and have him put into prison, but no one could steal his destiny. God had a plan for his life, and He would fulfill His purposes in Joseph's life no matter what others did.

Jacob made many mistakes as a father, but he did at least one thing right—he taught Joseph to believe in his God-given dreams, and more important, to believe in the God who brings those dreams to fruition. That's the key, isn't it? If we can keep believing in our future, in the God who gives dreams and then makes them come true, then we can endure any hardship, survive any tragedy.

As Joseph told his brothers, "But as for you, you meant evil against me; but God meant it for good, in order to bring it about as it is this day, to save many people alive" (Gen. 50:20; see also Gen. 45:4–8). What others intend for our harm, God will turn to our good. His plans will ultimately triumph. This conviction (i.e., divine perspective) has consistently helped the oppressed to rise above their troubles even when it seemed they were about to be overwhelmed.

Concern for Others

Although Joseph had every reason to feel sorry for himself, there is no evidence that he ever succumbed to self-pity. Only once does he mention his plight. "But remember me when it is well with you," he told the king's butler after interpreting his dream, "and please show kindness to me; make mention of me to Pharaoh, and get me out of this house. For indeed I was stolen away from the land of the Hebrews; and also I have don' nothing here that they should put me into the dungeon" (Gen. 40:14–15).

Instead of complaining about how unfair life was, he trusted himself to the faithfulness of God. Rather than bemoaning his miserable state, he did everything in his power to make life better for everyone around him. As a result he found favor with those in authority: Potiphar (Gen. 39:4) and the keeper of the prison (Gen. 39:21–23). I cannot help but believe that Joseph's faithfulness under the most adverse circumstances helped prepare him for the huge responsibilities God had in store for him. And in the process he found meaning, even contentment, in the most adverse circumstances.

At nineteen Marc Buoniconti had "the world by the tail" so to speak. He was a starting linebacker on the Citadel football team, with plans to follow in his father's footsteps and become a star in the National Football League. All of that changed in an instant when he tackled East Tennessee State's Herman Jacobs. Subsequent medical tests revealed that he had dislocated two vertebrae in his neck, wrenching and twisting millions of nerve fibers in his spinal cord. The robust young football player who ran onto the Astroturf that afternoon in 1985 was now a quadriplegic fighting for his life.

Once his life was assured, Marc's family gathered in his hospital room for a family conference. After closing the door they huddled around Marc, who described what happened next: "As we saw it, I had two choices. I could withdraw, close the door on life, and feel sorry for myself. Or I could decide to use my life to help others who had suffered spinal cord injuries similar to my own."

Marc chose the latter. With the assistance of his father, he met with Dr. Barth Green, an internationally recognized expert in the field of spinal cord injury and the founder of the Miami Project to Cure Paralysis. Subsequently, the Buonicontis formed the Buoniconti Fund to Cure Paralysis as a fund-raising organization devoted to raising money exclusively for the Miami Project.

The past ten years have seen significant strides in the treatment of paralysis, convincing Marc that a "cure" will be discovered within the next decade. Should that happen, no little credit will go to Marc and the Buoniconti Fund for helping raise the capital needed to finance a project of this magnitude.

Although Marc remains a quadriplegic, confined to a wheelchair that he maneuvers by blowing into a tube, he is an inspiration to thousands. Even if he never walks again, he has found purpose and a sense of fulfillment that might have eluded him had he achieved his dream of playing in the NFL. Recently he told an audience at Miami–Dade Community College that before his injury he was self-centered and obsessed with football. In spite of the fact that he was living his dream, he was unfulfilled on the inside. Now he devotes much of his life to helping others, and in the process he has discovered the secret of fulfillment. "When you do something good for someone other than yourself," he says, "you experience something real."

Like Joseph of old, Marc Buoniconti has found fulfillment under the most adverse circumstances by focusing on the needs of others.

A Willingness to Forgive

The final characteristic that enabled Joseph to transcend all the negative, degrading ramifications of slavery and imprisonment was his willingness to forgive those who had wronged him. Although the Scriptures say nothing about his forgiving Potiphar or his wife, I have no doubt that he did. Unforgiveness is a poison that infects every part of a person, not only his personality, but his spirit and his mind as well. Soon he spends every waking moment nursing his grudge. Over and over he relives the injustices he has suffered at the hands of others, dreaming of the day when he will finally take revenge. It is all he can think about, the subject of his every conversation.

Does that describe the Joseph we see in the Scriptures? Hardly! Such a man would never have found favor in the eyes of those he served or been promoted to a place of trust as Joseph was. We know Joseph released his hurt and anger, we know he forgave his brothers, Potiphar, even Potiphar's conniving wife, because he never talks about the things he suffered at their hands. Nor does he spend time or energy plotting revenge or dreaming about what might have been.

By forgiving those who had wronged him, Joseph freed himself from the pain of the past. When he did, life opened up for him. God gave him beauty for ashes, the oil of joy for mourning, and the garment of praise for the spirit of heaviness (see Gen. 41:41–50 and Isa. 61:3). In what must be the original rags-to-riches story, he went from a trustee in prison to the second most powerful man in all of Egypt in a single day. Then it was only a matter of time until the dreams God had given him when he was a boy were literally fulfilled. Soon his estranged brothers were bowing before him (see Gen. 43:28; 44:14; 50:18). What God had promised He brought to pass! Though the enemies of Joseph tried to derail God's plan, He turned the tables on them. The very things they intended for Joseph's destruction God used to fulfill His own purposes.

Victor or Victim

Like Joseph, you may be in a prison of pain right now. Someone you loved and trusted has betrayed you, and you are tempted with anger and bitterness, perhaps even despair. Don't give in to those feelings or you will destroy yourself. Instead do what Joseph did. Let go of your hurt and anger. Forgive those who have wronged you. It is the only way to be free. Remember you can never experience the abundant life as long as your life is filled to the brim with bitterness. Anger and vindictiveness leave no room for joy and love. Hands clenched, ready to take revenge, can never reach out and receive the blessing of God.

Don't worry if you don't know how to go about forgiving those who have betrayed you. I will give you some specific instructions in Chapter 8 when I deal with forgiveness in depth. For now simply confess your feelings to the Lord. Admit that you don't know how to forgive those who have hurt you. Maybe you really don't want to forgive them. If that is the case, confess that as well. Now give God permission to change your feelings. Ask Him to replace your hurt and anger with His unconditional love.

Remember, while you cannot control how others will treat you, you can choose how you will respond. You can give up in despair and take your own life like the husband who shot and killed himself, or you can trust God as Joseph did. You can allow the degrading deeds of others to define who you are, or you can allow God's plans and promises to determine your destiny. You can be a victim or a victor. The choice is yours.

> Remember, while you cannot control how others will treat you, you can choose how you will respond.

Chapter 7

WHEN LIFE
ISN'T FAIR

In the long scope of history, 1954 was not a momentous year, though it did include some significant events. The most notable probably being the Supreme Court decision in the *Brown vs. Board of Education of Topeka, Kansas,* prohibiting racial segregation in public schools. Other note-worthy events included the launching of the first nuclear submarine—the *Nautilus*—on January 21 and the nationwide testing of the Salk antipolio vaccine. On the world scene, Gamal Abdel Nassar ousted General Muhammad Nuguib as president of Egypt, and the Geneva Convention established the partition of Vietnam into North and South. In sports news, Roger Bannister ran the first sub–four-minute mile. No event, how-ever, so captured the nation's imagination as did the July fourth murder of thirty-one-year-old Marilyn Sheppard—the wife of Cleveland osteopath Sam Sheppard—who was found bludgeoned to death at the couple's sub-urban Bay Village home. Subsequently Dr. Sheppard was convicted of sec-ond-degree murder and sentenced to life in prison. Ten years later the U.S. Supreme Court overturned his conviction. Following a second trial in 1966 he was acquitted.

Welcome though Dr. Sheppard's acquittal was, there was little it could do to undo the damage done by his earlier conviction. Both of his parents were dead—having died shortly after he was found guilty—and their deaths were no doubt hastened by grief over the plight of their son. He was alienated from Marilyn's family, who believed he was guilty. Sam

Reese Sheppard—his only child—was living with his brother. Financially he was destitute. His health was broken, and four years later he would be dead at the age of forty-six.

That should have been the end of the story, but it wasn't. Nearly fifty years later, the case is still making the news. The driving force behind the ongoing effort to prove Dr. Sheppard's innocence is his son, who is suing the state of Ohio, alleging wrongful imprisonment. He contends that his motivation is not money, but the desire to prove his father's innocence and restore his good name.

I am inclined to think he is wasting his time. Dr. Sam Sheppard is dead. That is a tragedy to be sure, especially if his death was a result of a miscarriage of justice, but there is nothing anyone can do to change that now.

Yet, on another level, I find myself empathizing with Sam Reese Sheppard, or at least with the seven-year-old boy he was when it all happened. Overnight his entire world was shattered. In a single stroke he lost both of his parents. His mother was brutally murdered, and his father was sentenced to life in prison. That single event became the defining moment of his life, determining, to no small degree, the person he is today.

However well-intended, his efforts will likely be futile. He may well prove his father's innocence, even win his lawsuit against the state of Ohio, only to discover that his victory is hollow. Restoring his father's good name will not bring his mother back, nor return his lost childhood. The best he can hope for is some kind of closure to the tragic event that has dominated his entire life.

Although the Sheppard case is extreme, it does graphically illustrate the devastating impact the actions of others can have on our lives and well-being. While most of us will never experience a personal tragedy of this magnitude, many of us will suffer injuries at the hands of others. Not infrequently these hurts will be administered by the very ones we love and trust, inflicting emotional wounds that can leave us crippled for life.

For some of you, the crippling wounds may have come as a result of your parents' divorce. They went their separate ways, and you were left to live with the consequences. Even now you struggle with feelings of insecurity. Sometimes you awake in the middle of the night, gripped with the same fear you felt the day your father walked out. Though your husband has given you no reason to doubt his love, you still find yourself fearing that he will leave you.

Or maybe you were sexually molested as a child, leaving you with a barely concealed self-loathing. Try as you might you can't help blaming yourself. Though he was an adult and you were just a child, you still feel guilty, as if it were somehow your fault. Even now, these many years later, the long shadow of that shameful experience casts its gloom over all the relationships of your life.

The hard truth is life isn't fair! You may do everything in your power to live an exemplary life and still suffer from the trouble others bring. Is there an answer, a way of overcoming the wounds of our past?

Yes!

> The eyes of the LORD are on the righteous,
> And His ears are open to their cry . . .
> The righteous cry out, and the LORD hears,
> And delivers them out of all their troubles.
> The LORD is near to those who have a broken heart,
> And saves such as have a contrite spirit.
> Many are the afflictions of the righteous,
> But the LORD delivers him out of them all. (Ps. 34:15, 17–19).

Those words were penned by David, and they grew out of his own experience with both the injustices of life and the faithfulness of God. At the time he composed this psalm he was a fugitive fleeing for his life. Although he had served King Saul faithfully (see 1 Sam. 22:14) Saul was jealous of him and determined to kill him (see 1 Sam. 18:9–19:12). Yet for all of his military might, Saul did not prevail. The Lord delivered David out of Saul's hand and established him as the king of Israel.

Principles to Live By

While God was the source of David's deliverance, He did not arbitrarily rescue him. Had David allowed bitterness and hatred to take root in his heart, the Lord would have been hard-pressed to work on his behalf, at least until David invited him to deal with those destructive emotions. But because David maintained a pure spirit God was able to work both in him and for him. That is not to say that David was never tempted with hard feelings toward Saul, for he was, but he resisted them. If they began to take root in his spirit, his heart troubled him and he repented (see 1 Sam. 24:5–7).

As we look at David's experiences we will identify the principles he lived by—principles that enabled him to overcome the trouble others brought on him. Pay particular attention to his self-honesty. Notice how he continually searched his own heart to make sure his spirit remained pure before the Lord. Also note how he repeatedly refused to let the evil actions of Saul turn him into something he wasn't. David was not a vindictive person, and he refused to repay evil with evil. Bottom line—he rested his case with God. He trusted the Lord to fulfill His purposes in his life (see Ps. 138:7–8).

By studying the way David responded to the trouble Saul brought on him, we can find resources to help us overcome the trouble we suffer at the hands of others. With these thoughts in mind, let us turn our attention to David's story.

A Jealous King

David first came to the attention of King Saul as a result of his musical ability. There was magic in his fingers. He could do things with a harp like no one else. Whenever the king was troubled in his spirit, he sent for him. As David's fingers caressed the harp strings, music filled the palace—sweet music, soulful music. Almost immediately the king's depression lifted. Little wonder the Scriptures say, "Saul liked him [David] very much" (1 Sam. 16:21 NIV).

Then came the event that triggered David's fall from favor: his triumph over the Philistine champion Goliath.

When the men were returning home after David had killed the Philistine, the women came out from all the towns of Israel to meet King Saul with singing and dancing, with joyful songs and with tambourines and lutes. As they danced, they sang:

"Saul has slain his thousands,
and David his tens of thousands."

*Saul was very angry; this refrain galled him . . . From that time on Saul
kept a jealous eye on David.* (1 Sam. 18:6–7, 9 NIV, emphasis mine).

Saul's jealousy reminds me of a tragic story that came out of the South
during those dark days when segregation and racism were rampant.
According to the story, an industrious colored sharecropper managed to
buy a mule to plow with. Once he had his mule he worked harder than
ever, becoming even more successful. He mistakenly believed his success
would win the respect and acceptance of his white neighbors.

Unfortunately his modest prosperity only further alienated them. To
their way of thinking he was "uppity"—an unpardonable sin for a black
man in those days.

One especially destitute farmer could hardly contain his jealousy. Seeing that colored man plowing with a mule, when he did not have one himself, nearly drove him mad. One night he slipped into the pen where the
mule was kept and poisoned his feed. Later he justified his actions to his
young son. "If a man ain't no better than a colored boy," he said, "then he
might as well be dead."

David's "sin"—the thing that drove Saul absolutely mad—was his
success. No matter what Saul commanded him to do he succeeded: "In
everything he did he had great success, because the LORD was with him"
(1 Sam. 18:14 NIV).

Unfortunately David was in a no-win situation. If he failed then the
king would be "justified" in dismissing him or having him executed. If he
succeeded, Saul's jealousy would rage out of control, causing him to hate
David all the more. There was nothing David could do to mitigate the situation because the problem did not lie with him, but in the heart of the king.

The Wrath of Saul

Twice Saul tried to kill David with a spear (1 Sam. 18:11). Failing there, he
decided to make him the commander of a thousand men and send him to

fight in the most dangerous campaigns, reasoning, "I will not raise a hand against him. Let the Philistines do that!" (1 Sam. 18:17 NIV).

To the king's growing consternation, "David met with more success than the rest of [his] officers, and his name became well known" (1 Sam. 18:30 NIV). "When Saul realized that the LORD was with David . . . [he] became still more afraid of him, and he remained his enemy the rest of his days" (1 Sam. 18:28–29 NIV).

Finally, Saul laid aside any pretense of being David's friend and mentor. This was all-out war and he ordered "his son Jonathan and all the attendants to kill David" (1 Sam. 19:1 NIV) on sight. Desperately Jonathan attempted to reason with his father, winning a temporary reprieve (1 Sam. 19:4–10). In short order, however, Saul's murderous jealousy returned and he dispatched a team of assassins to David's home to kill him. When Michal learned of her father's plans she was torn between loyalty to him and love for her husband. At last she decided to help David escape. In the dead of night she lowered him from a high window, and he slipped out of the city undetected.

The Fugitive

From the night Michal helped David escape until the day, many years later, when he became king of Judah (2 Sam. 2:4), he was a hunted man. For months at a time he hid in caves like an outlaw. Sometimes he took refuge in the forest of Hereth (1 Sam. 22:5). At other times he fled to the desert of Ziph or Maon (1 Sam. 23:14, 25) in hopes of escaping the relentless pursuit of the king. No matter where he fled Saul hunted him down. Finally he was forced to become an expatriate living among the Philistines at Ziklag (1 Sam. 27:6–7).

David's fall from grace was all the more painful because he had done nothing wrong. One moment he was an insider, a member of the king's trusted inner circle. The next he was an outcast, a pariah. A price was placed on his head—he was wanted dead or alive.

Desperate though David's physical circumstances were, they are not our primary concern. Few, if any of us, will ever be forced to live the life of a fugitive, but who among us hasn't been misunderstood? Who hasn't been falsely accused, misrepresented, or betrayed by someone we loved and trusted?

The powerful emotions that struggle inside of us in response to the injustice of it all are what links us to David. Like us, he struggled with feelings of self-pity, despair, even anger. There were moments when he was tempted to take matters into his own hands, to respond in kind to the cruelties thrust upon him, but to his everlasting credit he did not yield to those self-destructive urges. Instead he put his trust in the Lord.

Self-Examination

The first step in dealing with the trouble others bring is self-examination. Hear David as he pleads with Jonathan: "What have I done? What is my crime? How have I wronged your father, that he is trying to take my life?" (1 Sam. 20:1 NIV). This was not a rhetorical question. David wasn't simply protesting his innocence. He truly wanted to know if he had somehow unwittingly brought this trouble on himself.

When trouble comes it is always wise to search our hearts before God. Like David, let us pray, "Search me, O God, and know my heart; / Try me, and know my anxieties; / And see if there is any wicked way in me" (Ps. 139: 23–24).

Should the Lord reveal some inappropriate behavior, or even something in our attitude that may have wounded our brother, it is our responsibility to make things right. Jesus said, "If you bring your gift to the altar, and there remember that your brother has something against you, leave your gift there before the altar, and go your way. First be reconciled to your brother, and then come and offer your gift" (Matt. 5:23–24).

Two Dangers: Self-Deception and Self-Blame

As we examine ourselves, we must always guard against self-deception. Since our hearts are deceitful by nature (see Jer. 17:9) it is easy to minimize our sinful shortcomings or to overlook them altogether. Therefore it is often beneficial to seek the counsel of a trusted friend—someone who loves us enough to tell us the truth. In David's case that friend was Jonathan. Although David had examined his life without finding any reason for Saul's murderous hatred, he sought outside confirmation of his innocence. He was dealing in matters of life and death, and he could not afford to be wrong. Nor can we.

Inherent in self-examination is a second danger: self-blame. We are often tempted to blame ourselves when, in fact, we are not responsible. The spouse whose partner has been unfaithful is especially vulnerable to this danger. She is often only too ready to blame herself for his philandering. It is common for her to think, if only I had been more attentive to his needs he would not have strayed. Or, if I had taken better care of myself he would not have been attracted to someone younger. Or, if I had not spent so much time with the children. The list is endless, and while there is probably some truth in it, the fact is, her husband was unfaithful because he chose to be unfaithful.

This second temptation appeals to us because it seems to put us in control. If our spouse is unfaithful because we are overweight, then all we have to do is lose those extra pounds and everything will be all right. If King Saul is seeking David's life because David has done something worthy of death, then all David has to do is to change his behavior and he will be back in the king's good graces. Unfortunately that is seldom the case. Let David change his behavior, and Saul will just find another reason for taking his life. Let the overweight spouse return to her wedding-day size, and the wandering husband will simply find another excuse for his philandering.

Succumb to this second temptation, and you will soon find yourself living in a cycle of ever-deepening depression. No sooner do you correct one "fault" before you discover another. No matter how much you change, your relationship continues on the same destructive path. Before long you see yourself as a walking fault, as someone deserving of the mistreatment you are suffering.

As is often the case, the correct response lies in the tension between self-deception and self-blame. We dare not minimize our responsibility lest we become self-deceived: "A man's own folly ruins his life, / yet his heart rages against the LORD" (Prov. 19:3 NIV). At the same time, we must be careful not to accept blame when it is undeserved, lest we are overcome with condemnation. Like David, you may well discover that the mistreatment you are suffering is totally undeserved. In that case you must commit yourself to the Lord. "Do not take revenge, my friends, but leave room for God's wrath, for it is written: 'It is mine to avenge; I will repay,' says the Lord" (Rom. 12:19 NIV).

Don't Become a Monster in Order to Destroy a Monster

Several years ago a dear friend of mine went through an extremely difficult time. His youngest child suffered a bitter divorce. Hard on the heels of that heartbreak he developed some serious health problems. In a span of twelve months he underwent four angioplasty procedures. On top of everything else the congregation where he served as senior pastor forced him to resign.

Although the experience was nearly unbearable, I never heard him utter an unkind word. Through the whole miserable experience he never complained or spoke evil of anyone. One day, while we were having coffee, I ask him how he managed to maintain such a positive attitude. Without a moment's hesitation he replied, "I've never been a bitter or vindictive person, and I'm not going to let anyone make me into something I'm not!"

My friend refused to respond in kind. He would not become a monster in order to destroy a monster. His integrity was more important to him than either his life or his reputation.

Well do I remember talking with a young woman who had suffered a grievous wrong at the hands of her mother. With tears staining her cheeks she said, "I was the perfect daughter, or at least as close to perfect as a human being can be. Not once did I give my mother a moment's trouble. My grades were excellent. I was active in church. I even married a man she approved of. So why did she do this to me?"

Her poignant question hung in the air between us for what seemed a long time. Her eyes begged me for an answer, but what could I say? I had no answer, no explanation, beyond the deceitfulness of sin and the depravity of the human heart. What her mother had done simply could not be explained any other way.

The real question for her was not "Why?" but "What?" Not, why did my mother do this to me? But, what am I going to do about it? For weeks she was torn between love and anger. She loved her mother, but everything within her screamed for revenge. Her mother deserved to be punished, but she could not bring herself to harm her. From childhood she had been taught to honor her father and mother, and she could not bring herself to violate the teachings of Scripture no matter what her mother had done.

David's Dilemma

David undoubtedly struggled with similar feelings. He had done everything King Saul required of him and more, yet Saul vowed to kill him. Hear him as he pleads with Saul: "Why is my lord pursuing his servant? What have I done, and what wrong am I guilty of?" (1 Sam. 26:18 NIV).

Of course Saul had no answer, for his motivation was rooted in passion rather than reason. Nor was there any way for him to explain his jealousy or hatred or fear. Those are the kinds of emotions that consume a person. They turn him into something he is not. They make him behave in ways that cannot be explained.

The temptation we face, of course, is to respond in kind. Instead of turning the other cheek, we are tempted to take an eye for an eye and a tooth for a tooth. Sometimes it even seems as if life has conspired to make it easy for us to take matters into our own hands. For instance, while David was hiding in a cave just below the Rocks of the Wild Goats, King Saul entered the cave to relieve himself. Seeing the king in that unguarded position, some of David's men urged him to strike quickly. "This is the day of which the LORD said to you, 'Behold, I will deliver your enemy into your hand, that you may do to him as it seems good to you'" (1 Sam. 24:4).

Who knows what thoughts raced through David's mind in that moment? Undoubtedly he was tempted to end Saul's life, and who could blame him? Soundlessly he slipped out of the darkness of the inner recesses of the cave. With the grace of a huge cat he crept up behind Saul without making a sound. His razor-sharp dagger glinted for an instant in the faint light coming from the mouth of the cave. Now all David needed to do was jerk Saul's head back and cut his throat and all his troubles would be over.

Or will they? Can David stoop to Saul's tactics without becoming like Saul in his own heart? I think not. Well it has been said that we must not become a monster in order to destroy a monster.

In the darkness David's dagger flashed, but it was not Saul's throat he cut. Instead he trimmed a piece of material from the corner of the king's robe. Even that was too much for his conscience: "Now it happened afterward that David's heart troubled him because he had cut Saul's robe. And he said to his men, 'The LORD forbid that I should do this thing to my master, the LORD's anointed, to stretch out my hand against him, seeing he is the anointed of the LORD'" (1 Sam. 24:5–6).

Unfortunately not even David's mercy could change King Saul's hard heart. Although he initially "lifted up his voice and wept" (1 Sam. 24:16) when he realized David had spared his life, his change of heart was short-lived. As soon as he returned to his city he began amassing an army of three thousand choice men.

Once more he set out in pursuit of David and chased him into the wilderness of Ziph. When night fell, Saul and his army camped near the hill of Hachilah. After dark David and Abishai slipped into the camp where Saul lay sleeping. "Then Abishai said to David, 'God has delivered your enemy into your hand this day. Now therefore, please, let me strike him at once with the spear, right to the earth; and I will not have to strike him a second time!'" (1 Sam. 26:8).

If the evil one cannot get us to take revenge on those who have wronged us, he will tempt us to allow our loyal friends to do it for us. It is a subtle temptation, one that allows us to remain technically "innocent," even as we destroy those who have wronged us.

David was not fooled, and once more he resisted the temptation to take matters into his own hands. He would not allow himself to harm a hair of Saul's head, nor would he allow his men to lay a hand upon the king. It wasn't only Saul he was protecting, but his own heart and the hearts of his loyal followers as well.

> If the evil one cannot get us to take revenge on those who have wronged us, he will tempt us to allow our loyal friends to do it for us.

Instead of allowing Abishai to kill the king, David took Saul's spear and the jug of water that was beside his head. Once they were safely out of the camp, David and Abishai climbed to the top of a nearby hill and called out to Abner, the king's bodyguard. "As the LORD lives, you deserve to die, because you have not guarded your master, the LORD's anointed. And now see where the king's spear is, and the jug of water that was by his head" (1 Sam. 26:16).

As soon as Saul realized that David had spared his life a second time he said to him, "I have sinned. Return, my son David. For I will harm you no more, because my life was precious in your eyes this day. Indeed I have played the fool and erred exceedingly" (1 Sam 26:21).

The Wisdom of David

Although David loved Saul and forgave him, he knew better than to trust him. It wasn't anger or unforgiveness that kept him from returning to Saul's service, but wisdom. As much as it pained him, David was forced to admit that Saul could not be trusted. He undoubtedly meant well, but his good intentions were just that—good intentions, nothing more. Until Saul produced fruits of repentance David refused to reenter a relationship with him. In fact he was convinced that Saul would never stop trying to kill him, his promises to the contrary notwithstanding (1 Sam. 27:1).

Many people cannot bring themselves to forgive those who have wronged them, not because they are unforgiving, but because they have confused forgiveness with trust. Somewhere they picked up the idea that if they truly forgive that means they will have to reenter the same destructive relationship. Not true! David forgave Saul but he "went on his way, and Saul returned to his place" (1 Sam. 26:25). It was not unforgiveness but wisdom that caused him to keep his distance.

Consider the dilemma faced by the victim of domestic violence. Almost without fail the abusive husband is contrite and loving following an outburst of violence. Realizing he has gone too far, he tries to make it up to his wife. Begging her forgiveness, he promises he will never lay a hand on her again. Often he reinforces his pleas with flowers and gifts. Not infrequently he also engages family and friends to help him plead his case. Unwittingly they tell his wife she is his only hope. Without her, he will be destroyed. What will happen to the children if she takes them away from their father? People can change.

Since she really does love her husband, she allows them to persuade her to forgive him and allow him to move back home. Of course the battering cycle—tension-building stage, battering incident, and loving contrition—begins again. A better response would be to forgive him but refuse to live with him until he has received professional help. Nor is it unreasonable for her to require verifiable evidence of change before resuming the relationship. The wise man said, "A righteous man is cautious in friendship" (Prov. 12:26 NIV). How much more a battered wife.

Forgiveness is something we give freely because God has forgiven us. Trust has to be earned, and we do not reenter the relationship until trust has been restored. By forgiving Saul, David was able to keep his heart pure. By keeping his distance he was able to escape the evil that still lurked in Saul's heart.

David Strengthened Himself in the Lord

Several actions enabled David to overcome all the trouble that Saul brought upon him: (1) *He examined himself.* He searched his heart before the Lord to see if there was any wicked way in him. (2) *He turned the other cheek.* He refused to become a monster in order to destroy a monster. (3) *He would not let others fight his battles for him.* God and God alone was his defender. (4) *He understood the difference between forgiveness and trust.* He forgave Saul, but he did not trust him. (5) And, perhaps most important of all, " . . . *David strengthened himself in the* LORD *his God*" (1 Sam. 30:6, emphasis mine).

I'm not sure how David encouraged himself in the Lord, but I know how it works for me. I call it "soul talk." Borrowing from the words of the Psalms I ask myself, "Why are you cast down, O my soul? / And why are you disquieted within me?" (Ps. 42:5).

Is God dead?

No!

Is my sin greater than His grace?

Absolutely not!

Has He forsaken me in my hour of desperate need?

No way!

Is there anything too hard for Him?

Not hardly!

There is nothing God cannot do. No sin He cannot forgive. No sickness He cannot heal. No relationship He cannot restore. No broken heart He cannot make whole. No wayward life He cannot redeem. No evil He cannot make work for our eternal good if we will but give it to Him.

Then, "Why are you cast down, O my soul? / And why are you disquieted within me? / Hope in God . . ." (Ps. 42:5).

For in the time of trouble
He shall hide me in His pavilion;
In the secret place of His tabernacle
He shall hide me;
He shall set me high upon a rock. (Ps. 27:5)

When my father and my mother forsake me,
Then the LORD will take care of me. (Ps. 27:10)

The LORD is my light and my salvation;
Whom shall I fear?
Though an army may encamp against me,
My heart shall not fear;
Though war may rise against me,
In this I will be confident . . .
Wait on the LORD;
Be of good courage,
And He shall strengthen your heart;
Wait, I say, on the LORD! (Ps. 27:1, 3, 14)

By looking my fears full in the face I realize they are no match for the Almighty. By confronting my troubles, even as I remind myself of God's goodness, I discover that I have little or nothing to fear. God is greater than all my problems, and He will not let me down.

In the end that is all we really need to know. Troubles will come, but God is greater than anything life can throw at us. Let us therefore strengthen ourselves in the Lord and say, "The LORD is my strength and my shield; / My heart trusted in Him, and I am helped" (Ps. 28:7).

I have no way of knowing what kind of relationship Sam Reese Sheppard has with the Lord. He may be a man of great faith, or he may blame God for the terrible tragedy that befell his family. Whatever the case, I cannot help thinking how different his life might have been if he had looked to the Lord for vindication rather than to the judicial system.

The real question, though, isn't what David did, or what Sam Reese Sheppard did, but what I will do. Will I trust the Lord to heal my hurts, to redeem my troubles, and to fulfill His purposes in my life, or will I take matters into my own hands? How we answer that question will determine both our emotional wholeness and our destiny, so choose wisely.

Chapter 8

FIVE STEPS TO FORGIVENESS

The moment Maria heard the car pull in to the driveway she felt herself relax. The tension that had frayed her nerves and knotted her muscles released her. How silly her fearful premonition seemed now that her son was home safely.

Turning over, she fluffed her pillow, seeking a more comfortable position. Preparing to give herself to sleep, she inadvertently brushed her husband's broad back. In an instant her anger returned, hot and suffocating. Without intending to, she found herself replaying their argument from earlier that evening. Like a rerun of a sitcom, she watched it being played on the screen of her memory.

"How dare you give my son permission to go out when I've told him he can't. You know how I feel about his so-called friends. They're a bad influence. What were you thinking, for heaven's sake?"

"Calm down, Maria. It's Friday night, and Danny is sixteen years old. He's a guy. He'll be fine. Let him grow up."

"Don't patronize me! You know I hate it when you do that."

"I'm not patronizing you. I'm trying to reason with you."

"Well, don't do that either."

"Fine. I won't open my mouth."

"Now you're mad."

"A little maybe, but I think I'm more confused than angry. I don't know what you want from me."

"Support. That's what I want. When I tell him he can't do something, I expect you to back me up."

"Even when you're being unreasonable?"

"Absolutely. I'm his mother."

"And what am I, the man next door?"

The ringing of the doorbell jerked her back to the present. Hastily she flung back the covers and reached for her robe.

"What is it?" Ron asked, sleep blurring his words.

"It's Danny," she said. "He must have forgotten his keys. I'll let him in."

Opening the front door, Maria gasped. A dreadful fear took her by the throat. In an instant she knew her son was dead. Though she did everything within her power to push that terrible certainty from her mind, it would not budge.

"Are you Ms. Robbins?" the police officer asked, his voice coming to her as if from a great distance.

Numbly she nodded.

"Is Danny Fernandez your son?"

"Yes, he is," Ron answered from the staircase as he came to stand beside Maria.

"May I come in?"

"Certainly," Ron said, motioning him toward the family room.

Once they were seated the officer pursed his lips and took a deep breath. Finally he said, "I'm afraid I have some very bad news. There's been a drive-by shooting, and your son is dead."

"No!" Maria wailed, her eyes darting wildly about as if looking for a way of escape. Finding none she cried, "There must be some mistake. Danny can't be dead. He can't!"

"I'm sorry, ma'am."

Lunging off the couch, she stumbled blindly into the kitchen where she stood at the bar sobbing, her face pressed against the wall.

"He's too young to die," she lamented, sorrow soaking every word. "Too young!"

Holding her stomach, she doubled over in pain. Rocking back and forth, her nearly soundless sobs giving way to a grief-stricken wail, she screamed, "No! Not Danny! Not my sweet Danny!"

Ron had followed her into the kitchen, and now he moved to comfort her. Gently he took her in his arms, drawing her close. For a moment she buried her face against his chest, then in a flash her grief gave way to a tormented rage.

"It's your fault," she screamed, pounding his chest with her fists. "If it wasn't for you Danny would still be alive."

For a moment he just stood there, too stunned to speak. Finally he said, "Maria, please . . ." only to be cut off in midsentence.

"I told Danny he couldn't go out with his friends," she hissed through clenched teeth, "but you knew better. 'Let him grow up,' you said. 'He's a guy. He'll be all right.'"

Her rage spent itself as quickly as it came, leaving her sick with sorrow. For a moment it seemed she might faint, then with an effort she steadied herself. As she turned to go, Ron reached for her, his hand tugging at the sleeve of her robe. Jerking her arm free she said, "Don't touch me."

Grief and Rage

Thus began an odyssey of grief and rage in which Ron and Maria found themselves together, but alone. As the months passed Maria seemed to retreat ever deeper within herself. For a time Ron attempted to reach her, but there was simply no getting past her grief-stricken rage. She wore her angry pain like a suit of armor and, try as he might, he could not touch her. After a while he simply stopped trying.

It wasn't, as Maria told her pastor, that she wanted to be angry, but rather that she couldn't help it. "Every time I looked at Ron," she explained, "I was engulfed with an anger so immense that it eclipsed everything else. It was all-consuming—blocking out all reason, compassion, everything. I'm sure Ron must have been hurting too, but I didn't care. As far as I was concerned, if it weren't for him Danny would have still been alive."

Of course Maria's anger wasn't limited to her husband. In fact she had more than enough to go around. She raged at the incompetency of a police department that couldn't protect her son, or find his killer. Once they finally did make an arrest, she turned her wrath on a justice system that seemed to require the prosecutor to jump through hoops in order to get a conviction. And when she learned the identity of the boy who was charged with killing her son, she focused her full fury on him. She hated him with an altogether perfect hatred. There was no room in her heart for compassion—not for him, nor for his mother who seemed to die a little each day.

Most of all she was angry with God.

"I couldn't admit that at the time," she confided, "not even to myself. Instead I told myself I was disappointed with God. When pressed, I once admitted to my dearest friend that, while I still loved God, I didn't trust Him the way I once did.

"If the truth be known," she continued, "I blamed God. Even more than I blamed Ron. Ron made an error in judgment. God was negligent. At the time I couldn't explain Danny's death any other way. God was supposed to be watching over him, protecting him. But when push came to shove, God was nowhere to be found.

"I think that is when I stopped praying. Well do I remember thinking, *if God isn't going to look after things then there really isn't much sense in praying.*"

As the date for the trial approached, Maria became obsessed with "justice." Her only son was dead, and someone had to pay. She convinced herself that once justice was served she would get on with her life. Little did she realize how hollow justice would be. José, Danny's killer, was found guilty as charged, but beyond a momentary sense of triumph nothing changed for Maria. Danny was still gone, and she remained a desolate woman, estranged from her husband, grief-stricken and filled with rage.

A Prison of Pain

As I think of Maria, I find myself asking what she can do to escape her prison of pain. Grief and rage are eating her alive, turning her into a mere shell of the woman she once was. Surely there must be something she can do to save herself.

Nor is it just Maria I'm concerned about, for she is only one tormented soul in a cast of millions. The penitentiary of pain is immense, yet each inmate suffers in solitary confinement, isolated by hurts they often cannot talk about. The abused are here and the abandoned, victims of rape and incest, those who have been betrayed by parent or spouse. Prisoners, each and every one, locked in a dungeon of hurt too deep for words.

Others put them here. The incestuous father who crept to his daughter's bed under the cover of night. The weak and fearful mother who pretended not to see. The unethical counselor who violated the trust of his needy client. The faithless friend who slept with his neighbor's wife. The manipulating spouse who never missed an opportunity to put her husband in his place. The colleague who lied about you, the coworker who stole your ideas and passed them off as his own, the manager who repaid your hard work and loyalty by choosing a young upstart with an M.B.A. over you.

Others put you in your prison of pain, but they cannot keep you there. You hold in your hands the key to your freedom. No, it is not revenge, for while revenge may provide a temporary release from your all-consuming pain, it is simply sickness of another kind. Nor is justice the key that unlocks the prison of your past. Justice may punish the evildoer, but it does nothing to heal the terrible wound in your soul. As the great Jewish philosopher Hannah Arendt concluded, there is only one power that can stop the inexorable stream of tormenting memories: the "faculty of forgiveness."[1]

But to forgive another is not easy. Indeed, it may seem impossible, especially if the perpetrator neither acknowledges his sins, nor seeks your forgiveness. Still, it is the only way. Nothing else will release you from your painful past, nor empower you to begin living again.

Five Steps to Forgiveness

Forgiving those who have wronged us is a process rather than a single event. It involves at least five steps: (1) Identify your feelings; (2) Confess your feelings; (3) Invite God to change your feelings; (4) Pronounce forgiveness specifically; and (5) Release your feelings. The sequence is important, for if we try to pronounce forgiveness before we have worked through the steps it will only be an empty act, nothing more. It is also important to remember that we often cannot deal with

> Forgiving those who have wronged us is a process rather than a single event.

more than one incident at a time. Therefore this process may need to be repeated again and again, over a period of weeks and months, as God brings us to the place where we can deal with each incident in the long list of hurts we have suffered.

1. Identify Your Feelings

Murder statistics tell a tragic tale. Most victims are killed by someone close to them—a friend or family member. So it is with the hurts that imprison us. More often than not they are inflicted by those we love. Occasionally a stranger sorely wounds us, as in Maria's case, but not usually.

When the perpetrator is someone we love and trust, we are torn by conflicting emotions. Love and hate coexist within our hearts like Siamese twins. We love them for who they are, or at least for who we thought they were, but we hate them for what they did to us. Not infrequently we want things to be the way they were before any of this happened. We may want it so badly that we become self-deceived, denying the truth in order to pretend nothing evil happened. The truth is simply too painful to bear so we "forget" or repress our memories.

Should the memories be too graphic to repress we may attempt to rewrite them. Your father does not come to your bed in the dark hours after midnight because he is evil, but because you are. If he hurts you, shames you, it must be because you deserve it. Child though you are, the fault lies with you. Now you hate yourself for what you are, and for what you have made of your father.

After years of practice you are a master at pretending. You pretend to be happy when you are not happy at all. No matter how much you are hurting on the inside, that smile never leaves your face. You pretend to have it all together when in reality you are clinging to your sanity by your fingernails. If the truth be known you are nearly mad with pretending, and if something doesn't give soon you are going to explode.

Terrifying though it may be, the time has come for you to honestly face your feelings, even the ones you are sure you shouldn't have. Name them: shame, hurt, anger, hatred, self-loathing, guilt, disgust, and fear. Each emotion is rooted in a painful memory or in a combination of memories. In order to truly forgive and receive the liberating miracle that forgiveness produces you must now revisit each hurtful experience. Of course, it is likely that you will not have the emotional energy to visit more than one memory at a time, making it necessary for you to repeat the process over a period of time until each incident has been revisited.

2. Confess Your Feelings

True biblical confession happens on at least two levels: facts and feelings. The facts are confined to the objective details of the incidents and experiences that have wounded us, the things others have done to hurt us. The feelings, on the other hand, focus on our involuntary response to their hurtful actions—how they made us feel.

As a pastor, I often have ministered to people who could dispassionately tell me the painful details of the injustices they had suffered at the hands of others. Try as I might, though, I could not break through their defenses in order to help them get in touch with their feelings. They could handle the facts, but they were not about to deal with their feelings.

Then there were their counterparts, those desperately hurting people who could not escape their pain. Because the facts of their memories were too painful to bear, they had simply repressed them. That is they refused to recall the events that were the source of their painful feelings. While they had conveniently "forgotten" the cause of their pain, they could not escape the emotional fallout.

Many wounded souls can deal with either the facts or the feelings, but most have difficulty integrating the two. Unfortunately, it is only when we are able to honestly confess both the facts and the feelings that we experience the healing work of the Holy Spirit. That which we deny, either the facts (conscious memory) or the feelings (emotional pain), is beyond the reach of His healing touch.

To help people make an honest confession, I often ask them to write an uncensored letter to God. Since the Lord already knows our deepest thoughts and feelings (Matt. 9:4) there is nothing to be gained by editing the truth. In fact, it is only as we honestly acknowledge the thoughts and intents of our heart that God can heal us.

> It is only when we are able to honestly confess both the facts and the feelings that we experience the healing work of the Holy Spirit.

Since writing a letter of this significance can be a demanding experience, I suggest that the writer block off a two- or three-hour period when she can be alone, without distractions or interruptions. Before she begins the actual writing, I encourage her to prayerfully seek the help of the Lord Jesus, inviting Him to be with her and to help her honestly relate the details of her painful past.

The actual writing of the letter requires detail and clarity. Whereas our thoughts may be vague and indistinct, the discipline of writing forces us to clearly state exactly what we mean. For example, Maria's letter might say something like this:

Dear God:

The night Danny was murdered was the night from hell. When the cop gave me the news it felt like my life ended. I only wish it had. Instead I have to go on living in a world where there is no joy, no sunshine, no Danny, and no God I can trust. You let me down. I counted on You to protect Danny and watch over him, and You failed me. Once I was a happy person, a lover of life, but that woman is dead and in her place there lives a bitter woman, sick with hatred.

It has to be someone's fault. Someone has to pay. Someone has to take responsibility for the insane act that took my son from me.

In a way I blame Ron, Danny's stepfather. If he hadn't given Danny permission to go out with his friends, after I told him he couldn't go, none of this would have happened. He blames himself too. I can see it in his eyes. It shames me to admit it, but I take a perverse pleasure in witnessing his pain.

A saner part of me knows that it isn't his fault, but I can't get free of my anger. Every time I look at him I want to kill him. There, I've finally said it—I want to kill him!!!!

Then there is the stupid jerk who pulled the trigger. When I think of him I am seized with feelings so black, so evil, that they leave freezer burns on my soul. I comfort myself with the knowledge that he will burn in hell for ever and ever.

Oh no, I just had a horrible thought. What if José gets saved? What if that murdering *#*# calls on the name of the Lord Jesus Christ? That better not happen, that's all I've got to say. Hear me, God. If You forgive José, I will never forgive You.

Oh God, I can't believe I said that! I'm surprised You don't strike me dead. Or would that be too kind? Better to let me suffer this living death, isn't it?

Is that what this is about God, my punishment? Did you let Danny die to punish me? Well that's sick! Really sick! What kind of God would punish the innocent instead of the guilty?

The letter writer continues in this vein until she has recalled every hurtful experience, until she has relived every painful moment, until she has honestly expressed everything she thinks and feels. Then, and only then, does she stop. Having exhausted both the *facts* and the *feelings* of her painful past, she is finally ready to move to the next step.

3. Invite God to Change Your Feelings

Writing the letter will likely be an emotionally wrenching experience, the reliving of memories you have long refused to recall. The initial wounding experiences were painful beyond telling. Now you are living them again, and the pain has not diminished a single bit. It cut you to the core when it happened, and the memory of it cuts you to the core now. The only difference: that initial wound was a killing blow designed for your destruction. This is a surgical wound administered by the Spirit. It is painful to be sure, but one that brings healing rather than death.

Having gotten in touch with your true feelings, it is now time to do something about them. In prayer, acknowledge that while you don't like what you are feeling, nor do you want to feel this way, you are, however, powerless to change the way you feel. Now invite the Lord to change your feelings. Ask Him to replace your anger with compassion, your hatred with love, your bitterness with a sweet spirit.

At this point, it is often helpful to remember that God loves those who have abused us, every bit as much as He loves us. Jesus died for their sins just like He died for ours. Therefore let us pray, "Oh, Lord, give me eyes to see my enemies as You see them. Give me a heart to love them as You love them. Help me to remember how they are made, that they are weak and sinful as all men, and in desperate need of forgiveness (see Ps. 103:10–14). Give me now, I pray, a compassionate heart, full of mercy and ready to forgive. Amen."

Sometimes God answers our prayer instantly. Hardly have we finished speaking before we sense the bitterness and hurt draining out of us. More often it is a gradual process requiring our persistent prayers over a period of days, sometimes weeks.

4. Pronounce Forgiveness Specifically

It is now time to review your letter. With pen in hand and a notepad handy, work your way through your letter, identifying each person who has wronged you. Make three columns on your notepad. In the left-hand column put the name of the person who wronged you. In the center column note the specific way they sinned against you. And in the right-hand column identify how it made you feel and what you would like to do to them.

Using your list, forgive each sin specifically. Remember, you were not sinned against generally, but specifically, therefore you must forgive in the same way. For example, Maria might pray: "God, by the power of Your Holy Spirit, I forgive my husband for the role he played in Danny's death. I forgive him for his poor judgment. I release my anger and resentment toward him."

Regarding the young man who murdered her son she might pray: "God, by the power of Your Holy Spirit, I choose to forgive José. I choose to release my anger, my hatred, and my all-consuming desire for revenge."

The incest victim might pray: "God, by the power of Your Holy Spirit, I choose to forgive my father for betraying my trust and stealing my innocence. I choose to forgive him for destroying my childhood and staining my soul with a shame so deep that it is with me to this day. I forgive him for creating in me a distrust for all men. I forgive him for haunting my marriage bed and for robbing me of the sexual joy I should share with my husband. I forgive him for destroying my self-confidence and for stealing my joy. Most of all, I forgive him for acting like it never happened, for never apologizing or seeking my forgiveness."

Regarding her mother she might pray: "God, by the power of Your Holy Spirit, I forgive my mother for not protecting me from my father. I forgive her for turning a blind eye, for not listening when I tried to tell her what was happening, for pretending she didn't know."

The betrayed spouse might pray: "God, by the power of Your Holy Spirit, I choose to forgive my wife for violating our marriage vows. I forgive her for lying to me about her relationship with my friend, the man who became her lover. I forgive her for sharing her most intimate thoughts and feelings with him rather than me. I forgive her for shattering our world, for embarrassing me, and for hurting our children. By an act of my will I let go of all my hurt and anger. I choose to love and cherish her rather than punish her."

Regarding his wife's lover he might pray: "God, by the power of Your Holy Spirit, I choose to forgive the man who stole my wife's affections. I forgive him for using the guise of friendship to worm his way into our family. I forgive him for all the lies and deceptions he perpetrated upon me and my children. By an act of my will I release all of my hatred and bitterness."

As you can see, forgiving is not an easy thing. It is hard work, and the feelings of forgiveness almost never precede the act of forgiving. Were it not for the presence of the indwelling Christ in our lives, expressing His love and forgiveness through us, none of us could forgive those who have trespassed against us. But with His help we can do all things, even this (see Phil. 4:13).

5. Release Your Feelings

Now we are ready to release our feelings. We have hugged our hurts and made a shrine out of our suffering for far too long. Our anger and bitterness has hurt no one quite so much as it has hurt us. It's time to let it go. By forgiving those who have sinned against us, we are now free to put the whole nasty experience behind us.

But what of those who have wronged us? Should they get off scot-free? If we don't hold them accountable for their sins, who will?

To which I reply: Sin is its own punishment. In due time they will pay, either in this world or the next. If they do not throw themselves upon the mercies of Jesus they will surely be punished for all their sins, including their sins against us. And if they do seek forgiveness from the Savior, who are we to hold their sins against them? Indeed, if He has forgiven them, then we should forgive them as well. The apostle Paul exhorts us to "forgive whatever grievances you may have against one another. Forgive as the Lord forgave you" (Col. 3:13 NIV).

The longer I live the more I realize the great power there is in ritual and symbolic acts. That is why the last step in forgiveness is a symbolic one, a faith ritual, in which I urge the participant to get rid of both his letter and his list of grievances.

There are two ways I suggest he do this, both being symbolic of the spiritual work being done in his innermost being. He may burn them if he has a fireplace or a wood-burning stove. Or he may cut them up or shred them. As he is placing them in the fire, or dropping the shredded pieces into the trash, he should declare in prayer: "God, by the power of Your Holy Spirit, I release all of my negative feelings. I let go of every hurt, every hateful thought, every desire for revenge, every thought of getting even or making the other person pay."

When we forgive those who have sinned against us, those who have wounded our souls in crippling ways, we perform spiritual surgery on our hearts. No longer do we define ourselves by what others have done to us. The one who sinned against us may not be changed, but we are. The door to our prison of pain has been opened, and we walk out of our past into a new life. Through the miracle of forgiveness we are free to become the person God has called us to be.

Let me remind you once more that forgiveness is a process. Sometimes the five steps must be repeated again and again—not because they don't work, but because many of us have been wounded by a number of people over a long period of time. God in His wisdom knows that we cannot bear the emotional strain of dealing with everything at once so He allows us to deal with one or two things at a time. After a period of rest, in which we enjoy the benefits of forgiving those who have wronged us, He then brings another set of issues to the forefront and we begin the process again.

> God in His wisdom knows that we cannot bear the emotional strain of dealing with everything at once so He allows us to deal with one or two things at a time.

In a perfect world forgiveness would always result in reconciliation. Of course we do not live in a perfect world, or else there would be no need for forgiveness in the first place; therefore, forgiveness often stops short of reconciliation. Not because we refuse to restore the relationship, but because the wrongdoer neither acknowledges his sin, nor receives our forgiveness. While this ongoing brokenness in the relationship may cause us distress, it in no way minimizes the reality of our act of forgiveness, nor does it jeopardize our personal wholeness.

Beyond Grief and Rage

As Maria worked through her terrible grief and rage she was finally able to forgive not only her husband, but her son's killer as well. Blinded by bitterness and hatred, she had painted José with a broad brush, making it impossible to separate the person he was from what he had done. To her way of thinking he had no redeeming qualities. He was not a person, but a killer—the murderer of her son.

But once she was able to forgive him, even though he did not deserve to be forgiven, she began to see him through God's eyes. In her hatred she wanted to believe he was all bad, but that was not the case. He had done a bad thing to be sure, a terrible thing, a thing that could never be undone, but that was not the whole truth, not the deepest truth about him.

For the first time she was able to see the person who lived beneath the cloak of his wrongdoing. And the truth was, he was a weak and needy human being, not unlike herself. This revelation in no way excused his criminal behavior, but it planted a seed of compassion in Maria's heart. Daily she watered it with prayer. Little by little it began to grow until one day she realized that she was thinking of José without rancor. Forgiveness had done its healing work.

Then she had a new thought. Maybe she should go to the penitentiary where José was incarcerated and tell him she had forgiven him. It seemed such a ludicrous idea that she tried to put it out of her mind. Yet it would not go away, and the more she prayed about it, the more convinced she became that the idea was from God. After a number of telephone calls and a mountain of red tape she finally secured permission to visit him.

Sitting in the visitor's center, waiting for José to be brought from his cell, Maria was suddenly overwhelmed with uncertainty. What if she hadn't really forgiven him? What if the sight of him brought a rush of hatred? For a moment she considered walking out, but before she could leave José was brought in.

How young he looked, how vulnerable, sitting there in his ill-fitting prison garb. Gone was the defiant young man who had sat sullenly throughout the trial. Suddenly Maria was seized with an overwhelming feeling of compassion. Quickly she glanced away, giving herself a moment to get her feelings back under control. When she looked at José again he could not meet her eyes, instead he looked down, seeming to study his hands.

They were separated by a glass partition, their only means of communication via a telephone headset. Picking up the receiver, Maria motioned for José to do the same. Reluctantly he placed the receiver against his ear and waited for her to speak. The carefully rehearsed phrases now fled her mind leaving her struggling for something to say. The silence stretched between them, painfully unbroken. At last she heard herself speaking in a voice that sounded only vaguely familiar.

"José," she said, "I am here to ask your forgiveness. I have hated you. I have cursed you and prayed for your death. I only hope you can find it in your heart to forgive me."

Slowly José lifted his head and looked at her, his eyes filled with surprise and suspicion. Although he had not known what to expect from their meeting, it was apparent he had expected anything but this. Not knowing what to say, he said nothing.

Once more a heavy silence lay between them. Now the rehearsed phrases filled Maria's mind, but she could not bring herself to speak them. Try as she might the words stuck in her throat. Bowing her head, she prayed silently for strength to do what she had come to do.

"José," she said, her voice hardly more than a strangled whisper, "I have come today to forgive you for murdering my only son. I do not have the goodness within myself to forgive you, but my Savior, the Lord Jesus Christ who lives within me, gives me the power to forgive you. I don't hate you. I don't wish you evil. In fact I am praying for your salvation."

The intensity of her words were too much for José. Dropping the receiver, he lunged to his feet and started toward the door leading back to the cell block. As the guard came to escort him back to his cell, he glanced at Maria once more. His eyes were filled with pain and confusion and the tiniest flicker of hope.

In the months that followed Maria continued to journey to the penitentiary to visit José, sometimes weekly, sometimes biweekly. Under the most difficult circumstances they slowly forged a relationship of mutual trust. She read the Scriptures to him and prayed with him, but he steadfastly refused to receive Jesus as his Savior. "Sometimes," she told her husband, "I'm tempted to give up."

Then came the day that made it all worthwhile. As soon as José stepped into the visitor's center she knew something had happened. Grabbing the receiver he started talking excitedly. "I did it," he said. "I did it!"

Though Maria knew exactly what he was talking about she wanted to hear it from him. Smiling, she asked, "What exactly did you do?"

> Forgiveness does not always end in reconciliation, but it always produces new life and freedom.

"I prayed the sinner's prayer. I asked Jesus to come into my heart and be my Savior!"

As we've already noted, forgiveness does not always end in reconciliation as it did in Maria's case, but it *always* produces new life and freedom for the one doing the forgiving. It does not change the past—nothing can do that, not even God—but it does something better. Forgiveness unlocks the future!

Chapter 9

REBUILDING
YOUR LIFE

Unlike Maria, most of us will never have to try to rebuild our life after losing a child in a drive-by shooting. The things that shatter our worlds will likely be more common, but devastating nonetheless: A beloved parent succumbs to cancer and dies before you graduate from high school. A family member despairs of living and takes her own life. Your second child is born with crippling birth defects. Your spouse of nearly thirty years divorces you for a younger woman. Your company is downsizing, and you suddenly find yourself unemployed at age fifty-five.

Regardless of what brings your world crashing down, the rebuilding process will not be easy. If you have prepared for this moment by building your life on Jesus Christ, the only sure foundation (see Matt. 7:24–27), you will have nothing to fear. Although the experience will likely be stressful, you are well equipped to withstand the storm. While the circumstances may differ from situation to situation, the principles that facilitate the rebuilding process will be the same. First, you weather the storm. Next, you come to grips with the reality of your present circumstances. Then you maintain hope in even the most despairing circumstances. Finally, you have to pick up the pieces and start over.

Thankfully, God promises to be with us through the entire process, from the beginning to the end. "Be strong and of good courage, do not fear nor be afraid of them; for the LORD your God, He is the One who goes with you. He will not leave you nor forsake you" (Deut. 31:6).

Weathering the Storm

Recently I received a letter from a young woman named Carrie detailing the events that had shattered her world. She wrote:

In a voice filled with cruelty, he rasped, "Welcome to hell . . ." and shattered my world. He told me of infidelities, alcohol abuse, and prescription drug addiction. My mind was reeling, my heart was breaking. "No . . . no . . . no . . ." I screamed rushing out into the night. I made it as far as the front yard before collapsing in despair. "No, no, no . . ." I continued to moan.

He came and touched me on the shoulder and I repulsed at his caress. "Come inside," he whispered, "you shouldn't be out here in the dark."

Groggily I stumbled into the house and up the stairs to our bedroom. Collapsing on the bed, I drew myself into a ball wanting to disappear, wanting my innocence to be restored, needing to be ignorant once again.

I felt his weight on the bed and winced at the thought of what he might say next. "You can't tell a soul about this. No one, do you understand? Not your mom, not your dad, and not your best friend." He paused for effect, "If you do, I'll kill myself and you'll be responsible for my death." With those words, he penetrated my fog, and I looked at him and wondered, what more could he take from me.

The rest of the night passed in a haze of pain and denial. My dreams were filled with torment, death, and a sense of loss so deep I couldn't imagine how I could go on living. How could I pretend everything was OK? How could I face my parents knowing what I now knew? How could I pull off this facade? For the first time in my life, I began to dread being with my family. He had done this to me. He had done this to my family.

All of this occurred three days before my twenty-third birthday. I had to face my parents at my birthday party and pretend like everything was perfect. I had to pretend my heart hadn't been shattered. I had to pretend my life wasn't reeling out of control and that I didn't wish to die.

But in the midst of my despair, in the darkest time of my soul, when my earthly father could not be there for me, I reached for my Heavenly Father and He was there. When I needed arms to comfort me and strength to face another day, He was there. When fear and confusion shrouded my soul like a blanket, smothering the very life out of me, He was there. When suicide beckoned to me, promising the only escape from my tormented world, He was there.

One particularly difficult night I grabbed my Bible and crawled help-lessly into the bathroom crying out to Him. "God," I sobbed, "I need You now more than I've ever needed You before. I must have a word from You or I cannot go on living.

Randomly I opened my Bible to the 71st Psalm. Instantly my eyes were drawn to verses 20 and 21: "Though you have made me see troubles, many and bitter, you will restore my life again; from the depths of the earth you will again bring me up. You will increase my honor and comfort me once again."

Astounded, I read it once more and a fragile hope was birthed in me. In gratefulness I clung to it. It became my shelter in the storm. I wrote it on yellow stickies and pasted it everywhere. In my room, on my mirror, on my books, in my purse, everywhere. That was my word from God and I clung to it for dear life. My circumstances didn't change immediately. My bitter pain didn't go away that night, nor for a long time afterwards, but I knew I was going to make it. God had given me His word!

The first time I read Carrie's letter I was moved to tears, both by her pain and by God's eternal faithfulness. Well do I remember thinking that there was life in that tragic account. Despair yes, and unspeakable pain, but more than that there was hope! God spoke to her out of the storm, fierce though it was, giving her a word to cling to until it finally blew over.

When a storm first strikes it can be a mind-numbing experience, especially if you are not expecting it. Suddenly your orderly world is topsy-turvy. Nothing makes sense any more. You may find yourself think-ing, *This can't be happening to me. It's a bad dream. Any minute now I'll wake up and everything will be all right. It's a sick joke. Would someone laugh? Please?*

But it *is* happening to you. No one's laughing. Little by little the terrible reality of your situation begins to sink in. You have been blindsided by a terrible storm. Your world has been shattered. The best you can hope for, right now anyway, is to survive the storm—to hang on until the worst of it blows over and then you can assess the damage and begin thinking about rebuilding your life.

Coming to Grips with Reality

Tucked in the Old Testament, between Judges and 1 Samuel, is a wonderful little book called Ruth. It is a story of survival, and the heroines are Ruth and Naomi. Because of their steadfastness in the face of terrible adversity, they found favor in the sight of the Lord and He delivered them out of all their trouble.

While Naomi was still a relatively young woman, a severe famine spread throughout the land of Judah, reaching as far south as Bethlehem where she dwelt with her husband and two sons. Rather than trust the Lord to meet their needs, Naomi's husband Elimelech decided to take his chances in Moab. After selling the family property to finance his ill-conceived venture, he set out, taking Naomi and their two sons with him.

Although there was bread enough and to spare in Moab, it was richly seasoned with bitterness. First Elimelech died, leaving Naomi a widow. Shortly thereafter both of her grown sons died as well. Though they had each married, neither had fathered a child. Now Naomi was alone in a foreign country, without family or any visible means of taking care of herself.

Like many of us, she found herself in a precarious position through no real fault of her own. People and events seemed to have conspired against her. First there was the famine, then Elimelech's decision to take his family to Moab, and finally the untimely deaths of her husband and sons. Little wonder that she laments, "The hand of the LORD has gone out against me!" (Ruth 1:13).

Yet, in the midst of her trouble, God provided a source of strength in the person of Ruth, her daughter-in-law. Ruth loved Naomi with a selfless love. A widow herself, she committed her life to taking care of her widowed mother-in-law. Though Naomi entreated her to return to her own family, Ruth replied,

Entreat me not to leave you,

Or to turn back from following after you;

For wherever you go, I will go;

And wherever you lodge, I will lodge;

Your people shall be my people,

And your God, my God.

Where you die, I will die,

And there will I be buried.

The Lord do so to me, and more also,

If anything but death parts you and me. (Ruth 1:16–17)

Unlike Elimelech, who apparently trusted his own resourcefulness more than God's faithfulness, Naomi decided to return to her homeland and take her chances on God's provision. Better, she may have reasoned, to perish among her own kinsmen than to die a stranger in the land of Moab. More likely, hope was kindled in her heart when she heard that, "the LORD had visited His people by giving them bread" (Ruth 1:6).

The years of suffering and grief had taken their toll, etching a painful story in Naomi's pinched features. The vivacious young woman who set out for Moab ten years earlier was gone, replaced by a stranger with sadness in her eyes and a certain weariness in her step, causing the women of Bethlehem to exclaim, "Is this Naomi?" (Ruth 1:19).

She said to them, "Do not call me Naomi [which literally means "pleasant"]; call me Mara [which literally means "bitter"], for the Almighty has dealt very bitterly with me. I went out full, and the LORD has brought me home again empty. Why do you call me Naomi, since the LORD has testified against me, and the Almighty has afflicted me?" (Ruth 1:20–21)

Naomi was nothing at all if she was not a clear-eyed realist. Her situation was desperate, and she made no bones about it. She was widowed and childless, without sons or grandsons to continue the family name. Yet, beneath her clear-eyed realism there was an unwavering faith. The God of Abraham, Isaac, and Jacob would not fail her. Even then, He was arranging circumstances and events to meet her needs. That she believed this should be readily apparent. Why else would she have returned to Bethlehem?

The balance she managed between realism and faith was not an easy one. More often than not we come down on one side or the other. Either we are realists to the point of despair, or we think we must deny reality all together if we are to be people of faith. Naomi avoided both extremes. She honestly acknowledged the painful truth of her situation, even going so far as to "blame" God for her sufferings. Yet on a deeper level, her faith never wavered. No matter what happened she was absolutely convinced that God had everything under control.

Rebuilding our lives requires that kind of faith. Only when we trust God enough to honestly accept the painful reality of our shattered world can we begin the excruciatingly slow work of rebuilding. It is not faith but fear that causes us to declare that things are not as bad as they appear. This kind of "faith talk" may provide a temporary relief, but in the end it only delays the rebuilding process.

Consider the situation in which Weldon and I found ourselves when a sudden storm caused us to lose our way while fishing for halibut in the Gulf of Alaska. After wandering through the trackless waters for nearly three hours, without so much as a compass to help us chart our course, a fishing trawler suddenly emerged from the fog. In that moment we had a choice.

> Only when we trust God enough to honestly accept the painful reality of our shattered world can we begin the excruciatingly slow work of rebuilding.

We could have pretended that we were not lost, that our situation was not really critical, or we could face reality and signal the fishing trawler for help. Thankfully we swallowed our pride and admitted how desperate our situation was. In a matter of minutes the captain of that fishing boat had us back on course, and we returned to Sitka without further trouble. But I would hate to think what might have happened had we been too proud, or too stubborn, to face the reality of our situation and seek his help.

Unfortunately, over the years I have ministered to a number of people who simply refused to come to grips with the reality of their situations. Even as they watched their beloved die, a little each day, they refused to acknowledge that death was imminent. As a consequence, when death came, they were ill-equipped to handle it, nor had they prepared their family. The resulting grief and anger were often debilitating. How much better it would have been to have honestly acknowledged the seriousness of the situation and faced it together. Their grief may not have been any less, but at least they would have been better prepared to handle it.

The same kind of thing often happens in the case of infidelity. Though the signs are all present, the betrayed spouse simply refuses to face the facts. Even when the unfaithful partner discloses the truth and seeks a divorce in order to marry the other person, the betrayed spouse may still stubbornly cling to the hope that their marriage can be saved. In extreme cases, they may refuse to give up hope even after the divorce is final, even after their "ex" has remarried. Unfortunately God cannot help us rebuild our shattered world until we honestly acknowledge the reality of our circumstances and take appropriate steps to deal with them.

Maintaining Hope

From Ruth and Naomi we not only learn the importance of confronting reality, but also how to maintain hope in the most despairing of circumstances. Yes, they were widows, having neither husbands nor children, yet their faith did not fail. He who is "A father of the fatherless, [and] a defender of widows" (Ps. 68:5) will take care of them, of this they were sure.

In order to fully appreciate their story we must have at least a rudimentary knowledge of the customs of that day. First is the law of the harvest. God commanded His people to leave the corners and the edges of their fields for the poor and the alien (see Lev. 23:22 and Deut. 24:19–22). Therefore it was common to see widows and aliens following behind the reapers, gleaning what they missed. It was meager fare to be sure, but when the harvest was abundant it allowed the poor to subsist.

Next, we must understand the "kinsman-redeemer" law. According to it, the property each family received upon entering the promised land was theirs forever. Should they fall upon hard times and find it necessary to "sell" their land, they still retained the right to redeem it (buy it back) at any time. If neither they nor a close relative (kinsman-redeemer) redeemed the property before the year of Jubilee (every fiftieth year, see Lev. 25:8–28) the land automatically reverted to them or their descendants.

To these first two laws must be added a third levitical provision known as "levirate marriage" (from the Latin word *levir*, meaning brother-in-law). This refers to the provision in Jewish law for a man to marry the widow of his deceased brother if no heir has been born. The widow was not to remarry outside the family, but the brother of the deceased husband was to raise up an heir for his dead brother so that his name might be perpetuated and his family inheritance continue to be possessed."[1] (See Deut. 25:5–10).

Against the backdrop of these three customs, we find the story of God's provision for Ruth and Naomi lived out. Hardly had they arrived in Bethlehem before we see the hand of God working on their behalf. Not in overtly obvious ways, but subtly. He choreographed circumstances and events that brought Ruth into contact with those He had appointed as her helpers.

The central figure in God's plans for restoring their fortunes was a wealthy landowner named Boaz. He just "happened" to be a close relative (kinsman-redeemer) of Naomi's late husband Elimelech. When Ruth went into the fields to glean after the reapers "she *happened* to come to the part of the field belonging to Boaz" (Ruth 2:3). She did not consciously choose his field; rather, the Lord directed her steps, albeit without her knowledge, but not without her consent. When she told Naomi, "Your people shall be my people, / And your God, my God" (Ruth 1:16), she made a conscious choice to follow the Lord God Almighty. When she just "happened" into the field of Boaz, it was simply a natural consequence of that earlier decision.

"Now behold, Boaz came from Bethlehem" (Ruth 2:4) to the field where Ruth was gleaning. Almost immediately he noticed her and asked his servants, "Whose young woman is this?" (Ruth 2:5).

Again we see the hand of God in Boaz's impromptu visit. Had he visited his fields a day earlier Ruth would not have been there. Had he come a day later, Ruth might have already moved on to someone else's field. Oftentimes, the destiny of God's chosen ones hinges on just such "chance" happenings. It is not chance, however, but divine providence. When one's life is directed by God, these kinds of divine coincidences seem to have a way of occurring with comforting regularity.

And as you read earlier in Carrie's letter, at the point of her deepest despair Carrie just "happened" to open her Bible to the Seventy-first Psalm. Her eyes just "happened" to fall on verses 20 and 21. Those verses just "happened" to be exactly what she needed to see her through the storm: "Though you have made me see troubles, many and bitter, / you will restore my life again; / from the depths of the earth / you will again bring me up. / You will increase my honor / and comfort me once again" (NIV).

The same sort of thing happened when Weldon and I were lost in the Gulf of Alaska. Once we finally acknowledged how desperate our situation was, and cried out to God for help, a fishing trawler just "happened" to emerge from a fog bank and cut across our path. A coincidence? Hardly. Though we were unaware of it, the Lord who directs the steps of His people had brought us to that place at that precise moment in order to save us from a night at sea or worse. "If the LORD delights in a man's way, / he makes his steps firm; / though he stumble, he will not fall, / for the LORD upholds him with his hand" (Ps. 37:23–24 NIV).

> When one's life is directed by God, divine coincidences seem to have a way of occurring with comforting regularity.

As Paul Tournier has said:

God guides us, despite our uncertainties and our vagueness, even through our failings and mistakes . . . He leads us step by step, from event to event. Only afterwards, as we look back over the way we have come and reconsider certain important moments in our lives in the light of all that has followed them, or when we survey the whole progress of our lives, do we experience the feeling of having been led without knowing it, the feeling that God has mysteriously guided us.[2]

Starting Over

Upon learning that Ruth was the daughter-in-law of Naomi, Boaz invited her to glean only in his fields, promising her the benefit of his protection. Overcome with gratitude, she bowed before him with her face to the ground. "Why," she asked, "have I found favor in your eyes, that you should take notice of me, since I am a foreigner?" (Ruth 2:10).

> And Boaz answered and said to her, "It has been fully reported to me, all that you have done for your mother-in-law since the death of your husband, and how you have left your father and your mother and the land of your birth, and have come to a people whom you did not know before. The Lord repay your work, and a full reward be given you by the Lord God of Israel, under whose wings you have come for refuge. (Ruth 2:11–12)

God caused the paths of Boaz and Ruth to cross, but that would have been of little consequence had Ruth not been the kind of person she was. Had she become bitter or self-serving as a result of her grievous misfortunes, Boaz would have likely paid her no mind. From her experience we see how important it is to maintain a right spirit regardless of the trouble that comes our way. We can be sure that God is at work on our behalf, but He can only work with the raw materials we give Him.

Being a mother in Israel and a true woman of faith, it was not hard for Naomi to discern the hand of God in the events that had transpired. Nor was it difficult for her to sense God's continuing guidance. To her way of thinking, God did not bring them back to Bethlehem to live out their days on the subsistence they could glean by following the reapers. God had a better plan, of that Naomi was sure.

Using the events that had already transpired as "clues," Naomi began to put things together. *Since God brought Ruth and Boaz together,* she may have reasoned, *perhaps he is to be our salvation. After all he is a kinsman-redeemer, albeit not our nearest relative, but a close one. Did not Ruth find favor in his sight? If this is not divine providence, then it is the closest thing to it.*

Following the accepted customs of their day, Naomi instructed Ruth regarding the proper way to approach Boaz. Although the law permitted a public appeal, Naomi did not think that would be wise. Having no desire to put their benefactor in an awkward position, she instructed Ruth to approach him privately. To her credit Ruth responded, "All that you say to me I will do" (Ruth 3:5).

On the night that the barley harvest ended, Ruth followed Boaz to the threshing floor as per Naomi's instructions. As soon as he fell asleep, she slipped in and uncovered his feet. Lying down she placed them against her body in an act of submission. At midnight Boaz rolled over and realized he was not alone. Startled, he asked, "Who are you?" (Ruth 3:9).

So she answered, "I am Ruth, your maidservant. Take your maidservant under your wing, for you are a close relative." (Ruth 3:9)

When Ruth said "for you are a close relative," Boaz understood that she was making a proposal of marriage in keeping with the law. Since her husband had died without giving her a child, it was the responsibility of a close relative to marry her in order to provide an heir of her deceased husband (see Deut. 25:5–10).

Some may see the actions of Ruth and Naomi as forward, even manipulative, but surely that was not the case. To my way of thinking, Naomi was simply "following after God." She was trying the door that seemed to be opening to them. She had no intention of trying to "make" something happen. Her sole purpose was to discover what God was doing on their behalf. Had Boaz been unreceptive to their proposal, Naomi would have accepted that as the will of the Lord.

But Boaz was not unreceptive. Indeed he welcomed Ruth's proposal with an enthusiasm that suggests his feelings for her were already well developed.

Then he said, "Blessed are you of the LORD, my daughter! For you have shown more kindness at the end than at the beginning, in that you did not go after young men, whether poor or rich. And now, my daughter, do not fear. I will do for you all that you request, for all the people of my town know that you are a virtuous woman. Now it is true that I am a close relative; however, there is a relative closer than I. Stay this night, and in the morning it shall be that if he will perform the duty of a close relative for you—good; let him do it. But if he does not want to perform the duty for you, then I will perform the duty for you, as the LORD lives! Lie down until morning." (Ruth 3:10–13)

The next day, while Ruth and Naomi anxiously awaited the outcome, Boaz met with the relative who had the first right to redeem Naomi's land. He refused to exercise his right of redemption, leaving Boaz free to act as the kinsman-redeemer.

So Boaz took Ruth and she became his wife; and when he went in to her, the LORD gave her conception, and she bore a son. Then the women said to Naomi, "Blessed be the LORD, who has not left you this day without a close relative; and may his name be famous in Israel! And may he be to you a restorer of life and a nourisher of your old age; for your daughter-in-law, who loves you, who is better to you than seven sons, has borne him." (Ruth 4:13–15)

Nowhere in all the Scriptures is there a more fitting picture of God's faithfulness. Naomi and Ruth were not spiritual giants. They were just ordinary people, yet God intervened on their behalf. They returned to Bethlehem totally destitute without anyone to rely on except the Lord. Nor did the Lord fail them. Ruth was now married to one of the most influential men in the city and was the mother of a handsome son. The family property had been redeemed, and Naomi was firmly ensconced in the honored position of grandmother.

Nor do these kinds of things only happen in the Bible. In fact God has a long history of restoring broken people. Take Carrie (the young lady who wrote the heartbreaking letter at the beginning of this chapter). After God gave her the promise of Psalm 71:20–21, she clung to it as if her life depended upon it. At first she thought it meant that the Lord was going to restore her marriage, and she prayed desperately to that end. But as the months passed and her estranged husband continued in his self-destructive lifestyle, she came to realize that what God had promised to restore was her life.

After weeks of agonizing soul-searching she decided to file for a divorce. Although she had clear, biblical grounds it was still a heartbreaking decision. Initially the divorce decree brought no relief, just a new kind of pain. It was all-consuming. It came at her from all sides. Sometimes she felt like a failure—if only she had tried harder, been more sensitive. Sometimes she felt like she had committed the unpardonable sin, like she would never be without shame again. And sometimes it felt like death. In fact it was a death—the death of her marriage. The death of her hopes and dreams. The death of what was and what could have been.

Then God intervened again. While attending a concert, Carrie just "happened" to run into an old friend from high school. On the surface it appeared to be nothing more than a chance encounter, but don't be fooled—this was no accident. He who orders the steps of the righteous (see Ps. 37:23) caused their paths to cross.

Though Carrie had not seen Kent in more than five years, they immediately hit it off. The next night they went to dinner and talked for hours. Though Carrie was distrustful at first, and afraid of being hurt again, over the next several weeks her feelings for Kent continued to grow. Here was a man who not only seemed to enjoy her company, but who also valued her opinions. He didn't try to tell her what to think or how to feel. Not once did he put her down or try to change her.

As the months passed they began spending more and more time together. Though Carrie had been married for more than five years, she had never felt this close to a man. Kent opened his heart to her, and she shared hers with him. Little by little she began to feel lovable again. *Maybe,* she thought, *just maybe there is life after divorce.*

Remember the four principles for "starting over" that we learned from Ruth and Naomi? First, you weather the storm. Second, you come to grips with the reality of your present circumstances. Then, you maintain hope in even the most despairing of times. And, finally, you pick up the pieces and start over.

Well, applying those same principles to Carrie, we can see that she has weathered the storm. She came to grips with the reality of her circumstances. She found a way to maintain hope even during the darkest of times, and she is now picking up the pieces and moving ahead. In a very interesting way, as you can see, she is now poised to either make good on her efforts or simply slide into a plateau of mundaneness. An interesting corollary now exists between Carrie, who is beginning to believe that God does have a better future for her than she dared imagine, and Ruth, who presumed to dream that through prostrating herself at the feet of Boaz she could have a brighter future than just the place of a preferred beggar in the fields.

Both Carrie and Ruth faced the ultimate test in starting over, and they both passed with flying colors. What is that test? Why, it is the test of vulnerability, is it not? To successfully start anew when we have ex- perienced "undeserved hurt" from others requires that we display ultimate faith in God by making ourselves available to His grace and redemption. For you see, God's redemption and grace in our daily lives is most often realized through those He brings closest to us—a new husband for Carrie and Ruth. How truly marvelous is the redemptive power of our God.

> To successfully start anew when we have experienced "undeserved hurt" from others requires that we display ultimate faith in God by making ourselves available to His grace and redemption.

Just a postscript for you to consider. Some months later Kent and Carrie were married in a small but elegant ceremony, and in a few weeks they will be celebrating their fifth anniversary. Carrie has never been happier. God has fulfilled His promise to her. He has restored her life. From the depths of despair, He raised her up. She is honored by her husband and secure in his love. Surely God has comforted her once again, just as He promised in His Word.

Chapter 10

THE ULTIMATE
LESSON

Now that we have reached the midpoint of this book, I find myself reflecting back on the people we have met, on the stories they have shared, and the lessons we have learned. People like Marc Buoniconti, Helen Roseveare, Barbra Russell, Jim and Dolly Gilbert, Maria, José, Carrie, and others. They come from all walks of life and from various parts of the country. Some are nationally known figures, but most are just ordinary people like you and me. They all have at least one thing in common—with God's help they have overcome the worst life could throw at them. There is much we can learn from them, but if it were reduced to a single axiom I believe it would be this: *Have faith in God.*

While serving as a medical missionary to the Belgian Congo (now Zaire) in the mid-sixties, Helen Roseveare begin reading *Foxe's Book of Martyrs.* Given the political climate at the time, it seemed a prudent thing to do. Fearing she might one day be required to lay down her life for her faith, she hoped it might encourage her. Unfortunately it had just the opposite effect. It made her sick. After reading it she was so agitated that she couldn't sleep at night. Finally she put the book away, concluding that she wasn't made of the stuff of martyrs. Clearly she remembers thinking, "If God should ever ask me to be burned at the stake I will do it, but I sure won't be singing."

Six months later she was one of seven missionaries standing before a firing squad of rebel soldiers. "They were ordered to take aim," she said, "and we were singing our savior's praises." Thankfully Dr. Roseveare's life was spared, and she has been used by God to inspire hundreds of new missionaries.[1]

What, you may be wondering, happened during the ensuing six months to change her? Nothing. But when the moment of need came, the God in whom she placed her faith was sufficient. It was not her faith that sustained her, but *God* in whom she placed her faith!

There is no formula for overcoming trouble, no pat answers for surviving the storms of life. There are some helpful principles to be sure. Important things to remember: be prepared, ask for help, persevere, and focus on God, not your problems. Still, if you put all of those principles together and shake them down, you will end up with one undergirding truth: *Have faith in God!*

As long as we have faith in God we can face anything. We can overcome any trouble. We can survive any storm. Consider the example of those who have gone before us.

> Who through faith subdued kingdoms, worked righteousness, obtained promises, stopped the mouths of lions, quenched the violence of fire, escaped the edge of the sword, out of weakness were made strong, became valiant in battle, turned to flight the armies of the aliens. Women received their dead raised to life again.
>
> Others were tortured, not accepting deliverance, that they might obtain a better resurrection. Still others had trial of mockings and scourgings, yes, and of chains and imprisonment. They were stoned, they were sawn in two, were tempted, were slain with the sword. They wandered about in sheepskins and goatskins, being destitute, afflicted, tormented—of whom the world was not worthy. They wandered in deserts and mountains, in dens and caves of the earth. (Heb. 11:33–38)

Unfortunately, trouble tempts us to doubt the character of God. It reminds us of all the pain and disappointment we have suffered in the course of our lives. Like an underground stream, silently cutting its way through the subterranean strata, it erodes our confidence in the Lord. So slowly, so silently, does it wear on us that we will likely not even be aware of it. Then one day we awake to discover, much to our dismay, that we no longer trust God. Somewhere among the long days of pain and disappointment we have lost our faith in God's goodness. We still trust Him for our salvation, but we are no longer confident that He will take care of the lesser matters.

That is how it often happens, but it is not inevitable. If we know in advance what to expect we can take steps to reinforce our faith. Even as concrete sea walls are erected to prevent the erosion of the shoreline, so can we construct barriers to protect ourselves from the ravages of trouble and disappointment. The first line of defense is an unwavering faith in the goodness of God. It must be built on nothing less than the infallible Scriptures.

Have Faith in God's Goodness

We can be sure God is good because Jesus gives Him an irreproachable character reference. The One who knows Him best tells us He is good, so good in fact, that in comparison to Him no one else can be considered good at all—not even Mother Teresa or Billy Graham.

> Now behold, one came and said to Him, "Good Teacher, what good thing shall I do that I may have eternal life?"
>
> So He [Jesus] said to him, "Why do you call Me good? *No one is good but One, that is, God.*" (Matt. 19:16–17, emphasis mine)

The Scriptures identify God as our heavenly Father, a fact that gives me no little comfort. Being a father myself I know the feelings a father has for his children. Nothing pains me more than seeing my daughter suffer, nor does anything bless me more than her happiness. Whatever touches her touches me. If I, a mere mortal, have these kinds of feelings for my daughter then I can only imagine how much more Father God cares for His children. "As a father pities his children, / So the LORD pities those who fear Him" (Ps. 103:13).

I am especially sensitive to this truth at the present time because my daughter is going through a difficult season in her life. She has suffered with chronic to severe TMJ for nearly five years. This is an especially painful condition caused when the jaw is improperly aligned or when the cartilage slips out of place, leaving the bones in the jaw joint to grate bone on bone. When this type of condition occurs in the knee the treatment of choice is knee replacement surgery.

Following her first onslaught of TMJ, Leah was fitted with a mouth splint designed to move the jaw back into alignment. In addition she had a saline solution and steroids injected directly into the jaw joint on two occasions. This is an extremely painful procedure and can only be done under anesthetic. While she did experience some temporary relief she was never free from pain.

In response to our prayers, God gave Leah a healing touch in the fall of 1995 and her jaw "popped" back into alignment. It was not a complete healing, as she continued to experience discomfort and sometimes fairly severe pain in her jaw, especially if she was under stress. Talking and singing continued to cause her pain, but nothing like it was before the Lord touched her.

In January of this year Leah was involved in an automobile accident in which she was hit from the back. Of course she suffered whiplash and the resulting trauma to her neck, back, and shoulders. In addition she noticed an increased sensitivity in her jaw, but thought nothing of it, considering her other injuries. In the months since the accident her jaw has caused her increasing discomfort, complicated, no doubt, by the fact that her job requires her to talk almost nonstop, eight hours a day. About ten days ago Leah yawned and something popped in her jaw, leaving her in excruciating pain. Since that time she has been unable to eat solid foods. She is now taking heavy doses of prescription pain medication plus a strong muscle relaxant to combat the pain.

Leah's problem is complex. She can no longer do her job because it involves talking on the telephone almost constantly. Unfortunately her company does not provide paid sick leave. Nor is the medical prognosis encouraging. There are really only two options: (1) Repeat the earlier procedures—i.e., mouth splint and steroid injections—though they were relatively ineffective. The dentists acknowledge that this is not a cure, but it could provide some relief from the extreme pain, at least temporarily.

(2) Undergo surgery, which has a less than 50 percent success rate. About half the time it does not correct the problem nor relieve the symptoms. On top of all of this is the insurance problem. No medical insurance policy covers TMJ. Although Leah's husband works for a good company with major medical benefits, treatment for TMJ problems are excluded. When Leah considered surgery four years ago the cost was in the $15,000 range. Who knows what it will cost now.

No matter what I am doing, Leah's situation is never far from my mind. When I lie in bed at night awaiting sleep, my mind is searching for solutions. My first thought upon waking in the morning is a prayer for her. When I pray, her needs take precedence over almost everything else. I am her father, and I am touched by the feelings of her infirmities. What hurts her hurts me. Her pain is my pain.

Is not my concern for Leah but a dim reflection of the Father's concern for His own? Isn't this what He is talking about when He says, "Can a woman forget her nursing child, / And not have compassion on the son of her womb? / Surely they may forget, / *Yet I will not forget you.* / See, I have inscribed you on the palms of My hands" (Isa. 49:15–16, emphasis mine).

It is nearly inconceivable that a nursing mother could forget the child at her breast, after all she went to the very doorway of death to bring that new life into the world. That tiny bundle of humanity, so fragile, so dependent, is flesh of her flesh. Surely nothing short of death itself could make her forget him. Yet in extreme cases mothers have been known to forsake their children. It is unnatural. It goes against everything that a mother is. Still it does happen.

But Father God could never forget one of His own. He has made us a part of Himself. We are engraved on the palms of His hands. As Matthew Henry notes, "God's compassions to His people infinitely exceed those of the tenderest parents towards their children. What are the affections of nature to those of the God of nature!"

Or as Jesus said,

What man is there among you who, if his son asks for bread, will give him a stone? Or if he asks for a fish, will he give him a serpent? If you then, being evil, know how to give good gifts to your children, *how much more will your Father who is in heaven give good things to those who ask Him*! (Matt. 7:9–11, emphasis mine)

Again He said,

And do not seek what you should eat or what you should drink, nor have an anxious mind. For all these things the nations of the world seek after, and *your Father knows that you need these things.* But seek the kingdom of God, and all these things shall be added to you.

Do not fear, little flock, for *it is your Father's good pleasure to give you the kingdom.* (Luke 12:29–32, emphasis mine)

In addition to the testimony of Jesus and the witness of Scripture, Father God reinforces our faith in His goodness in other ways. Sometimes He surprises us with an epiphany. I had such an experience a few weeks ago while attending church with my daughter and her husband. We had arrived early in order to get a seat near the front. As I was sitting quietly, waiting for worship to begin, the lady seated beside me introduced herself. I responded in kind. Upon hearing my name she became visibly excited. And then this is the story she told me.

"Thirteen years ago," she said, "God used you to save my life!"

I must have looked baffled because she reached over and patted me on the arm before continuing. "My husband was a mean man, cruel and abusive. It gave him great pleasure to cause me pain. He fed on my fear. I wanted to leave him, but I couldn't. I felt trapped.

"According to my pastor, God required me to stay with my husband no matter what he did. Though my pastor saw my bruises and undoubtedly sensed my fear, he did nothing but tell me to read and obey 1 Corinthians 7:13: 'And a woman who has a husband who does not believe, if he is willing to live with her, let her not divorce him.'

"As far as my pastor was concerned I had no choice in the matter. He had me convinced that if I divorced my husband I would be sinning against God. Though I was dying a little every day, I couldn't risk God's disapproval, not in the state of mind I was in."

By now she had my attention, and I was listening intently for some clue as to the role I had played.

"One Sunday night," she said, "I locked myself in the bathroom and turned on the radio. The sounds of 'Straight from the Heart' with Richard Exley filled the room. That night you were doing a program on domestic violence. Over and over I found myself weeping with the women who called. Their situations sounded so much like my own. I was tempted to call, but I couldn't risk leaving the bathroom, so I just listened.

"Not once did you refer to 1 Corinthians 7:13, but you did talk about the biblical grounds for divorce. I don't remember everything you said, but I do know that you said God does not require us to stay with a spouse who is physically abusive. By the time you finished I had made my decision. When morning came I was leaving.

"Shutting off the radio, I tiptoed out of the bathroom toward the bedroom. I didn't dare wake my husband who had fallen into a drunken stupor on the couch. With freedom this close, I couldn't risk another beating. Thankfully he never stirred from the couch all night. As soon as he left for work the next morning I packed a few things and moved out. If I hadn't left when I did, I'm sure I would be dead."

Giving my hand a final squeeze, she turned toward the chancel as the pastor called us to worship. Standing beside her I found myself marveling at the goodness of God. With more than two thousand worshipers present, what were the chances that I would sit beside the one woman whose life the Lord had allowed me to touch in a profound way? My brother Bob has a name for moments like that: he calls them "postcards from heaven."

Have Faith in God's Sufficiency

It is comforting to think of God as our heavenly Father, good and merciful, gracious and kind, but it is not enough. Given the troubles we face we need not only a heavenly Father who cares, but One who also has the power to do something about our situation. Not infrequently our troubles are so deep that apart from a divine intervention we have no hope of recovery. Thankfully our heavenly Father is not just good, He's great! He is capable of delivering us from all of our troubles. From our human perspective our situation may seem hopeless, but "with God all things are possible" (Mark 10:27).

What would you do if your husband of nearly twenty-seven years told you he wanted a divorce? Suppose he went on to say that he did not love you and in fact had never loved you. Imagine that he admitted to a three-year affair with one of your friends, whom he intends to marry as soon as his divorce from you is final. Suppose he ordered you and your seventeen-year-old daughter to move out of the house that very day.

That is exactly what happened to Martha. What did she do? She threw herself on the mercies of God. Like David of old, she said, "My soul finds rest in God alone; / my salvation comes from him. / He alone is my rock and my salvation; / he is my fortress, I will never be shaken . . . / Trust in him at all times, O people; / pour out your hearts to him, / for God is our refuge" (Ps. 62:1–2, 8 NIV).

Though her world was falling apart, she experienced a kind of relief. For three years she had known something was going on, but her husband had denied it. It was her imagination, he said. Her illness was making her paranoid. She was jealous. She didn't trust him. The stress was unbearable, causing her lupus to flare up. She wondered if she was losing her mind. Now at last she was vindicated—it hadn't been her imagination.

The weeks immediately following their separation were filled with terrible pain and desperate hope. Bit by bit the details of her husband's deceit came out. The scope of his sin was much greater than she had imagined. Still, she was ready to forgive him, ready to rebuild their marriage. God could restore their love, of that she was sure. But her husband would have none of it. His words were biting and cruel. It was all her fault. She was responsible for destroying the marriage, such as it was. He could not imagine living with her under any circumstances. Little by little her hope faded, then died. The divorce was granted. Her marriage was over.

Did God fail her? Was her faith in His sufficiency misplaced? No. Though God is all-powerful, He will not violate our human will. If we are determined to destroy ourselves and those who love us, He will not override our will. He will deal with us, be it ever so severely, in an attempt to bring us to our senses, but in the end the choice is ours. God did not fail her, but her husband did. He broke faith with her. He sinned against their marriage. He divorced her.

Now, nearly five years later, Brenda and I were sitting with Martha in the sunlit breakfast nook at her home in Durango, Colorado. As we listened she recounted the saga of God's faithfulness. "During those dark days immediately following my divorce, the Word of God was my only hope. With only a high school education and limited secretarial skills, my chances of landing a decent job were not good. When you throw in my age—forty-four—and my poor health, things really looked grim. I was suddenly poor, a single parent, with little hope for brighter days ahead.

"Not only was I dealing with my own grief, but I was trying to help my children deal with theirs. Night after night I had to listen to Jody cry herself to sleep. She had idolized her father, and his actions had left her devastated. It was bad enough that Roger should do this to me, but how could he do it to the children?

"The only way I could go to sleep at night was to listen to the Bible on cassette tape. I literally filled my mind with the Word of God. It became my meat night and day. One of the passages that spoke most clearly to me comes from Isaiah 54."

Picking up her Bible, she opened it and began to read, beginning with verse 4:

"Do not be afraid; you will not suffer shame.
    Do not fear disgrace; you will not be humiliated.
You will forget the shame of your youth
    and remember no more the reproach of your widowhood.
For your Maker is your husband—
    the LORD Almighty is his name—
the Holy One of Israel is your Redeemer;
    he is called the God of all the earth.
The LORD will call you back
    as if you were a wife deserted
        and distressed in spirit—
a wife who married young,
    only to be rejected," says your God.

For a brief moment I abandoned you,
  but with deep compassion I will bring you back. (Isa. 54:4–7 NIV)

Pushing her Bible across the table toward Brenda and me she said, "Look at verse 5: 'For your Maker is your husband—.'

"That verse was particularly comforting to me because Jody was planning to be married in just a few weeks, and I had no way to pay for the wedding. If God was truly my husband then He would provide. With that promise in mind we planned the wedding as if we had the money in the bank. Nothing elaborate, mind you. In fact our plans were rather modest; still, they were beyond our means.

"One Saturday morning Jody and I went to a sidewalk sale. While we were browsing through the sale racks, in search of a bargain we could afford, she spied a bridal shop. In an instant she lost all interest in the sidewalk sale. Now she had eyes only for one thing—bridal gowns.

"Turning to me she said excitedly, 'Can we just look Mom, can we?'

"I had to bite my tongue to keep from saying, 'Why torment yourself, honey? You know we can't afford a wedding gown.' Instead I smiled at her and said, 'Of course we can.'

"While she was looking at the gowns, I was fuming on the inside. Had it not been for Roger's pigheaded selfishness Jody could have had a bridal gown for her wedding.

"'Mom,' she called from across the shop, holding a dazzling gown up against her, 'can I try it on?'

"I smiled an answer, and she disappeared into the dressing room. A few minutes later she stepped out looking absolutely stunning. The gown looked like it had been made for her. The naked desire in her eyes made my heart hurt.

"I walked across the shop to stand beside her as she admired herself in the mirror. Trying to appear nonchalant, I reached for the price tag hanging from the sleeve. To my amazement it had been marked down from $700 to $100.

"*There must be some mistake,* I thought. I'd never heard of a bridal gown costing only a hundred dollars. Turning to the clerk I asked, 'Is this price correct?'

"'Yes it is,' she said.

"Nervously I began examining the gown more closely. Unable to spot any obvious flaws I asked, 'Why is it so inexpensive? Is there something wrong with it?'

"'It's what we call a model gown,' the clerk explained. 'We've used it in several style shows. We're now closing out that line and have no further use for it.'

"Without a moment's hesitation, I said, 'We'll take it,' luxuriating in the look of pure joy that flooded my daughter's face.

"While waiting for the clerk to ring it up, I made my way to a close-out table near the door where I discovered a matching veil for ten dollars. Although I only had $122 in my checking account, it was just enough. With tax, the total came to $118.80.

"If I live to be a hundred I don't think I will ever be as happy as I was that day! Though Roger had failed both Jody and me, our heavenly Father—my eternal husband—had provided."

We talked for a long time that morning, marveling at the way God had restored her life. Her health was better than it had been in years. According to the doctor her lupus was in full remission. She was remarried to a wonderful Christian man who was devoted to her. Financially she was more secure than she had ever been in her life.

Still, as I think about all God did for Martha I keep returning to that bridal gown. It wasn't the most significant thing He did, not by a long shot. In fact it's hardly worth mentioning when compared to either the physical or emotional healing He had worked in her life. Maybe its very insignificance is what makes it stand out to me. If God is concerned about a "little thing" like that, then surely He will not rest until He has taken care of the really big things that concern us.

Have Faith in God's Willingness

Believing that God is omnipotent—that He is all-powerful, that He can do all things—is easy enough for most of us. Believing that He cares takes considerably more faith, especially in light of the persistent suffering so evident in our world. It is harder still to believe that He is willing to intervene on *our* behalf. We know He has done it for others, but believing He will do it for us often seems just out of our reach.

Herein lies the tension in which we live. On the one hand we have the clear teaching of Scripture portraying God as an all-powerful heavenly Father who is anxious to intervene on behalf of His suffering children. On the other hand we are confronted with the reality of painful situations that seem immune to our most desperate prayers. If God genuinely cares, if He is truly touched by the feelings of our infirmities, then why doesn't He do something?

I'm caught in this very tension right now. With all my heart I believe that Father God loves my daughter Leah more than I do. As much as I am concerned about her TMJ problem, I believe that He is even more concerned. I care about her, but He cares more. Here's my problem: If God loves her so much, if He really cares about her, then why doesn't He do something? If I had the power I would heal her jaw and be done with it. As it is I am ready to do anything within my power to get her whatever medical treatment she needs. If I have to take a second mortgage on my house to pay for corrective surgery I will. Should it be necessary for me to supplement their monthly income until she can go back to work I will do that as well.

Since God loves her more than I do, since His resources are so much greater than mine, why does He do nothing while I scramble to do whatever I can? *Because He sees the big picture while I am focusing only on the immediate problem.* My concern is for Leah's immediate comfort and physical well-being. God is concerned with her character and eternal well-being. He loves her enough to let her suffer for a season, if need be, in order to fulfill His purposes in her life. Still, having said that, I have to admit that I cannot imagine what eternal purpose could possibly be served by Leah's TMJ.

As I grapple with such thoughts, I'm reminded of a young couple in our congregation who were expecting their first child. They wanted everything to be perfect and prayed accordingly. They prayed that the baby would have perfect health, a gentle disposition, and a spiritual aptitude. According to their theology, this should have assured them of a perfect child. Imagine their bewilderment when their newborn daughter cried incessantly. In addition to the obvious concern they had for her well-being, they were also tormented with self-doubt and questions regarding their faith.

Needless to say, all of this was more than they could bear. In desperation they came to see me. "Why," they demanded, "did God not answer our prayers? We prayed in faith. We did everything we were taught to do, so why didn't it work?"

The answers I could have given them might have technically answered their questions, but they would not have resolved the real issue. Consequently, I chose to simply assure them of God's love and faithfulness.

A few weeks later the doctor discovered that their baby had a hernia, and surgery was scheduled. The appointed day arrived, and I went to the hospital to be with them. Long before I located the parents I could hear the baby wailing. Her anguished cries echoed forlornly down the long hospital corridors. Turning a final corner, I saw the young mother nervously pacing the hallway trying to comfort her baby, while her husband looked on helplessly.

Approaching her I asked, "What seems to be the problem?"

"She's hungry," the distraught mother replied. "The doctor told us not to feed her after ten o'clock last night."

"Surely you're not going to let that stop you?" I asked with a straight face.

"What do you mean?" she asked, puzzled.

"Your baby is obviously hungry and not to feed her is terribly cruel."

She looked at me like I had lost my mind. Finally she said, "It's dangerous to have surgery on a full stomach, especially for a baby."

Without giving her a chance to finish I interrupted. "Well, at least explain that to her. She must think you are a sadist. You carry her in your arms next to your breast, but you won't feed her. As young as she is she knows you could feed her if you wanted to, if you really cared."

"Don't be silly," she said with forced calmness, "you can't explain something like this to a three-month-old baby."

Gently I said, "I know what you are doing is an act of love. I know you have your baby's best interest at heart. But she doesn't understand that, and you're right, there's no way you can explain it to her."

Understanding began to brighten her tense features, so I continued, "That's the way it is with God. He is too wise to ever make a mistake and too loving to ever cause one of His children needless pain. Still, He must sometimes risk our misunderstanding in order to do what's best for us. And we are simply too 'young,' too finite, to comprehend His infinite wisdom."

Like that young couple, you may be facing a crisis right now, and like them you may be asking why. You may even be tempted to rail at God about the apparent injustice of life, the unfairness of it all. Don't. That is just an exercise in futility. Instead, encourage yourself in the Lord (1 Sam. 30:6). Strengthen your faith by affirming your confidence in God's goodness, in His sufficiency, and in His willingness to do what is best for you. Accept the fact that in this life we only "see through a glass darkly . . . [we only] know in part" (1 Cor. 13:12 KJV). Do this, and God will grant you a supernatural peace that is based on trust rather than understanding.

> God must sometimes risk our misunderstanding in order to do what's best for us. And we are simply too "young," too finite, to comprehend His infinite wisdom.

Strength for the Storms We Bring on Ourselves

After living more than half a century, and having made more than my share of blunders, here are some of the lessons I have learned:

1. *Every action has a consequence—some good, some bad.* Some poor decisions lead to painful but temporary embarrassments, while others have permanent, life-altering consequences. Although God always stands ready to forgive our sinful mistakes, not even forgiveness can change the past.

2. *Every experience—good or bad—can be redeemed.* God has a long history of redeeming our failures, turning our worst blunders into opportunities for personal growth and spiritual development. Whatever your failures, you need not despair. With God's help you can overcome them.

3. *Every mistake can become a lesson learned.* What a thought! I can learn from this

tragic experience. It need not destroy me. This pain, this awful, unrelenting pain, can be made an ally. Yes, failure is a harsh teacher, but her very harshness sensitizes us to lessons we might otherwise never learn.

4. *God always forgives, but life doesn't.* Don't waste time on either bitterness or regret. Accept your situation and move on.

5. *God's grace is always greater than our sin.* The roll call of the redeemed is filled with scoundrels and con men, philanderers and prostitutes, drunks and derelicts, not to mention ordinary sinners like you and me.

Chapter 11

HOW COULD I HAVE
SEDUCED BATHSHEBA?

In all of Scripture only one man has ever been called a man after God's own heart (Acts 13:22). Not Enoch, who walked with God and "was not" because God took him (Gen. 5:24). Not Abraham, by whose name God chose to identify Himself (Ex. 3:15). Not Joseph, a man to whom God granted favor (Gen. 39:21). Not Moses, who talked with God face-to-face (Num. 12:8), nor Joshua, nor Samuel, nor Solomon, nor Elijah, nor even Daniel. The only man God ever called a man after His own heart was David the son of Jesse.

Although I am quite sure I do not fully comprehend what it means to be a man after God's own heart, I have no doubt it is the highest compliment a man can receive. No doubt David was deserving of it. He was, after all, one of the most spiritually sensitive men in all of Scripture. His psalms soar with insight. They throb with spiritual passion. To this day they are a source of strength and comfort to all who read them.

Of one thing I am sure, however; being a man after God's own heart does not mean that David was a perfect man. In fact the very hand that penned the best known of all psalms—"The LORD is my shepherd" (Ps. 23:1)—is the same hand that wrote the letter ordering the death of Uriah the Hittite, one of his loyal officers (2 Sam. 11:14–15). And the lips that continually praised the Lord (Ps. 34:1) also seduced Bathsheba, the wife of Uriah.

As a writer I have often wished that I could interview David. I would like to look him in the eye and ask him what went wrong, where he got off track. I would like to ask him how a man after God's own heart could do what he did, how he could stoop so low.

Of course that is not possible. David lived and died nearly three thousand years ago. To understand what happened—not just the actual events, but the underlying forces that motivated them—we will have to rely upon the Scriptures and whatever insight the Holy Spirit can give us into the heart of David the king.

With your permission I would like to recreate those fateful events through the experiences of David himself. Within the factual framework of Scripture, I will give my imagination free rein to create a first-person account as seen through David's eyes. As a knowledgeable reader, you will readily recognize where Scripture ends and imagination begins. Yet because I have made my creativity congruent with the facts, I believe you will also recognize the reality of this account.

Now let us turn our attention to "David: A Case Study in Self-Destruction." During his lifetime he weathered every kind of storm imaginable—the vicissitudes of life that come to us all, the trouble others bring—but nothing was as devastating as the trouble he brought upon himself and those he loved through his irresponsible and sinful choices.

Without Excuse

I am an old man without long to live. Though I have amassed both wealth and power, they cannot help me now. In the end death comes to all men, and I am no exception. I am not afraid to die, but I cannot say that I relish it either. Before I depart this world I would like to set the record straight concerning the great tragedy of my life. Lest I be misunderstood, let me say right up front that there is absolutely no excuse for what I did. The responsibility is totally mine. I made a series of sinful choices, each more serious than the last, setting in motion a chain of events that continue to this day. This, the worst of all the troubles in my long life, I brought on myself.

As I have already said, there is no excuse for what I did, no extenuating circumstances. There were reasons for my actions, to be sure, but they in no way excuse what I did. I will mention them only as a way of alerting you to the pressure they can bring to bear upon a man, a pressure few of us are prepared to handle.

Looking at me now, emaciated as I am, my old skin hanging like a poorly fitted garment over my stooped frame, you would never know that I was once a handsome man, but I was. In those days my shoulders were broad and my legs strong. Though I was nearing the midpoint in my life I had lost none of my strength. I was still a match for any man.

It was the time of the year when kings go forth to battle, but I decided to stay in Jerusalem (2 Sam. 11:1). Having risked my life on the battlefield more than any man I knew, I felt I deserved a break. Besides, Joab was a capable general. He could handle the campaign against the Ammonites, of that I was sure. Unfortunately I was ill-prepared to handle the temptations that came my way. I was a man of action with time on my hands, a warrior king who now took naps in the afternoon.

I was restless, bored. Having achieved more than I ever dreamed possible, I discovered I did not feel the way I thought I would feel. The self-doubts I had worked so hard to dispel were back with a vengeance. It seemed I always needed a new achievement, a fresh conquest to keep them at bay.

Whatever the case, I found myself pacing on the roof of the palace. Maybe I went there to enjoy the evening breeze or perhaps in search of inspiration for a new psalm. Who can remember after all these years? Anyway, out of the corner of my eye I caught sight of a woman bathing. Instantly I turned away, not wanting to invade her privacy. I should have returned to my chambers, but I walked to the other side of the roof instead.

Gazing across the valley below, as the evening sun washed the harshness out of the sky, I had eyes only for what I saw in my mind. Without consciously deciding to do so I found myself retracing my steps. A part of me hoped she had finished with her bath and was gone, while a more carnal part of me hungered for another glimpse of her beauty. Though I knew in my heart that what I was doing was wrong, I couldn't seem to help myself.

That night I could not sleep. Every time I closed my eyes I saw her. I willed myself to put her out of my mind, but the harder I tried the clearer her image became. By morning I was obsessed with her. I had to know who she was.

Much to my disappointment I learned that she was married, the wife of Uriah the Hittite, an officer in the Israelite army. I knew that what I was thinking, what I was feeling, was wrong. The commandment was clear: "You shall not covet your neighbor's wife" (Ex. 20:17). Still, I could not get her out of my mind.

Against my better judgment I sent a messenger to invite her to take dinner with me in my private chambers. Although I tried to convince myself that my intentions were honorable, I knew better. No matter how you rationalize it, it is never honorable to share a private dinner with another man's wife. Nor was that all I had in mind. Though I could not admit it to myself, in my heart of hearts I knew I was going to make love to her.

Once my passion had spent itself, I was sick with guilt. It is a terrible thing to discover you are not the man you thought you were. I had prided myself on being an honorable man, a man of integrity. Never had I cheated another man or taken something that did not belong to me. Now I could not bare to look at myself in the mirror. I was a purple hypocrite. At the core of my soul I was dead. Where once there burned a holy fire, now there were only ashes.

Just when I thought things could get no worse, the woman sent word to me telling me she was pregnant. Now I faced a serious dilemma. If I did nothing it would only be a matter of time until her pregnancy became public knowledge. Once Uriah learned of his wife's unfaithfulness he would take her outside the city gates and stone her. The commandment was clear. There were no exceptions: "If a man is found lying with a woman married to a husband, then both of them shall die—the man that lay with the woman, and the woman; so you shall put away the evil person from Israel . . . you shall bring them both out to the gate of that city, and you shall stone them to death with stones" (Deut. 22:22, 24).

Being king, I was obviously in no danger, but Bathsheba clearly was. Immediately I dispatched a messenger to Joab, ordering him to send Uriah to the palace. When he arrived I questioned him at length regarding the siege of Rabbah, then I sent him to his house with a gift of food. *Let him enjoy the comforts of his wife,* I thought, *and tomorrow I will send him back to Joab and all of our problems will be over.*

Awaking the following morning I felt better than I had in some days. On an impulse I climbed to the roof of the palace to enjoy the sunrise in solitude. Walking to the edge of the roof I looked down and spotted Uriah sleeping among the servants at the gate to the palace. To my dismay I learned that he had spent the night there.

When I questioned him about it he said, "The ark and Israel and Judah are dwelling in tents, and my lord Joab and the servants of my lord are encamped in the open fields. Shall I then go to my house to eat and drink, and to lie with my wife? As you live, and as your soul lives, I will not do this thing" (2 Sam. 11:11).

There was a time when I would have admired that kind of devoted service, but that time was long past. Now I saw it as nothing more than an obstacle to be overcome. I ordered him to remain in Jerusalem another day, and that night I invited him to dine at my table. Every time he sipped from his goblet of wine I nodded to the servant, who refilled it. By the time the meal was finished, Uriah was drunk, and I ordered two of my men to take him to his house.

Sleep did not come easy that night. Mostly I tossed and turned, tormented by thoughts too evil to put into words. I was up with the first hint of daylight, and, just as I feared, Uriah had not gone home. Once again he was sleeping on a mat among the servants.

He left me no choice. Returning to my chambers I dashed off a note to Joab, telling him to put Uriah at the front of the battle, where the fighting was the fiercest. I could have left it at that. Chances are that Uriah would have been killed, but I couldn't risk it. Taking a deep breath, I continued writing: "Retreat from him, that he may be struck down and die" (2 Sam. 11:15).

I despised myself for what I had done, but what choice did I have? It was his life or hers. Sealing the letter with my royal seal, I commanded a servant to take it to Uriah to be delivered to Joab. It seemed poetic justice to have Uriah deliver his own death sentence, seeing that his own obstinateness made his death mandatory. Had he been a less rigid man he might have lived a long and prosperous life.

Looking at it now I can see how twisted my thinking had become, but at the time I almost convinced myself that the fault was his and not mine.

Having started down sin's slippery slope the evening I first saw Bathsheba bathing, I now discovered there was no turning back. In short order, sin had taken me farther than I ever intended to go, and in the end it would cost me far more than I ever intended to pay.

A few days later I received a casualty report from General Joab in which he said, "Your servant Uriah the Hittite is dead also" (2 Sam. 11:21). I should have felt guilt, or at least grief, but all I felt was relief. After the time of mourning was over, I brought Bathsheba into the palace, and she became my wife. To this day I do not know if she realized the part I played in her husband's death. She did not ask nor did I tell her. Though we never talked about it, it lay between us like a piece of broken furniture in the soul of our relationship. Every time we tried to get close to each other, we bumped into it.

God Is Not Mocked

The months immediately following Uriah's death were some of the worst of my life. Try as I might, I could not get him out of my mind. My sleep was fitful, tormented, haunted by bloody dreams of battle. They were filled with smoke and fire, the clatter of armor, the clashing of swords, the grunts of straining warriors, the sorrowful groans of the dying. Then there was silence as still as death. A chill wind carried steamers of black smoke over the battlefield, cloaking it in gloom. Through the gathering darkness I saw Uriah. He was sorely wounded. In his eyes there was a look of startled surprise that gave way to disbelief as I watched. Just before he died he said, "No. Not you, my lord."

In those days I came to hate myself. I wore shame like a hair shirt. My heart hurt. I was filled with self-loathing. If you have ever lived a lie you know what I'm talking about. You despise yourself. Shame has made you sick. Fear eats at your belly. Depression dogs your days. You feel trapped, and you are tempted to run away, but where can you go to escape yourself? Thoughts of suicide tempt you, but fear of the eternal consequences stay your hand.

In those dark hours I penned some of my most tormented psalms:

My guilt has overwhelmed me
    like a burden too heavy to bear.
My wounds fester and are loathsome
    because of my sinful folly.
I am bowed down and brought very low;
    all day long I go about mourning.
My back is filled with searing pain;
    there is no health in my body.
I am feeble and utterly crushed;
    I groan in anguish of heart. (Ps. 38:4–8 NIV)

Then one day Nathan the prophet appeared at the palace. He requested a private audience with me, which I granted, of course, seeing he was my spiritual adviser. Besides, if I were to be called to account for my sins, I would rather it be done without an audience.

Upon entering my chambers, he immediately launched into an account of a civil dispute between a wealthy landowner and a poor man. As he talked I allowed myself to relax. Apparently the Lord had not sent him to confront me. The complaint he brought was hardly the kind of thing that required the king's attention, but since it was Nathan, I indulged him.

There were two men in one city, one rich and the other poor. The rich man had exceedingly many flocks and herds. But the poor man had nothing, except one little ewe lamb which he had bought and nourished; and it grew up together with him and with his children. It ate of his own food and drank from his own cup and lay in his bosom; and it was like a daughter to him. And a traveler came to the rich man, who refused to take from his own flock and from his own herd to prepare one for the wayfaring man who had come to him; but he took the poor man's lamb and prepared it for the man who had come to him. (2 Sam. 12:1–4)

As I listened I grew more and more angry. I simply could not abide that kind of behavior. If there was one thing I hated it was the abuse of power. Finally I stood to my feet and thundered, "As the LORD lives, the man who has done this shall surely die! And he shall restore fourfold for the lamb, because he did this thing and because he had no pity" (2 Sam. 12:5–6).

All the color drained out of Nathan's face, and a terrible sorrow filled his eyes. In a voice that was hardly more than a whisper he said, "You are the man!" (2 Sam. 12:7).

Shame, as black and deep as outer darkness, descended upon me, and I felt like I was smothering. I couldn't get my breath. It caught in my throat. Staggering backwards, I collapsed on the throne, fighting to breathe. As if from a great distance I heard Nathan's voice going on and on, his words like body blows driving me to my knees.

> Thus says the LORD God of Israel: "I anointed you king over Israel, and I delivered you from the hand of Saul. I gave you your master's house and your master's wives into your keeping, and gave you the house of Israel and Judah. And if that had been too little, I also would have given you much more! Why have you despised the commandment of the LORD, to do evil in His sight? You have killed Uriah the Hittite with the sword; you have taken his wife to be your wife, and have killed him with the sword of the people of Ammon. Now therefore, the sword shall never depart from your house, because you have despised Me, and have taken the wife of Uriah the Hittite to be your wife." Thus says the LORD: "Behold, I will raise up adversity against you from your own house; and I will take your wives before your eyes and give them to your neighbor, and he shall lie with your wives in the sight of this sun. For you did it secretly, but I will do this thing before all Israel, before the sun." (2 Sam. 12:7–12)

How vile my sin now seemed. How unspeakably degenerate, how foul. *So this is what I have become,* I thought, *an abuser of power, an adulterer, and a murderer.* With my face pressed to the floor, I gasped, "I have sinned against the LORD" (2 Sam. 12:13).

My awful pain must have touched my friend's heart, for he knelt beside me and put his hand upon my shoulder. In a voice filled with compassion, but terribly sad, he said, "The LORD also has put away your sin; you shall not die" (2 Sam. 12:13).

Getting to his feet he continued, his voice resounding with awesome finality: "However, because by this deed you have given great occasion to the enemies of the Lord to blaspheme, the child also who is born to you shall surely die" (2 Sam. 12:14).

Without another word he turned and left, his sandals echoing forlornly in the empty room. *Is this how King Saul felt,* I wondered, *when Samuel told him the Lord had torn the kingdom from him and given it to another?* (See 1 Sam. 15:26–29.) Suddenly I had a vision of Saul bereft of the Spirit of the Lord (1 Sam. 16:14). Is that how I would live out my days, abandoned by God, driven mad by evil spirits? *It would be better to die,* I thought, *than to live without His Spirit.*

From the depths of my soul I cried unto the Lord. My lips gave birth to broken sobs of confession:

Have mercy on me, O God,
    according to your unfailing love;
according to your great compassion
    blot out my transgressions.
Wash away all my iniquity
    and cleanse me from my sin.

For I know my transgressions,
    and my sin is always before me.
Against you, you only, have I sinned
    and done what is evil in your sight . . .

Hide your face from my sins
    and blot out all my iniquity.

Create in me a pure heart, O God,
    and renew a steadfast spirit within me.
Do not cast me from your presence
    or take your Holy Spirit from me. (Ps. 51:1–4, 9–11 NIV)

Suddenly there came a loud rapping on the door to my chamber. Getting to my feet, I tried to compose myself as best I could before calling, "Come in."

The door was opened and a distraught servant hastened into the room. Bowing, he said, "It is your son, my lord. He has taken deathly ill."

"Take me to him," I commanded.

As we hurried through the palace, Nathan's words were going over and over in my mind: "The LORD also has put away your sin; you shall not die. However, . . . the child also who is born to you shall surely die" (2 Sam. 12:13–14).

Entering Bathsheba's private quarters, I rushed into the child's room and threw myself facedown on the ground. For seven days and nights my son's body was wracked with terrible convulsions and raging fevers as he battled for his life. During that entire time I fasted and prayed, imploring the Lord for my son's life. But the Lord had spoken, and on the seventh day my son died.

What did I learn during those dark nights of painful intercession? I learned that God is not mocked and that the wages of sin is death. My son's death was my punishment, not his. He was taken from this vale of tears, spared the sorrow and suffering that is so often the lot of mankind. I had to live with the pain of his death, knowing that had it not been for my sin none of this would have happened. In the years to come I would wish a hundred times that I might have died in his place, for I was to suffer a judgment worse than death. God did not punish me; life did. By my willful disobedience and reckless sin I had set in motion forces that I could not reverse. Forces that would nearly destroy both my family and my kingdom.

Chapter 12

INTEGRITY: Doing the Right Thing
After You Have Done the Wrong Thing
Even When It Is the Hardest Thing

"We don't read the Bible," said Kierkegaard. "It reads us." And so it does, doesn't it? Reads us like an open book.

The Scriptures are not simply a revelation of God but of human nature as well. With uncanny accuracy they lay bare our deepest desires, our most real selves. Suddenly the temptation story is not just a narrative of Adam's fall. Now it's my story, and yours too, for who among us hasn't fallen prey to the beguiling lies of the tempter? And it is not just Adam and Eve's story either. I see something of myself in nearly every biblical account.

Jacob is a conniver, a manipulator; so am I. Moses loses his temper and makes a mess of things; me too. Elijah falls prey to depression; I've been there. Peter is impulsive; I can identify with that. On and on it goes, revealing human nature at its best and at its worst. Not just in the biographies either, but in the poetry and the parables as well, even the prophecies.

From my perspective no biography is more revealing than David's. It encompasses the whole gamut of human experience. In him, and in those who play supporting roles in his story, we see both the best and the worst of ourselves. Nowhere else are the consequences of one person's sin revealed in such tragic detail. Nor is there any place else in all of Scripture where the grace of God manifests itself with such persistent determination. David sinned, he sank to the depths of despair, but God would not let him go. He sinned greatly, but God's grace was greater still.

With these thoughts in mind let us return to "David: A Case Study in Self-destruction." As we examine his experience, let us not simply seek to understand how he could do what he did, but what it reveals about us as well. In this section we will pay particular attention to how David's sin affected the members of his own family and others who were close to him.

> As we examine David's experience, let us not simply seek to understand how he could do what he did, but what it reveals about us as well.

From his tragic experience may we realize afresh the tremendous power our actions have on others, both for good and evil.

Like Father, Like Son

Following the death of the baby born to Bathsheba and me, an uneasy calm settled upon the palace. Infant mortality rates were high in those days, and the death of a child was not uncommon. Still, everyone seemed to sense that this was no ordinary death. By now, rumors filled the palace and spilled over into the city. Though no one dared approach me directly, I would have had to be blind and deaf not to realize what was going on.

Therefore I was not surprised when Ahithophel, my long-time friend and wisest counselor, approached me. As was his custom he came directly to the point. "Tell me it isn't true," he said, his voice thick with feeling. "Tell me you didn't lie with my granddaughter. Tell me you didn't use your power as king to take advantage of her. Tell me you didn't arrange for the death of her husband."

His intense eyes bored into my own, daring me to lie even as they begged me to tell him it wasn't so. Though it was all I could do, I forced myself to meet his gaze. In that moment I saw myself as he saw me, and it wasn't a pretty sight. Sighing deeply, I said, "I only wish I could."

In his heart he must have already known, still hearing it from my lips removed all doubt. For a moment I thought he might strike me. Then something seemed to die inside of him. Without a word he turned and walked toward the door, leaking sorrow from every pore. When he reached the door he paused, then turned toward me one last time, his face full of anguish. "How could you?" he asked. "How could you?"

God knows I have asked myself that same question more times than I can count. How could I? How could I lie with my neighbor's wife and mock the commandment of my God? How could I order the death of her husband in a futile attempt to cover my own sin? How could I think I could get away with it? How could I . . . ?

I can only conclude that there is, in each of us, a nearly unlimited capacity for evil. Should we ever open the door to it, even just a crack, it is almost impossible to close it again.

Though my days assumed a normal routine, I was not fooled. My troubles were not over, of that I was sure. I knew it was just a matter of time until tragedy struck again. Unfortunately nothing in my experience prepared me for the form it would take.

Amnon, my firstborn son and heir apparent to the throne, was taken ill or so I was led to believe. Given my state of mind I could only imagine the worst. Rushing to his bedside I found him ailing, but not really sick. Relieved that he was in no immediate danger, I prepared to go. As I was leaving he said, "Father, may I ask you for a favor?"

"Certainly, my son."

"I would like my sister Tamar to come and make some special bread in my sight, so I may eat from her hand" (2 Sam. 13:6 NIV).

In retrospect it seemed an odd request, but I thought nothing of it at the time. Without a moment's hesitation I ordered Tamar to her brother's house, never realizing I was sending her to a fate worse than death. I don't know how I could have known what Amnon was planning; still, I cannot help feeling responsible for what happened.

It pains me to admit that I did not learn of the incident until several days after it happened. When rumors of the thing finally reached my ears, I went immediately to the home of Absalom, Tamar's brother, where she was living. At the sight of her I thought my heart would break. She had hacked off her beautiful hair, her face was empty, her eyes dead. That was all the proof I needed. She had suffered a wound from which she would never recover, of that I was sure.

Once we were alone, Absalom gave me the details, in terse sentences, punctuated by short bursts of anger. "Amnon took advantage of her," he said. "Being stronger than she was, he had his way with her. Then he threw her out. Though she begged him to marry her and remove her shame, he refused. Instead he ordered his servant to drag her out of the house and bolt the door."

Leaving Absalom, I hastened to the house of my firstborn son. When I confronted him he became angry. Turning on me with thinly disguised contempt, he said, "How dare you talk to me about morals! You of all people. Do you really think no one knows about you and Uriah's wife? How low can a man sink? While Uriah is on the battlefield risking his life for you, you're bedding his wife. And then there's the disgusting spectacle you put on when your love child died. You not only made a fool of yourself, but of all of us as well."

Turning on his heel, Amnon stormed out of the room, leaving me stunned by the force of his anger. Then the weight of his words hit me. He was only doing what he had seen me do. As far as he was concerned the way he had used Tamar was no different from the way I had treated Bathsheba. Nor could I correct him. By my sin I had forfeited all moral authority. I could speak, but my words would carry no weight as far as he was concerned.

Unable to sleep, I paced the floor of the palace in the lonely night watches, ruminating on my failures. God had forgiven me, of that I was sure. "As far as the east is from the west, / So far has He removed our transgressions from us" (Ps. 103:12). Nonetheless I was finding it difficult to forgive myself. I had sown to the wind, and my family was reaping the whirlwind. Amnon was a willful man, lustful and bitter. Tamar was a desolate woman, doomed to live out her days in the house of her brother, never to know the joy of marriage or a family of her own. And it was my fault. All my fault.

The Wages of Sin Is Death

For two years life in the palace assumed a fairly normal routine. Bathsheba gave birth to our second child, another son whom we named Solomon.

Later God sent word through Nathan the prophet telling us to name him Jedidiah, which literally means "Beloved of the Lord." That was a real encouragement to both of us, but the words of judgment were never far from my mind: "This is what the LORD says: 'Out of your own household I am going to bring calamity upon you'" (2 Sam. 12:11 NIV).

When tragedy finally struck it wore a frighteningly familiar face. As Amnon had taken my lust to a new level in dealing treacherously with Tamar, so did Absalom take another of my faults and refine it. Watching my sons destroy themselves was in many ways like reliving my own sins. By my sin I had not only opened a door to the evil within, but I had also given the enemy a foothold in my family.

From the moment Absalom learned of his sister's disgrace he began plotting his revenge (2 Sam. 13:22). As cleverly as ever I plotted Uriah's death, so did he plan his brother's murder. When the time finally arrived he sprang the trap with consummate skill. At a banquet to celebrate the annual shearing of sheep in Baal Hazor near Ephraim, a cadre of his hand-picked men murdered Amnon. They waited until he was well on his way to being drunk, then at Absalom's signal, they killed him (2 Sam 13:28–29).

The first report I received said all my sons had been killed and not one of them was left alive except the murderer himself (2 Sam. 13:30). It was the worst possible news. Tearing my kingly robes I flung myself face-down on the ground. "Oh, Lord," I cried, "my punishment is more than I can bear!"

Later I learned that only Amnon had perished. Although I was relieved to discover that my other sons were alive, that information did little to mitigate my grief over Amnon's death. He was my firstborn, the heir apparent to the throne. From the day I became king I had groomed him to be my successor, and now he was dead. Like Jacob of old, my children were bringing my gray hair down to the grave in sorrow (see Gen. 44:29).

In a single day I lost my two most promising sons: Amnon who died at the hand of his brother, and Absalom who killed him. Fearing for his life, Absalom had fled to Geshur where he lived with his grandfather the king. For the next three years there was not a single day when I did not grieve for them both (2 Sam. 13:37–38). As time passed I found myself yearning more and more to be reconciled with my son. Unfortunately, I saw no way for that to be accomplished unless he threw himself on my mercy, a highly unlikely possibility given his stubborn pride.

This painful impasse was finally broken when General Joab intervened on behalf of the young man. Even then I found myself torn by conflicting emotions. I loved Absalom as I loved myself, yet I couldn't just ignore the terrible thing he had done. The law demanded an eye for an eye. Yet who was I to execute justice? My hands too were covered with blood—Uriah's blood. In many ways what Absalom did was far less odious than my own sin. I had Uriah killed to protect myself. He murdered Amnon to avenge his sister.

Finally I found a compromise I could live with. Absalom could return to Jerusalem without fear of prosecution, but he could not see my face. He would not be allowed in the palace. He would have to live in his own house. As I think about it now I am not sure whom I was punishing—him or me. I know I suffered at least as much as he did. Without a doubt I deserved it more.

The Final Chapter

Little did I realize that the worst was yet to come. In my darkest imaginings I could never have conceived of the pain and sorrow that lay ahead. Even now, these many years later, the memories are so painful that I can hardly speak of them. But speak of them I must. How else will you know the terrible things we bring on ourselves and those we love?

The memories I have of that dreadful time are fragmented and disjointed. If it is a coherent account you want, given in chronological detail, I cannot help you. My recollections are like jagged pieces of glass, sharp and piercing, but disconnected one from the other.

In the first I am fleeing from Jerusalem with my entire household. Absalom my son has incited a rebellion, and he is marching on the city with a great army. As I ascend the Mount of Olives, I am weeping. My head is covered. I am barefoot, and my feet are bleeding. *So this is what it has come to,* I remember thinking. *Father against son. Brother against brother. Friend against friend. And it is all my doing.*

Over and over again I heard the words of the prophet: "You struck down Uriah the Hittite with the sword and took his wife to be your own . . . Now, therefore, the sword will never depart from your house . . . This is what the LORD says: 'Out of your own household I am going to bring calamity upon you'" (2 Sam. 12:9–11 NIV).

The roadside was lined with loyal citizens. As we fled they were weeping, their tears mingling with our own. Runners continued to bring me reports on the progress of the rebellion. By now Absalom had entered the city and taken possession of the palace. Another runner arrived and informed me that Ahithophel, my former friend and counselor, was with Absalom. At this news a sense of doom settled upon me. Absalom was clever, but he was not wise. Left to his own devices he would likely self-destruct and bring the rebellion down with him, but that would not happen if he heeded the counsel of Ahithophel whose advice was "as if one had inquired at the oracle of God" (2 Sam. 16:23).

Suddenly I was assailed with a host of bittersweet memories. Ahithophel and I were taking sweet counsel together, we were walking to the house of God in company. Then we were sharing a meal, breaking bread together. The memories were nearly more than I could bear. In the agony of my soul I cried, "Oh Lord, if an enemy were reproaching me I could bear it. But it's not an enemy. It's my own familiar friend in whom I trusted—my companion, my acquaintance. He has lifted up his heel against me."

Another memory superimposes itself on the first. It is morning, and the sky is a soft blue above the muted colors of the city. Absalom is standing on the roof of the palace, silhouetted against the burnt orange streaks that now lay like bright bars above the horizon. Behind him is a cluster of shamefaced women huddled near a tent. His heavy hair is blowing in the wind, and in a rich voice he addresses the throng who have gathered in the streets below.

"I stand before you this day as a fulfillment of the judgment that Nathan the prophet pronounced against my father, David, when he sinned against God by laying with the wife of Uriah the Hittite. On the day he confronted the king, Nathan prophesied:

'Thus says the Lord: "Behold, I will raise up adversity against you from your own house; and I will take your wives before your eyes and give them to your neighbor, and he shall lie with your wives in the sight of this sun. For you did it secretly, but I will do this thing before all Israel, before the sun"'"(2 Sam. 12:11–12).   •

With that he turns toward the women who cower before him. Taking one by the arm he draggs her into the tent. For a moment there was stunned silence from the watching throng, then a single voice shouts, "Long live the king!" He repeats it, and his voice is joined by another, and then another, until the whole crowd is shouting, "Long live the king!"

That was not Absalom's doing, of that I am sure. He had no stomach for that sort of thing. Sexual abuse of any kind was abhorrent to him. It reminded him too much of what his sister suffered at the hands of Amnon.

That barbaric act reeked of Ahithophel. Hatred and bitterness had made him mad. He would stop at nothing to destroy me, never mind who got chewed up in the process.

Another memory breaks loose from the dark mass and floats toward the surface of my mind. In it we are approaching Bahurim, where a man named Shimei, the son of Gera, comes out to meet us. As we draw near he begins to curse and hurl stones at me.

> You bloodthirsty man, you rogue! The LORD has brought upon you all the blood of the house of Saul, in whose place you have reigned; and the LORD has delivered the kingdom into the hand of Absalom your son. So now you are caught in your own evil, because you are a bloodthirsty man! (2 Sam. 16:7–8)

Some of my loyal officers were incensed and wanted to kill him but I stayed their hands. As far as I was concerned there was nothing he could say to me that I had not already said to myself, no curse that he could call down on me that I had not called down on myself. Who knows, he may have been the instrument of God for my chastisement. God knows I deserved whatever judgment befell me. Besides, what were a few stones when my own son who came from my body sought my life?

Finally there comes the darkest memory of them all, the one I could never put to rest no matter how hard I tried. I am sitting between the two gates of the walled city of Mahanaim on the far side of the Jordan. All day my armies have fought a running battle with the forces of Absalom in the woods of Ephraim. Then late in the afternoon I see a runner approaching. Though I long for news of the battle, my first concern is for Absalom. If something has happened to him, the kingdom will mean nothing to me.

The runner is an African slave, a Cushite, and as he draws near he calls out, "There is good news, my lord the king! For the LORD has avenged you this day of all those who rose against you" (2 Sam. 18:31).

Perhaps I should have felt a sense of triumph, but I didn't. No matter what happened that day there would be no joy for me. Even if I regained the kingdom I would still lose, for in order to do so I would have to destroy my own son.

A painful heaviness filled my chest then, while my heart beat a slow rhythm in my ears. Trying to keep the fear out of my voice, I asked, "Is the young man Absalom safe?"

Gasping for breath the Cushite replied, "May the enemies of my lord the king, and all who rise against you to do you harm, be like that young man!" (2 Sam. 18:32).

All the pain I had suffered until now was as nothing compared to this. Sorrow took me to a place I had never been—a wasteland so desolate it made the valley of the shadow of death seem like the Garden of Eden. This was the land of the dead and everywhere I turned I was confronted with death. My newborn son was there, his tiny body forever frozen in the throes of a final convulsion. And Jonathan, my one true friend, whose love to me was wonderful, surpassing the love of women.

It was too much, I could not bear it, I had to escape that dreadful place. Staggering to my feet, I lunged toward the stairs leading to the chamber over the gate. Someone reached out a hand to comfort me, but I slapped it away. My son was dead, and I would not be comforted.

Staggering up the stairs, I heard myself wailing, "O my son Absalom— my son, my son Absalom—if only I had died in your place! O Absalom my son, my son!" (2 Sam. 18:33).

Once again I found myself in the wasteland of sorrow, surrounded by the dead. Amnon was there, the shock of death painted on his face like a tragic mask. Turning away, I saw the body of a man hanging from a rafter.

I watched it slowly rotate until I saw the face of Ahithophel, grotesque in death.

Those were my accusers. Their blood was upon my hands, and now I had to give an account to them for the things I had done. Had it not been for me, for my sins, they would all likely still be alive. When I was sure that I could bear no more I found myself staring in horror at the body of Absalom my son. His handsome body, limp in death, hung from a tree, an arrow protruding from his chest.

As if from a great distance, I hear a voice screaming. Though I cannot make out the words there is no denying their pain. I will myself not to hear, but there is no escaping that haunting cry. In the gathering darkness it echoes with the torments of the damned. Only later did I realize the voice was mine, the voice of one crying in the wasteland of sorrow, a place where I am ever dying but never dead.

The Mercies of the Lord

Thankfully David's story does not end here. Through the mercies of God his sins were forgiven, and his kingdom was restored. Hear him as he praised the Lord for all His goodness:

> Bless the LORD, O my soul;
> And all that is within me, bless His holy name!
> Bless the LORD, O my soul,
> And forget not all His benefits:
> Who forgives all your iniquities,
> Who heals all your diseases,
> Who redeems your life from destruction,
> Who crowns you with lovingkindness and tender mercies,
> Who satisfies your mouth with good things,
> So that your youth is renewed like the eagle's . . .
>
> The LORD is merciful and gracious,
> Slow to anger, and abounding in mercy.

He will not always strive with us,
Nor will He keep His anger forever.
He has not dealt with us according to our sins,
Nor punished us according to our iniquities.

For as the heavens are high above the earth,
So great is His mercy toward those who fear Him;
As far as the east is from the west,
So far has He removed our transgressions from us.
As a father pities his children,
So the LORD pities those who fear Him.
For He knows our frame;
He remembers that we are dust.

As for man, his days are like grass;
As a flower of the field, so he flourishes.
For the wind passes over it, and it is gone,
And its place remembers it no more.
But the mercy of the LORD is from everlasting to everlasting
On those who fear Him,
And His righteousness to children's children,
To such as keep His covenant,
And to those who remember His commandments to do them . . .

Bless the LORD, O my soul! (Ps. 103:1–5,8–18, 22)

We began this study on David by pointing out that he was called a man after God's own heart (see Acts 13:22). As we have learned, that obviously did not mean he was a perfect man, for he was the farthest thing from it. The fact that he could sin so terribly and still be loved by God should be an encouragement to each of us. By the same token, the reality of the terrible consequences that accompanied his sins should serve as a deterrent to all who are tempted.

Unlike so many who self-destruct, David never tried to put the blame on anyone else. When confronted with his sins, he never failed to take responsibility for his actions. Hear him as he prayed, "For I acknowledge my transgressions, and my sin is always before me" (Ps. 51:3). Because he took responsibility for his sins, God was able to forgive him. "If we confess our sins, He is faithful and just to forgive us our sins and to cleanse us from all unrighteousness" (1 John 1:9).

I have a pastor friend who defines integrity as doing the right thing after you have done the wrong thing even when it is the hardest thing. Perhaps that, more than any other single thing, is what makes David one of the most beloved characters in all of Scripture

> Integrity is doing the right thing after you have done the wrong thing even when it is the hardest thing.

and a man after God's own heart. Perhaps that is why he was able to survive the storms he brought upon himself and those he loved.

Chapter 13

TAKING RESPONSIBILITY FOR YOUR ACTIONS

Although David repented of his sin and received forgiveness, there was no way he could go back and undo the damage he had done. Uriah was dead; he would not live again. Bathsheba had been unfaithful to her husband, and that could not be undone. By his sin David set in motion a chain of events that caused himself and those he loved unspeakable suffering.

All of our actions have consequences; every mistake we make has a price. Some mistakes lead to painful but temporary embarrassments, while others produce consequences that alter a person's life from that point on. My brother Bob's decision, at the age of nineteen, to marry a girl he hardly knew was such a choice. It had a domino effect in his life: he was a father at twenty years of age, divorced by the time he was twenty-two, and divorced a second time when he was twenty-seven. That one decision changed the entire course of his life.

Nor did it affect only him. He writes,

> The consequences of this choice are far-reaching. They are being lived out through the life of my oldest son even as I write this. He struggles with being a young father of three children. Two of his children live with his first wife who is married for the second time. He too made a permanent life-altering choice that only he is responsible for, and yet, I suffer the consequences of his choice with him. I feel equally responsible. I also know that my parents struggle with feeling responsible for my poor choices.

They too, at times, fervently wish that they would have been more forceful in voicing their concerns.

For a long time, I blamed my parents for my failed first marriage, and in a strange but logical way, I also blamed them for the subsequent trouble that came into my life. Oh, I didn't say that to them or even voice it out loud at all, but, just the same, it was what I believed in my heart of hearts.

Heart of hearts, what an interesting term. In its simplest sense, one could define heart of hearts as the hidden but most true of our thoughts, feelings, and motives. It is that area of one's self where we rarely, if ever, allow others to visit. In fact, many of us refuse to even look candidly into this dark corner of our souls. Yet, if I am to honestly accept responsibility for my own choices, I must have the courage to peer into this forbidden zone.

Back to my tendency to blame my parents for the troubles in my life. You see, to my way of thinking, if my parents had been more firm in how they raised me, if they had said "no" to me more often, then I would have never married at nineteen years of age in the first place. And if I had not married I would not have divorced, and if I had not divorced . . .

I speak of this because it was not until I was brave enough to truly see my choices and actions for just that—my choices and actions—that I was able to accept responsibility for them.

Interesting isn't it, that Bob was able to get on with his life only when he accepted responsibility for his actions. As long as he blamed someone else he seemed doomed to repeat his mistakes. If we reexamine the account of King David and his family through this prism we will discover some interesting parallels.

For the sake of our discussion we will focus our attention on David and two of his sons—Amnon and Absalom. I have chosen them because they each played a key role in the complex series of events that comprise this tragic account. Of equal importance is the way each of them related to their individual actions and the consequences their respective approaches produced.

Amnon simply chose to put his sinful behavior out of his mind. If he "forgot" about it then as far as he was concerned it never happened. This is called denial. Absalom blamed others, particularly his father. It was never his fault. This is called self-deception. Finally there is David, who at times may have succumbed to both denial and self-deception, but in the end he always took responsibility for his actions. His was the way of self-honesty.

Amnon and the Fine Art of Denial

Most of us have any number of ways of dealing with our inappropriate behaviors. It is likely that Amnon was no exception. In addition to the fine art of denial he undoubtedly practiced self-justification, rationalization, and blame shifting. We cannot be sure, because the Scriptures are mostly silent in regard to the thoughts and intents of his heart. Still, it seems likely given human nature and his subsequent behavior.

Amnon was a sexual predator, and like most sexual predators he lacked all capacity for empathy. His feelings, his needs, his desires were all that mattered. In his mind, the one he preyed upon was there for no other purpose than to satisfy his desires. That his actions might destroy her life never entered his mind. It was simply no concern of his. This does not mean that he had no redeeming qualities or that he was not a likeable person, but only that he never allowed his good qualities to inhibit his sexual desires.

In this instance the object of his sexual obsession was his beautiful half-sister, Tamar. Had she been anyone else he probably would have sent for her like his father sent for Bathsheba. Being a virgin and the daughter of a king, however, she was carefully guarded because she had great value as a possible future wife to some political ally. In the language of the Scriptures: "It seemed impossible for him to do anything to her" (2 Sam. 13:2 NIV).

But he was not to be denied. With the help of his cousin Jonadab he concocted an elaborate scheme in which he pretended to be ill in order to get his father to send Tamar to his house. Once she arrived he ordered all of the servants out. As soon as they were alone he grabbed her and forced her to have sex with him.

"Don't, my brother!" she said to him. "Don't force me. Such a thing should not be done in Israel! Don't do this wicked thing. What about me? Where could I get rid of my disgrace? And what about you? You would be like one of the wicked fools in Israel. Please speak to the king; he will not keep me from being married to you." But he refused to listen to her, and since he was stronger than she, he raped her.

Then Ammon hated her with intense hatred. In fact, he hated her more than he had loved her. Amnon said to her, "Get up and get out!"

"No!" she said to him. "Sending me away would be a greater wrong than what you have already done to me."

But he refused to listen to her. He called his personal servant and said, "Get this woman out of here and bolt the door after her." So his servant put her out and bolted the door after her. She was wearing a richly ornamented robe, for this was the kind of garment the virgin daughters of the king wore. Tamar put ashes on her head and tore the ornamented robe she was wearing. She put her hand on her head and went away, weeping aloud as she went . . . And Tamar lived in her brother Absalom's house, a desolate woman. (2 Sam. 13:12–20 NIV)

There's not a person alive who hasn't done a bad thing, a bad thing that they are ashamed of and would give anything if they could just undo. That kind of bad happens mostly because people are weak, or in the wrong place, or lonely, or some such thing. They didn't consciously plan to be bad; it just happened. That in no way mitigates their guilt. It just explains the kind of people they are—more weak than wicked.

Then there are those who do bad things because they enjoy being bad. Their sins are well planned, carefully calculated, and premeditated. When they are finished they simply put it out of their mind. They do not grieve over it or feel any responsibility to make it right.

Since the Scriptures give no indication that Amnon ever regretted what he did or made any attempt to take responsibility for his actions, I can only conclude that he falls into this latter category. Tamar was devastated, David was furious, and Absalom was consumed with hatred (see 2 Sam. 13:20–21), but there is no indication that Amnon felt anything at all.

His response is not surprising given the nature of his sin. Although I have not had extensive experience in ministering to incest victims, those I have worked with, almost without exception, have told me the perpetrator never spoke of his sin. Even when he was confronted by the victim he refused to acknowledge wrongdoing or seek forgiveness. It is almost as if he believed that if he never acknowledged that it happened then it hadn't.

Such people are without shame. They have absolutely no qualms about holding high office or positions of leadership within the community or the church. They continue to go about their business as if they have done nothing wrong.

Such was the case with Amnon. For two years it was business as usual as far as he was concerned. So insensitive was he to the feelings of others that he never suspected a thing when Absalom invited him to a banquet to celebrate the annual shearing of sheep. It never occurred to him that Absalom might share Tamar's pain or seek to avenge her. The shamelessness that allowed him to abuse others without remorse now made him an easy prey. "So Absalom's men did to Amnon what Absalom had ordered" (2 Sam. 13:29 NIV).

To see all of this only as a bit of ancient history is to miss the point entirely. This is not just about Amnon and Absalom. It's about us and the way we deal with our failures and sins. If we practice the fine art of denial, pretending we have not failed, that we have not sinned, then we doom ourselves. Denial may be less painful in the short run, but in the end we pay a terrible price.

Spiritually and emotionally whole people grieve when they have sinned, sometimes almost to the point of self-destruction. Their wrongdoing causes them great pain, and they are anxious to make things right. Initially the response they have chosen seems to be more difficult, to require

> Spiritually and emotionally whole people grieve when they have sinned, their wrongdoing causes them great pain, and they are anxious to make things right.

more of them, but in the end it produces life and freedom. Having taken responsibility for their actions, they are free to get on with the business of living.

Absalom and the Fine Art of Self-Deception

There is a temptation when we look at Absalom, and even Amnon for that matter, to excuse their sinful choices because of the dysfunctional family in which they were reared. I have heard it said that Amnon can hardly be blamed for giving vent to his lustful passions considering the example his father set before him. If one accepts that argument, then who can fault Absalom for the course his life took?

As far as that goes one could use that same argument in David's defense. Being the youngest of eight sons he was hardly his father's favorite. In fact, it seems his father took so little thought of him that he didn't even bother to call him when Samuel came to Bethlehem to sacrifice to the Lord. Had Samuel not directed him to send for David, Jesse would have left him to tend the sheep while the rest of the family celebrated. Without a doubt that kind of thoughtless treatment leaves emotional scars resulting in lifelong self-doubt.

If anything, David's brothers' treatment of him was even worse. They made no attempt to conceal their contempt. When he came to the front lines to bring them provisions from their father they wasted no time ridiculing him.

> When Eliab, David's oldest brother, heard him speaking with the men, he burned with anger at him and asked, "Why have you come down here? And with whom did you leave those few sheep in the desert? I know how conceited you are and how wicked your heart is; you came down only to watch the battle."
>
> "Now what have I done?" said David. "Can't I even speak?" (1 Sam. 17:28–29 NIV)

On top of everything else there was the betrayal and mistreatment he suffered at the hands of Saul. In return for his loyal service, Saul did everything in his power to kill David. If anyone had a right to use the things they had suffered in their past as an excuse for their sinful mistakes it was David. The abuse he suffered makes anything Amnon or Absalom endured seem almost inconsequential.

That is not to say that the mistakes David made as a husband and a father did not contribute to the problems that his sons suffered, for they did. David's mistakes were a factor, but not the deciding factor. Ultimately we all must take responsibility for our own actions, no matter what has happened to us in the past.

Having said that, let us turn our attention to Absalom. To his way of thinking, David must have seemed a poor excuse for a father, not to mention a king. With his lips David honored God's law—"I rejoice in following your statutes as one rejoices in great riches" (Ps. 119:14 NIV)—but he did not live by the commandments. The law forbade adultery (Ex. 20:14), yet he lay with Bathsheba, the wife of Uriah the Hittite. The commandments also forbade murder (Ex. 20:13), yet he had Uriah put to death so Bathsheba could become his wife.

That was bad enough, but what really grated on Absalom was the way David refused to punish Amnon for raping Tamar. The law was clear: The man who lay with his sister was cursed (Deut. 27:22). If a man raped a woman he could be put to death (Deut. 22:25–27). At the very least he was required to marry her (Deut. 22:28–29).

David had several options for dealing with Amnon, but he exercised none of them. The reasons are not clear, but there are several possibilities. Being David's firstborn son, and the heir apparent to the throne, Amnon may have had a special place in his father's heart. Maybe David simply could not bring himself to deal harshly with his favorite son. Another factor may have been David's own guilt. It could not have been easy to punish his son for sexual sin when he had transgressed some of the same commandments.

Whatever the reason, David did nothing, and Absalom was left with a heart full of bitterness. Day after day he watched his beautiful sister wasting away, becoming, in the words of Scripture, "a desolate woman" (2 Sam. 13:20 NIV). For two long years his hatred ate on him. Tamar's life was ruined, but for Amnon nothing had changed. He was still David's firstborn son and the heir apparent to the throne of Israel. David had not disinherited him or punished him in any way.

Finally Absalom decided to take matters into his own hands:

> And it came to pass, after two full years, that Absalom had sheepshearers in Baal Hazor, which is near Ephraim; so Absalom invited all the king's sons. Then Absalom came to the king and said, "Kindly note, your servant has sheepshearers; please, let the king and his servants go with your servant."
>
> But the king said to Absalom, "No, my son, let us not all go now, lest we be a burden to you." Then he urged him, but he would not go; and he blessed him.
>
> Then Absalom said, "If not, please let my brother Amnon go with us." And the king said to him, "Why should he go with you?" But Absalom urged him; so he let Amnon and all the king's sons go with him.
>
> Now Absalom had commanded his servants, saying, "Watch now, when Amnon's heart is merry with wine, and when I say to you, 'Strike Amnon!' then kill him. Do not be afraid. Have I not commanded you? Be courageous and valiant." So the servants of Absalom did to Amnon as Absalom had commanded. (2 Sam. 13:23–29a)

This chapter is not about Absalom's sin, but the way he deals with it internally, in his heart of hearts. Unlike Amnon who simply ignored his sin, pretending nothing had happened, Absalom knew he had committed a crime, albeit he refused to accept responsibility for his actions. A court of law might have found him guilty, but as far as he was concerned the fault was David's, not his own. Had David fulfilled his duty and brought Amnon to justice, then he would not have had to take matters into his own hands.

This is a pattern we see repeated throughout his life. Nothing was ever his fault. When he set fire to the fields of Joab, it was Joab's fault for not responding to his summons (2 Sam 14:28–32). When he lay with his father's concubines, he was only following the advice of Ahithophel (2 Sam. 16:20–22). Hear him as he pleaded his case: "I want to see the king's face, and if I am guilty of anything, let him put me to death" (2 Sam 14:32 NIV).

"If I am guilty of anything." By now he has convinced himself that someone else was responsible for any and all wrongdoing.

Absalom's way of dealing with his sins can be called the fine art of self-deception. Here is how it works. When first confronted with our sin we are painfully aware of our personal responsibility. The thought of our sinfulness is so grievous, in fact, that we cannot bear it. But rather than face the hard truth about ourselves, we become involved in a massive cover-up. By the time we have finished "retouching" the sinful incident,

> When first confronted with our sin we are painfully aware of our personal responsibility. Rather than face the hard truth about ourselves, we become involved in a massive cover-up.

we are no longer to blame. The lie we tell ourselves concerning our "innocence" then becomes the "truth" we tell others. When Absalom protested his innocence and shifted the blame to others he was absolutely sincere. In his mind it was the truth.

Unfortunately self-deception is a dangerous and often deadly habit. Imagine the woman who discovers a lump in her breast. Immediately she is assailed with fear, imagining the very worst. Now she is faced with a critical choice. Should she schedule an appointment with her doctor and get to the root of this, or should she try to ignore it, try to put it out of her mind?

Suppose she decides to ignore it. Now she puts all thoughts of it out of her mind. She is careful never to touch it or to lay in such a way as to bring it to her attention. Finally she is at peace. She refuses to think about it.

But putting it out of her mind does not mean it is not there. Even as she goes merrily about her business, as if nothing were amiss, that deadly tumor continues to invade her body. What may have been a treatable cancer has now become a terminal condition. So it is with self-deception. It may provide temporary relief from the guilt feelings produced by our sinful actions, but in the end we suffer the consequences. Wrongdoing that could have been easily dealt with has now become a convoluted mess, making it nearly impossible for us to identify and acknowledge our sins.

Neither denial nor self-deception is an effective way of dealing with personal sin. Both Amnon and Absalom died violent deaths because they refused to take responsibility for their actions. David, on the other hand, owned his mistakes. When Nathan said, "You are the man!" (2 Sam. 12:7), then David said to Nathan, "I have sinned against the LORD" (2 Sam. 12:13). Because David took responsibility for his sins, Nathan said, "The LORD also has put away your sin; you shall not die" (2 Sam. 12:13).

Self-Honesty

Nearly all of us contend with self-deception to one degree or another. David was no exception. Self-honesty did not come naturally to him any more than it does to us. In fact, on at least two occasions his self-deception was so entrenched that God had to "trick" him into seeing the truth about himself. On both occasions David was asked to pass judgment on a matter that appeared to be totally unrelated to his own life. The first was when Nathan told him the parable of the rich man who took the poor man's one ewe lamb (see 2 Sam. 12:1–14), the second when a wise woman from Tekoa presented the dilemma of her two sons (see 2 Sam. 14:1–24). Each time David responded appropriately, only to discover that he was passing judgment on himself. Like us he seemed to see the sins of others more clearly than his own.

God often uses this same story technique to help us break through our self-deception. Sometimes it is the personal testimony of one who has walked this way before us. As they relive their story we see ourselves. At other times God may have to use more dramatic means to cut through our deeply entrenched self-deception, as He did when he spoke to my brother Bob through a prophetic dream. Here's how Bob tells his story:

It is May of 1992 and my entire family—my sister and her children, my older brothers and their children, and of course my mom and dad—as well as my wife's parents, aunts, uncles and grandmother have all gathered in Austin, Texas, for a truly momentous occasion. I am the first person in my immediate family to receive a doctoral degree. This is the same me who also failed twice in marriage and who has never really lived a consistent life for Christ. Yet, I have made it! I have done something no other individual in my or Anita's family has ever done—I will be awarded a Ph.D.

By this time, my wife and I are living in Miami, Florida, and I am employed by the most prestigious community college in the country. I have published a variety of articles and completed my master's thesis and my doctoral dissertation. I have served as the national president of a college honor society, and I have experienced the joy of presenting my research findings to regional, national, and even international scientific conferences. Yet, I remain haunted by uncertainty with regard to how I fit within my own family, and my life is devoid of any consistent contact with God or His church.

Two incidents happened which forced me to look into the true face of God. The first occurred during a discussion with my older brother Richard. We were sitting at the dining table of a condo at the Shores on Lake Travis talking about the importance of attending church. I said something like, "I bet you think that you are more spiritual than I am because you are in church every week and I'm not."

"I'm not convinced that it is because I attend church more often than you, Bob," he replied, "but, I do know that I am more spiritual than you are at this time in our lives."

The conversation petered out after that and it was not an acrimonious one in any sense anyway. In fact, it seemed quite unremarkable. When I speak with Richard about this conversation today, he does not even recall it. But, I certainly do because it was God's way of setting the stage for the next incident.

The second incident occurred about a week later after I had returned to Miami with my family. This is the only time in my entire life that I can say that God spoke to me through a dream, and the dream went like this:

I am alone in a private hospital room. Lying in bed with my entire body covered with large sores which ooze pus and infection. Open, running sores cover my entire face. I cannot bear to look at myself in the mirror. The doctor has just left after giving me the news that I have AIDS. I do not have long to live. I cannot believe that this is possible.

I shouted at him, "I can't have AIDS, I just got my doctorate."

No one will come into the room with me. I can hear my wife, Anita, and my children speaking in low voices in the hallway outside the door. I know that they are talking to other members of our families. *But, no one will come into the room! I am unclean, and so very alone!* I begin to cry uncontrollably.

At this point, my younger sister, Sherry, enters the room. Her eyes are filled with compassion and tears streak down her cheeks. She sits on the edge of the bed and gazes down on me. In a choked voice I say to her, "I can't have AIDS, I just got my doctorate. I have my whole career ahead of me, and I've worked so hard. I just can't have AIDS."

She just looks at me and nods her head in compassion. I begin to cry even harder. She places her hands on my shoulders, leans forward, and quietly speaks.

"You do have AIDS, and you will die. But, I love you and I will always be with you. I will not leave you."

Then, she pulls me to her in a hug. Wrapping her arms around me, she places her beautiful, soft, unmarked cheek directly against my cheek with its open, running sores. In her compassion and love, I sense a profound sadness that I am dying. And yet, even though she is helpless to prevent my death, she is never going to stop loving me.

At this point, I woke up in a cold sweat. I did not share this dream with Anita or anyone for a number of days. But, it did not take me more than a day or so to realize that the dream was directly from God and its meaning was quite clear.

My sister represented Jesus—because of all the people in my family only she can truly understand the emotional pain I have suffered. Only Sherry and I have experienced the trauma of divorce. She represented Jesus—because only Jesus has experienced everything I have experienced.

Jesus was saying to me that I was in the process of dying spiritually. He was telling me that although I had trusted Him with my salvation, my way of living life without Him was leading to my spiritual death. He was also telling me that He was still there and that He would always be there, even if that meant sitting at my deathbed until the bitter end.

Needless to say, I got the message. After sharing the dream with Anita, we decided that we were going to become involved in church. **We were going to GO TO CHURCH. Not visit a church or churches. But, simply go to church.** Within weeks we went to New Testament Baptist Church and we have been there ever since.

The road has not always been smooth, but it is the only road to be on for us. We have overcome our children's fear of new settings, our own preconditioned behavior patterns, the failure of our church leaders, the loss of new friends as they moved out of state, and many more daily crises. We have been challenged and tempted to slip back into old ways. But, we have remained steady. It has taken a significant amount of energy and changed how we live our lives.

That dream was key because through it I was finally able to take responsibility for my actions rather than blame others. I was set free to do this when I realized that God knew the worst there was to know about me and He loved me still. Coming to that realization shattered the bonds of avoidance for me. When I realized that God had no false assumptions about me, it allowed me to drop all of my pretenses and see my actions just as they are—the acts of a sinner saved by grace.

I cannot adequately express the feeling that I experienced then and the peace that I now know. For you see, I no longer have to worry about what is found in my heart of hearts—my selfishness, my uncertainty, my anger, my covetousness, my secret sins, nor my wildest hopes—because it is all covered by the grace of Jesus Christ. Once I comprehended this truth, then I became free to see my actions as my own because they are not going to separate me from Him since I have been forgiven. Knowing that I can now peer into my heart of hearts without fear of what I see, making it possible for me to accept that my mistakes can be forgiven. Something I could never really do as long as I avoided MY part in this drama of life.

If we can accept what we discover about ourselves as David did, as my brother did, then we too shall live. The Lord will take our sin away. How, you may be wondering, can you ever break through the layers and layers of self-deception that you have built up over the years? How can you undo all the lies you have told yourself? Only with God's help!

Let David be your model. Make his prayer your prayer:

O LORD, you have searched me
　and you know me.
You know when I sit and when I rise;
　you perceive my thoughts from afar.
You discern my going out and my lying down;
　you are familiar with all my ways.
Before a word is on my tongue
　you know it completely, O LORD . . .
If I say, "Surely the darkness will hide me
　and the light become night around me,"
even the darkness will not be dark to you;
　the night will shine like the day,
　for darkness is as light to you . . .
Search me, O God, and know my heart;
　test me and know my anxious thoughts.
See if there is any offensive way in me,
　and lead me in the way everlasting. (Ps. 139:1–4, 11–12, 23–24 NIV)

In the next four chapters you will learn to identify the hurtful habits that have short-circuited your best efforts to live an overcoming life. With God's help you can learn to forgive yourself and make restitution to those you have sinned against. Finally you will learn to walk in the light, to live transparently before both God and man. With God's help you can overcome the trouble and storms you have brought on yourself!

Chapter 14

IDENTIFYING HURTFUL HABITS

The last chapter contrasted the ways David and his two oldest sons each dealt with their own sin. Amnon, as you may recall, didn't deal with it at all. He simply pretended that it never happened. Absalom's way of dealing with his sin was hardly better. As far as he was concerned it was never his fault. Someone else was always to blame for his wrongdoing. Only David found forgiveness and new life. *He overcame the trouble he brought upon himself and those he loved, not because he was a better man, but because he found a better way of dealing with his sin—God's way.* David had a truth encounter. As a result he acknowledged his sins and threw himself upon the mercies of God.

Now it is time to go a step farther. Once we acknowledge that the trouble we are experiencing is of our own making, it is time to take a hard look at our lives. We are not simply looking for "sins" as much as attempting to identify hurtful habits (i.e., lifestyle). These habits represent the way we see ourselves and how we interact with others. For instance, what habits do you think David might have developed that made it possible (even likely) for him to do the things he did?

At this point you may want to jot down everything you know about David—youngest child, neglected by his father, ridiculed by his older brothers, anointed to be king, killed Goliath, etc.—as a means of identifying what character traits and personal habits he may have developed as a way of coping with his life. Because the traits and habits, or "coping mechanisms," were his own, they likely seemed normal to him, even healthy. Only later, after his tragic fall, did he realize how flawed his thinking was.

I begin with David for the same reason that Nathan began with a story about a rich man and a poor man (see 2 Sam. 12)—because it is almost always easier to see the faults of others rather than our own. But having examined David's life, we may very well discover that we have been looking into a mirror—that what we thought were flaws in his character were really a reflection of our own, and that the judgment we pass on David is really the judgment we are passing on ourselves.

Like most of us, David was a complex man, a mixture of dust and deity. One moment he was capable of extraordinary spiritual sensitivity, the next he might succumb to a wanton act of the flesh. It is this very complexity that makes it so difficult for us to come to grips with our sin. The spiritual part of us, the part that hungers after God, cannot bear the thought of our sinfulness. Therefore we begin to compartmentalize our lives. We are one person in a Christian setting and quite another person in a different setting. As far as we are concerned, the twain shall never meet.

Some may consider that hypocritical, but I don't think so. To be a hypocrite one must pretend to be something he is not. When we worship we are not pretending. The spiritual part of us really does love God. Our devotion is not an act. It is sincere. But because we have compartmentalized our lives, we almost never bring the sinful part of ourselves into the presence of God. Consequently there is no "cure" for us.

Redemptive Crisis

In His mercy God may precipitate a crisis—a crisis that forces us to confront the truth about ourselves. For David that crisis came in the form of a truth encounter with Nathan the prophet (2 Sam. 12:1–14). For my brother Bob the crisis came in the form of a prophetic dream. For me it came as a telephone call from my editor.

As kindly as he could he told me that my latest book was not selling nearly as well as they had hoped. The longer we talked, the more concerned

I became. I had been writing for more than ten years, and I knew if this book did not do well I might not get another chance with a major publisher.

> In His mercy God may precipitate a crisis—a crisis that forces us to confront the truth about ourselves.

His telephone call left me deeply disappointed (actually I felt like someone had kicked me in the stomach) and more than a little puzzled. This was my twenty-first book, and I truly believed it would be the one to finally enable me to take my place among the best-selling authors in Christendom. The publisher had done an outstanding job of producing the book: the editing was excellent, the cover was spectacular, the subject timely. So why wasn't it selling?

In desperation I fired off an E-mail to several close friends, asking them to pray with me regarding this matter. I specifically asked them to focus on four areas. I wrote:

1. If God is trying to tell me something by allowing me to experience this struggle then I want to hear and obey. In this regard pray that God will give me ears to hear, a heart to receive, a will to obey, and faith to act.

2. If there is something I need to do to make the book sell better ask God to make that clear to me so I can take the appropriate steps.

3. Ask God to give the book wings. May it literally fly out of bookstores.

4. Pray for every person who reads my book. Ask God to speak to the deep issues of his/her life. Pray for the Lord to make him/her an overcomer in every way.

Of course, I started praying in earnest myself. Almost immediately God began to deal with my heart. The things He showed me were far from flattering. Day after day He dredged up something else I had refused to deal with. Each time He revealed a problem area, I was faced with a choice.

I could acknowledge my need and receive God's provision, or I could pretend ignorance and continue the status quo. Though these prayer sessions were excruciatingly painful, often moving me to tears, I always sensed the Father's love. It was not anger that caused Him to deal with me ever so severely, but mercy.

First He dealt with me about prayerlessness. Even as I write this I am tempted to explain myself, to somehow cast my prayerlessness in a more favorable light. God forbid! Though I had made valiant efforts from time to time, and though there were periods of weeks, sometimes months, when I was fairly consistent in prayer, the truth is I have largely been a failure in this critical area. Only God knows how much kingdom good has been lost because I did not pray.

Not only have I been a failure at prayer in general, but in a very specific sense I have failed to cover my books in prayer. During the actual writing I frequently asked God to anoint my efforts, but once a book was completed I never prayed over it again. Not once did I ask God to help the art department create the perfect cover or to give the marketing team special anointing. Nor did I pray that my book might have special favor with the public.

Why? I would like to tell you it was because I thought it seemed self-serving and materialistic to pray for my own success, but I can't. Truthfully, I did have some concerns in those areas, but God knows that was not the real reason I failed to pray. Though it embarrasses me to tell you this, I must admit that I thought my books were good enough to make it without God's help. I was relying on my talent rather than His favor.

As my pride and self-reliance became ever more apparent, I humbled myself before the Lord and sought His forgiveness. "Change me, Lord," I prayed. "Forgiveness is not enough. I need to be transformed. Make me the man I ought to be."

This soul-searching continued day after day, for a week, then two, then three. I felt like Jacob on the bank of the Jabbok (see Gen. 32:22–31). I was wrestling with the Lord, and He would not let me go. I prayed for Him to bless me, to give my books favor, but He had something else in mind. Now He compelled me to look into the hidden depths of my heart of hearts. When I did, I discovered that my heart was full of jealousy and envy toward those authors whose books were selling better than mine.

Snide remarks that I had made now returned to haunt me. "He's a good communicator, but he's really not a writer." "Of course his books sell well. He's on radio (or television) every day." "He's not a real author, he has a ghostwriter." On and on it went, until I hung my head in shamefaced acknowledgment.

Desperately I prayed for God to change me, to save me from myself. Little wonder that God had not blessed my books with more than modest success. With a heart like mine, anything more would have surely made me intolerable.

As I prayed, a most amazing thing began to happen. God, in His mercy, let me see those gifted men and women through His eyes. He allowed me to love them the way He loved them. I felt like part of the family. They were my brothers and sisters. Their success was my success, and our success was God's success. With tears I found myself praying for them—thanking God for the contributions their gifts had made to the kingdom and to me personally.

God continued to dig deeper still, bringing up memories from my earliest days in ministry. Two leaped into my mind one after the other. So vivid did I remember them that they might have happened only yesterday. In the first I was performing a wedding for one of the wealthiest men in our town. I was barely twenty-one years old, just a kid preacher really, and more than a little intimidated by the splendor in which I found myself. The wedding came off without a hitch, due in no small part to my careful preparation, and I basked in the many compliments I received. Driving home, I permitted myself a sigh of satisfaction. I was sure I had made a good impression.

The second memory is not at all like the first, except in one aspect— I was once again the focus of attention, at least in my mind. A group of us were seated around a dining room table where I was holding court. With an exaggerated flair I was expounding the Scriptures, some Old Testament story, no doubt. For all of that this was not about the Scriptures. What I wanted these people to remember, especially one attractive woman in particular, was how clever I am. She did not disappoint me. When I finished she said, "You are so wise, I sometimes think you must have lived forever."

I was glowing as we drove home, but Brenda (my wife) was not impressed. Only now do I fully understand why.

Reliving those two incidents in the presence of the Lord, I was nearly undone. In the light of His glory my actions seem so vulgar, so self-serving. Though I professed to be an ambassador of Christ representing the kingdom of God, I was really promoting myself. Though I prayed, "Hallowed be Your name" (Matt. 6:9), it was my name I wanted people to remember rather than His.

All previous sins seemed nearly inconsequential in comparison to this. I fell on my face, literally, and begged for God's forgiveness. As always, His grace was greater than my sin. Forgiven, I am now praying every day for God to hallow His name in all that I do. May His name be hallowed in every sermon I preach, in every prayer I pray, in every word I write. May His name be hallowed in my marriage and in my family, in all the relationships of my life. May His name be hallowed in me!

Then the Lord brought to my memory something Max Lucado had written in the Acknowledgments in his wonderful book on Romans called *In the Grip of Grace.*

> And to you, the reader: I've prayed for you. Long before you held this book, I asked God to prepare your heart.[1]

What a novel thought—to pray for those who would read my books. Why hadn't I thought of that? I'll tell you why. That is, I will tell you what God revealed to me as I waited in His presence. It is not at all flattering, and it shames me to admit it, but I must. With dreadful clarity God showed me that I had never thought to pray for you, the reader, because in my mind the book was an end in itself.

Once more I repented. And again God graciously forgave me. Now I am praying for you every day and for every person who reads anything I have written. I want to promise you that I will continue to pray for you all the days of my life, but honesty forces me to admit that I don't have a very good track record when it comes to prayer. All I can really tell you is that I have prayed for you today, and with God's help I purpose to pray for you tomorrow and each day thereafter. Will I fail again? Perhaps, but if I do, I plan to get up and start praying again.

As I review the spiritual journey I have been on these past few weeks, two passages of Scripture come to mind. The first was penned by David, who wrote:

Before I was afflicted I went astray,
   but now I obey your word . . .
It was good for me to be afflicted
   so that I might learn your decrees. (Ps. 119:67, 71 NIV, emphasis mine)

As painful as this experience has been, as grieved as I am that my book did not get off to a better start, I am so thankful things have worked out as they have. Truly, "It was good for me to be afflicted" (Ps. 119:71 NIV). If I know my heart, I can truthfully say I would not trade a spot in *Book Store Journal's* top ten for the holy work God is doing in me.

The second passage of Scripture comes from 2 Corinthians 1:8–11 (NIV):

We do not want you to be uninformed, brothers, about the hardships we suffered in the province of Asia. We were under great pressure, far beyond our ability to endure, so that we despaired even of life. Indeed, in our hearts we felt the sentence of death. *But this happened that we might not rely on ourselves but on God,* who raises the dead. He has delivered us from such a deadly peril, and he will deliver us. *On him we have set our hope* that he will continue to deliver us, as you help us by your prayers. Then many will give thanks on our behalf for the gracious favor granted us in answer to the prayers of many. (emphasis mine)

Sometimes God has to allow us to be backed into a corner before we will truly rely on Him. I know that was true in my case. As long as I had the illusion that I had the talent to be a best-selling author I relied on myself rather than Him. Only when I was

> Sometimes God has to allow us to be backed into a corner before we will truly rely on Him.

brought face-to-face with my limitations did I turn to Him. I only pray that in the future I will not have to be "under great pressure, far beyond [my] ability to endure" (2 Cor. 1:8 NIV) before I rely on the Lord.

Faulty Assumptions

If our hearts are sensitive to the Holy Spirit, we need not be under duress in order to hear the voice of the Lord. For instance a few days ago I received some correspondence. As I was reading it, I immediately sensed the Lord speaking to me. Though this was a friend's story, God used it to speak to my heart. He wrote,

> I distinctly remember an event from my early childhood that demonstrates how easy it is to avoid accepting responsibility for our behavior. I could not have been more than four years of age when my family took a vacation to Arizona with my aunt and uncle. We were pulling a small travel trailer behind the family car. On this particular day, we had stopped for the evening in a campground somewhere in the Rockies. A small stream tumbled down the mountain side just a few hundred feet below the camp. My father and Uncle Roy took my two older brothers down to the stream but refused to take me along because I was too young.
>
> As was their habit, Dad and Uncle Roy had unhooked the safety chains from the trailer to the car, disengaged the latch which connected the trailer to ball of the trailer hitch, and lowered the support stand on the tongue of the camper. Thus, the car was separated from the trailer. The problem was the car had not yet been moved and the trailer tongue remained directly above the trailer hitch. Angry at being treated like a "little kid," I decided to see if I could prove how "big" I really was. Spying the trailer tongue, I managed to turn the handle and lower it back onto the hitch. Then, to my astonishment, I was able to re-engage the latch on the ball. No small feat as it took some real strength to do this. But when I tried to disengage the latch, I couldn't.
>
> A few minutes later my father, uncle, and brothers returned from the stream to find my mother and my aunt preparing dinner in the trailer.

Since dinner would not be ready for another thirty minutes, Dad and Uncle Roy decided to take us boys for a brief ride to see if we could spot some deer.

After we all piled into the car, Uncle Roy put it in gear and stepped on the accelerator. Almost instantly the car jerked and we could hear the ladies screaming from the trailer. Dinner was now all over the trailer and they were more than a little ticked.

The final scene remains vividly etched in my mind. I see my father angrily striding back to the car where I am sitting between my two older brothers on the back seat. He leans in over the front seat and says, "I want to know which one of you two boys hooked the trailer back up. I know it wasn't James because he isn't big enough to do it. Which one of you did it?" Well, as you know, I was indeed big enough. But, he had ruled me out so I wasn't about to say a word. Neither Robert nor Darrell was willing to confess to something they didn't do. Nor do I blame them. But, because of a false assumption, one that I could have corrected if I had so chosen, I was able to avoid taking responsibility for that action. I cannot recall what, if any, punishment my father meted out to my brothers, but I do remember getting off.

I shared this information with my Dad just a few years ago and we both had a good laugh, but it contains a painful truth for me. You see, I have re-enacted this same scenario in many different ways throughout my life. It has always been easier to let someone else assume something about me than it is for me to correct their faulty assumptions. Even though many of the assumptions were relatively minor, their combined impact was huge. This resulted in a horrific burden of guilt that I carried around with me on a daily basis. In order to cope with this burden, I became very adept at avoiding the reality in my heart of hearts.

There was more, but I read no further. Once again God was confronting me with a truth encounter. Vividly I recalled being introduced to a class where I was lecturing. In his introduction the teacher listed several things he admired about me. Among them was my generosity. He told the class that I gave more than 30 percent of my income to the work of the Lord. I winced as he said it, but I did not bother to correct him.

Nor did I correct him later when we were alone. I just let him assume I gave that much.

Now, more than a year later, it was back to haunt me. I had forgotten about it, but God had not. This was another moment of truth. Would I ignore the prompting of the Holy Spirit and let my friend go on believing I was more generous than I really am, or would I come clean with him? Thankfully I chose to pick up the telephone and call him to set the record straight.

You may think it silly for me to make such a fuss over something so insignificant, but I have learned that there are no insignificant misperceptions. Any time I allow others to believe I am better than I really am, I set in motion a force that is hard to reverse. Soon I am living a lie, pretending to be something I'm not. After a while the myth is so big I can't afford to admit the truth, not even to myself.

What starts out as a simple misperception soon becomes a role we play. If people perceive us as strong, then we dare not ask for help no matter how desperately we may need it. If they perceive us as being wise, as always having the solution, then how can we be otherwise? If others think we are more spiritual than we really are, how dare we disappoint them. By not correcting the misperception as soon as it occurs, we build a trap for ourselves.

A Better Way

Is this what happened to David? Did Jesse's youngest son, the keeper of the sheep, get so caught up playing the role of king that he couldn't admit, not even to himself, that on the inside he was still the insecure young man who hungered for his father's approval? To the populace he was the fearless giant killer, the warrior king who could do no wrong. But in his heart of hearts he knew better: "I'm only a poor man and little known," he said (1 Sam. 18:23 NIV).

Initially it is flattering to be seen as being bigger than life. Before long, however, trying to live up to those kinds of unrealistic expectations becomes an intolerable burden. Unless we can debunk those myths they will likely destroy us. It has even been suggested that some people have taken a fall in order to finally escape the pressure. Perhaps this is what happened to David.

I cannot help wondering how different his life story might have been if only he had prayed, "Search me, O God, and know my heart; test me and know my anxious thoughts" (Ps. 139:23 NIV), before he saw Bathsheba bathing rather than after Nathan confronted him. Be that as it may. This isn't really about David anyway. It's about us, it's about what is going on in our lives and more specifically, what is going on in our heart of hearts. In the twelve steps practiced by Alcoholics Anonymous this searching of one's soul is called a fearless moral inventory. As I understand it, the purpose is to identify and acknowledge all personal wrongdoing. For our purposes I would like to add a second goal: to attain a level of self-knowledge where we can come to a true and accurate understanding of our heart and motives.

In my experience this second goal is more difficult than the first—and more critical if we hope to deal with our issues before they manifest themselves in sinful actions that produce life-altering consequences. Only as we allow the Holy Spirit to reveal the hidden depths of our heart can we hope to identify and defeat these inner enemies of our soul.

While doing research for this book I interviewed a man who told me that for years he refused to examine his heart of hearts. To his way of thinking it was simply too painful. (Probably all of us can identify with that.) As a consequence he made many of the same mistakes over and over again. Only after he experienced the unconditional love of Jesus did he dare look within. With the help of the Holy Spirit he has been able to identify several hurtful habits. He wrote,

1. I demonstrated a consistent and *unhealthy dependence* on the fact that others would bail me out of any difficulty—this led me to make many unwise choices of which I never truly had to experience the full consequences.

2. I lived a life of *unrealistic optimism* where I developed a tendency to put off dealing with things in a realistic manner, e.g., spending money I didn't have (credit).

3. I had (still have) a tendency to speak too quickly and listen too seldom—*words can fix* anything.

4. I love the art of compromise—*avoiding rather than resolving conflict* led to an inability to truly develop my own set of core beliefs and values.

5. I had a need for approval at all costs. This led me to *try to be* what I thought others wanted me to be or what others would be proud of me being.

6. I developed an *overly strong ability to compartmentalize* parts of my life—the danger is that when things became too difficult I could "turn off" my caring for others and walk away.

7. Because I loved words, I developed the ability to *manipulate others* to see my point of view and I could *rationalize any choice* I made.

Because this man is now "walking in the light" (1 John 1:7) he is no longer being blindsided by his unhealthy coping mechanisms. Now he recognizes them for what they are—nothing more than a clever attempt to avoid responsibility for his behavior. Should he find himself reverting to one of his deeply ingrained and self-destructive habits, he deals with it immediately. He must, or he risks returning to the fruitless ways of the past.

Unfortunately, like David, he did not come to grips with these inner enemies until he had made some sinful choices that had life-altering consequences. Consequences that he is still dealing with today and will be for the rest of his life. He freely encourages me to share his story with you in order to help you deal with your issues before they manifest themselves in ways that have lifelong repercussions.

A Fearless Moral Inventory

Before we turn our attention to the next chapter I would like to encourage you to conduct your own fearless moral inventory. Begin by acknowledging in prayer that your heart is "deceitful above all things, / and desperately wicked" (Jer. 17:9). Invite the Holy Spirit to reveal what is in the hidden depths of your soul (Ps. 139:23–24).

If you are a Christian it is not likely the Lord will reveal obvious sins like adultery and stealing, though He may. Generally we are already aware of those kinds of things. The hidden things of our heart, the things that will do us in in the long run are more subtle. No less sinful, just more subtle.

In my life they include self-reliance, jealousy, envy, and self-promotion. My friend identified things like an inordinate need for approval, unrealistic optimism, strong ability to compartmentalize parts of his life, manipulation, and rationalization. Others have acknowledged such things as anger, fear of failure, greed, and self-centeredness, to name just a few.

It is almost impossible to truly search our hearts without writing out our thoughts and feelings. Often we have only the vaguest understanding of an experience or situation until we discipline ourselves to write it down. Once we put pen to paper, our elusive thoughts seem to crystallize. This is often referred to as journaling, but don't let that word intimidate you. All it means is an honest and uninhibited recording of the thoughts and impressions that come to mind as we wait before the Lord.

Madeleine L'Engle describes the importance of journaling for her personally when she said,

> If I can write things out I can see them, and they are not trapped within my own subjectivity . . .
>
> Not long ago someone I love said something which wounded me grievously, and I was desolate that this person could have made such a comment to me.
>
> So, in great pain, I crawled to my journal and wrote it all out in a great burst of self-pity. And when I had set it down, when I had it before me, I saw that something I myself had said had called forth the words which had hurt me so. It had, in fact, been my own fault. But I would never have seen it if I had not written it out.[2]

In addition to journaling, it is often helpful for me to work (pray) my way through a scriptural prayer like the Lord's Prayer (Matt. 6:9–13). As I pray and meditate upon the various petitions I sometimes sense the Lord speaking to me. For instance, much of what I related earlier in this chapter came to me as I was praying through this very prayer. Well do I remember praying, "Hallowed be Your name" (Matt. 6:9). No sooner had I said those words before I began to weep. My tears then gave birth to the shameful memories of those times when I had used the ministry to promote myself rather than Jesus. Nor was it simply the memory of past experiences, but the awful conviction that the same spirit of self-promotion was still at work within me. In His presence I confessed my sin and received His absolution.

Once we develop the habit of keeping short accounts with God, this soul-searching will become a regular part of our daily prayer life. Each time we meet with the Lord we will bare our hearts before Him and receive His healing grace.

Although the revelation of our sinfulness is capable of producing the most severe pain, it never leaves us feeling desolate. It is a healing pain, a redemptive pain, a purifying pain. It is not penance (self-punishment) but repentance wherein we see the error of our ways. Thus enlightened and empowered by the Holy Spirit, we make the appropriate behavioral changes.

> Each time we meet with the Lord we will bare our hearts before Him and receive His healing grace.

Some of you may feel it is already too late. Like David you have made a mess of your life. By your sinful actions you have loosed a storm of terrible consequences upon yourself and those you love. Even now the fierce winds of sin and death howl with a frightful fury. It may even seem that all is lost.

Don't give up! God's redemptive grace is greater than any storm you face. Through the sacrificial death of His Son on the cross He has already judged your sins. He stands ready to forgive and restore. Yes, scars may remain. We do reap what we sow, but out of the ravages of the storm can come new life.

You may be thinking that even if God could forgive you, you could never forgive yourself. Well, you are not the first person to feel that way, and you won't be the last. In fact, in the next chapter I am going to show you how others, whose sins were every bit as black as yours, learned to forgive

> Although the revelation of our sinfulness is capable of producing the most severe pain, it never leaves us feeling desolate.

themselves. If God could forgive them, He can surely forgive you! If they could learn to forgive themselves, then you can too. Remember, "the mercy of the LORD is from everlasting to everlasting" (Ps. 103:17), it "endures forever" (2 Chron. 7:3) and "His compassions fail not. / They are new every morning" (Lam. 3:22–23).

Chapter 15

FORGIVING
YOURSELF

Watching her beautiful, sixteen-year-old daughter take her place on the examining table, Diane was assailed with a plethora of emotions. With an effort she pushed them down and took Denise's hand. Unconsciously her other hand found its way to Denise's cheek where she traced the outlines of the red birthmark with her finger. It lay on her fair skin like a dark stain, reaching from just below her eye to under her ear. How Diane wished she could just make it go away.

The door to the examining room opened, admitting the doctor and two nurses. While he explained the laser surgery to Denise and her mother, the nurses prepared syringes for the local anesthetic. They had been over all of this before, still Diane listened intently trying to reassure herself. According to the doctor's instructions, she had given Denise a Valium before leaving the house. Now she wished she had taken one herself. She was having trouble breathing, her pulse was racing, and she felt like she might faint.

As the doctor picked up the first syringe, Diane willed herself to watch, though why she wanted to torture herself she did not know. Penance perhaps. As the needle pierced her skin, Denise flinched and tightened her grip on Diane's hand, but she did not make a sound. Swiftly the doctor inserted the needle around the edges of the birthmark, numbing the surrounding tissue. Watching her daughter grimace in pain, Diane thought, *This is my doing. It's all my fault.*

Once the doctor finished injecting the local anesthetic, a nurse helped Denise put on her tinted safety goggles to protect her eyes. Nodding at the technician, the surgeon picked up the laser wand and directed it toward the red birthmark on Denise's cheek. Almost instantly the air was filled with the unmistakable odor of burning flesh. Denise made no sound, but her body trembled with silent sobs, breaking Diane's heart.

Now Denise's tears seeped from under her protective goggles and ran down her cheeks, forcing the surgeon to stop. "Can you feel this?" he asked. When she nodded he called for more anesthetic and injected her face again. Each time the needle pierced her soft skin Denise seemed to shrink within herself, but there was no escaping the pain.

While waiting for the medication to take effect, Diane tried to get her nerves under control. *Why was this happening?* she wondered. The doctor had assured them that it was a relatively painless procedure—just some minor discomfort. And just underneath her anxious concern for Denise lurked the ever present guilt—the voice inside her head that kept telling her this was all her fault, that she had scarred Denise's face, brought this pain on her daughter.

Far too soon the doctor picked up the laser wand and turned his attention back to the task at hand. Once more the stench of burning flesh filled the air. Behind her tinted safety goggles, Denise's eyes begged her mother to do something. *Make him stop,* they seemed to say. *Make the pain go away.* But there was nothing Diane could do except hold Denise's hand and cry with her. The time when she could have done something, should have done something, was long past.

Twice more the doctor had to stop when the pain became too intense. Again he injected more anesthetic (more than sixty injections in all); still, he could not completely deaden the affected area. Taking a deep breath he picked up the laser wand one last time. There was nothing to do except finish the surgery. To stop now would only complicate matters.

Finally the torturous procedure was completed, and Diane held Denise while she sobbed and sobbed. "You were so brave," Diane told her. "You never made a sound until it was all over."

A few minutes later the nurse returned with some aftercare instructions and a follow-up appointment. It was nearly noon when Diane and

Denise finally exited the building. While they were driving home, the now familiar voice inside Diane's head returned to torment her. Cruelly it taunted her. "If Denise knew this was your doing," it seemed to say, "she would never forgive you."

The next few days were difficult. Denise's face swelled up, blistered, then turned black, followed by blue, then green, and finally yellow. According to the doctor's instructions they kept ice packs filled with frozen peas on her cheek. It helped relieve the pain, but nothing took it completely away.

Although Diane kept up a brave front, it was just that—a brave front. When she was alone she suffered a private anguish. Try as she might she could not escape her tormenting memories. Night after night they came to her, chasing sleep away. Alone in the darkness she hugged her knees and wept bitter tears of remorse, but felt no better.

Guilt

My heart goes out to Diane and her daughter. I cannot even imagine the kind of pain Denise experienced during laser surgery. Yet in many ways the pain her mother lived with was far worse. Physical pain, though severe, usually lasts only a short time. Our bodies have an enormous capacity to heal themselves. Spiritual pain, on the other hand, can linger for a lifetime. Untreated, it can kill you!

Come with me to Portland, Oregon, to the street beneath the Vista Bridge, just west of downtown. There you will see bloodstains on the pavement. They mark the spot where a middle school teacher died. After slashing his wrists he jumped off the bridge to his death. When he died he was free on $14,500 bail after being arrested and charged with three counts of second-degree sexual assault on children and ten counts of child pornography. Apparently living with what he had done seemed worse than dying, so he killed himself.

Come with me to the Eisenhower Tunnel near Loveland Pass in Colorado. Here a Vietnam veteran crashed his van into a concrete retaining wall while traveling at least eighty miles an hour. His friends described him as a tormented man. They say he could never forget the 114 enemy soldiers he killed or the friend who bled to death in his arms. In a desperate attempt to escape his spiritual pain he began taking tranquilizers and smoking pot. It didn't help. Nothing helped. When he could bear it no more he did what he thought he had to do—he ended his life in a violent crash near the top of the mountain.

Most of us are neither Vietnam veterans nor accused child molesters; still, who among us hasn't known the awful agony of guilt-infested memories? Maybe it's something you did, something for which you have never been able to forgive yourself. Or perhaps it was something that happened to you, something someone did to you, maybe even against your will; still, you feel guilty, as if it were somehow your fault.

"Would we were like animals," mused the poet Walt Whitman, "for I have not seen animals weep in the night because of the guilt of their sins. I have not seen them pour out their lives in remorse."[1]

But we are not animals, and guilt is a harsh reality among human beings. It is cruel and relentless. It refuses to be assuaged; it won't be put off. With Herculean efforts we may repress it for a time, but it always returns. It has the power to torment and immobilize. It can reduce a person to sleeplessness and tears and leave him an empty shell, only a shadow of his former self. Unresolved, it will eventually destroy him.

Consider David. Did not guilt pen some of his most poignant psalms? Hear his lament:

> I am worn out from groaning;
>> all night long I flood my bed with weeping
>> and drench my couch with tears.
>
> O LORD, do not rebuke me in your anger
>> or discipline me in your wrath.
> Be merciful to me, LORD, for I am faint;
>> O LORD, heal me, for my bones are in agony.
> My soul is in anguish.
>> How long, O LORD, how long? (Ps. 6:6, 1–3 NIV)

David was in agony, not only for what he had done, but for the fact that he could do it. Over and over he must have asked himself how he could have turned out this way—an adulterer and a murderer. Guilt had become a mirror revealing his inner self, and he could not bear what he saw. Nor was it only what he had suffered, but what his sinful actions had done to his family and closest friends as well.

No wonder Dr. Blanton writes, "Whether you consider conscience a divinely implanted mechanism, a dim echo of parental authority, or the ancient and collective taboos of the human race, it remains the device in human personality that triggers one of the most destructive of all emotions, guilt."[2]

Yes, guilt can be destructive, but it need not be. Like pain it is really just a signal that something is wrong. Ignore it, refuse to deal with the underlying cause (sin), and it will eat on you like a malignant tumor. There is only one cure—forgiveness. Not remorse, or penance, or self-flagellation—just forgiveness.

Since every sin is ultimately against God (see Ps. 51:4) it is His forgiveness we seek first. Having been forgiven by the Father (see 1 John 1:9), we must now forgive ourselves. If we continue to judge ourselves after God has forgiven us, we nullify the liberating power of His forgiveness. That is to say that while we will receive the eternal benefits of His forgiveness, we know nothing of the joy of a life lived without condemnation.

We cannot, however, simply decide to forgive ourselves. It doesn't work that way. First we must acknowledge our sins. Then we must allow God to forgive us. Only then are we in a position to

> Guilt can be destructive, but it need not be. There is only one cure—forgiveness.

forgive ourselves. Invert the order, try and skip a step, and any attempt to forgive yourself will be nothing more than an exercise in futility.

Step I: Acknowledge Your Sin

Return with me for a moment to Diane and her daughter Denise. It is obvious that Diane was struggling with guilt and that she had been for some time, perhaps years. Apparently she had been able to keep it at bay, under control, but Denise's surgery changed all of that. Then Diane had to deal with the guilt she had tried to ignore all these years.

Because I know Diane, I know her guilt is rooted in something that happened more than seventeen years ago when she was a very young woman. At the time she was in the middle of a painful divorce. Since she was broke and had no way to support herself, she moved home to live with her parents. Then to her dismay, she missed her period.

A few days later, she had an old school friend buy her a home pregnancy test kit. Back then it took two hours for the results, so she got up at 4:00 A.M. and did the test (so her parents wouldn't know). For the next two hours she sat in the dark and waited. At 6:00 A.M., just as the sun was coming up, she got the bitter news. The test was positive.

Of course she was hardly surprised, her body was changing. Still, this was proof positive, and she was devastated. She had already filed for a divorce and couldn't imagine reconciling with her estranged husband. Although she lacked absolute proof, all the circumstantial evidence indicated that he was involved in homosexuality. She already had one child who was not yet two years old, and now she was pregnant again. It was too much.

Emotionally, Diane was a wreck. She didn't have anyone to confide in, so she bottled all her fears and confusion inside of herself. Day after day she grew more depressed until one day she simply gave up. Here's how she describes what happened:

> One afternoon when I was putting my daughter down for a nap she wouldn't stop crying. I was in the bedroom with her and I was just going to let her cry herself to sleep, but my mother wouldn't hear of it. She marched into the room and picked Darlene up. As she was leaving she said something to me. I don't remember exactly what, but I interpreted it to mean that I was an unfit mother, a failure as a wife, and a disappointment as a daughter. In other words I wasn't good for anything!
>
> Sitting on the nightstand beside the bed was a bottle of prescription sleeping pills. Without really thinking about it I dumped all the pills into my hand, about fifty of them, I think. Then I went into the bathroom and got a glass of water and downed them all. I didn't consciously want

to die. I just wanted to sleep and sleep and sleep. I never again wanted to think about how messed up my life was, not ever.

A few minutes later my mom returned to the bedroom to put Darlene in her bed and found me passed out. Seeing the empty pill bottle she put two and two together and called 9-1-1. In a few minutes an ambulance arrived and I was rushed to the hospital. When I arrived at the emergency room my blood pressure was 60/40 and falling. They immediately pumped my stomach and induced vomiting. For the next two hours I puked my insides out.

Finally they put me in a semi-private room right next to the elevator. All that night and the next day I listened to the elevator door opening. Every time it did I expected my husband to walk in and tell me every-thing was going to be okay. But he never came, or even called. That's when I knew our marriage was truly over.

Later my obstetrician told me that the type of sleeping pill I had tried to overdose on could cause birth defects. If it did it would affect my baby's face. It could be anything from a cleft palate to birthmarks.

For the next seven months I lived with the terrifying possibility that I might have done something to scar my baby for life. When Denise was born I immediately put my finger in her mouth to make sure she did not have a cleft palate. Thankfully she was fine and for the first time in months I felt that awful fear leave me. Only later, after she was cleaned up, did I realize that she had a large birthmark on her face and several smaller ones. Now guilt took up residence where fear had once lived. How could I ever forgive myself for doing something so stupid?

As Denise was growing up I kept telling myself that makeup would cover it. She never said much about it so I tried to convince myself that it didn't really bother her. Now I wonder how I could I have been so blind, so insensitive to what she was feeling?

Anyway when she turned sixteen she asked me to check with a plastic surgeon to see if there was a way to have it removed. I think that was when I first realized I had only been fooling myself. A few days later, she told me that the reason she had never spent the night with any of her friends was because she was ashamed to let anyone see her without makeup. Hello guilt!

After learning that our insurance would cover laser surgery to remove birthmarks we made an appointment with a surgeon. The day they actually did the surgery was one of the worst days of my life. It was done in the doctor's office and I was on one side of the table holding Denise's hand and a nurse was on the other side holding her other hand. A second nurse was beside me holding me up. Denise was crying. I was crying. Even the two nurses were wiping their eyes. I have never witnessed such bravery as Denise exhibited, nor have I ever seen a child endure such pain.

And never had I felt such guilt, never! It was all my fault. I caused all this pain. Not God. Not nature. Me! I couldn't help wondering that if she knew, would she ever be able to forgive me? Maybe an even bigger question was, would I ever be able to forgive myself?

After seventeen years Diane had finally taken the first big step toward forgiving herself—she acknowledged her sin. No more rationalizing that makeup will cover it. No more pretending that her daughter is just shy and doesn't like sleeping over at her friends' houses. At last she was facing the painful truth—by her actions, however unintentional, she had scarred her daughter's face. Until now she could not receive God's forgiveness, nor forgive herself, because she could not bring herself to admit that her daughter's birthmark was her fault. In order to receive forgiveness she had to acknowledge her need to be forgiven.

I'm reminded of the woman who suffered a series of psychological problems following an abortion. Although she was treated by some of the best mental health professionals she only grew worse. In desperation she sought the help of a wise old pastor.

After listening to her recount her woes he said, "Your doctor said having an abortion was the right thing to do."

Sobbing, she nodded in the affirmative.

"Your husband said having an abortion was the right thing to do."

"Yes," she managed between sobs.

"Your doctor excused your abortion. Your husband excused your abortion. But God doesn't excuse it," he thundered. "God says abortion is sin!"

Doubling over as if in great pain, she rolled out of her chair unto the floor. Whimpering like a motherless child, she curled into a fetal position. Kneeling beside her the old pastor placed his hand on her arm. "God won't excuse your abortion," he said, "but He will do something better. He will forgive you!"

Though the road to spiritual and emotional wholeness was a long one, it began that afternoon. It started when she was finally able to acknowledge her sin. As long as everyone told her she had made the right decision, she was trapped in her guilt with no way to find forgiveness.

As you can readily see, few things in life are more painful than facing our sins. Stripped of the rationalizations and self-justifications in which we have cloaked, they are now revealed in all their self-serving vulgarity. Still, painful as it may be, it is a necessary first step. Whether we are talking about Diane, whose suicide attempt scarred her unborn child for life, or the lady who aborted her baby, or any one of us, the first step to redemption is always the same—the honest confession of our sins. Not in vague generalities, but in painfully specific detail.

> The first step to redemption is always the same—the honest confession of our sins. Not in vague generalities, but in painfully specific detail.

Step 2: Receive God's Forgiveness

Having finally faced our personal sinfulness in all of its tragic particulars, we must now be careful not to fall into despair. The damage we have done, the hurt we have caused, the ruin we have brought on ourselves and others are almost more than we can bear. No matter what we do now we cannot right the terrible wrongs we have done. Regret seeps into the very core of our soul, producing a black despair. Though the Bible clearly states that God stands ready to forgive our sins, we cannot imagine why He would.

The biblical word for what God does next is grace—unmerited favor. Although we deserve to die, He gives us life. Although we deserve to be punished for our sins, He forgives us. Although we should bear the shame of our past all the days of our life, He removes it from us.

> He does not treat us as our sins deserve
>> or repay us according to our iniquities.
> For as high as the heavens are above the earth,
>> so great is his love for those who fear him;
> as far as the east is from the west,
>> so far has he removed our transgressions from us. (Ps. 103:10–12 NIV)

Rachel was one of those people who loved Jesus with an unbridled enthusiasm. When she worshiped her faced glowed, her eyes sparkled, her entire being seemed to radiate the praises of her Lord. Then before our very eyes she began to change—to die, really. Over a period of weeks a deadness crept into her eyes. In unguarded moments her face wore a haunted look. Behind a smile that seemed forced there lurked a terrible sadness, a sorrow so severe it was painful to behold.

> Our only hope is the regenerative power of God's forgiveness.

Therefore I was not surprised when she made an appointment to see me. I only wondered why it had taken her so long. When she stepped into my office there was not even a hint of the vivacious young woman she used to be. For what seemed a long time she said nothing. She simply sat in a chair across the desk from me and looked at her hands. Then she began to cry, a soundless weeping that tore at my heart. I wanted to reach across the desk and comfort her somehow, but there was something about her pain that pushed me away. It was a private thing, and until she chose to share it I dared not intrude.

Finally she seemed to gather herself, then she spoke in a voice I had to strain to hear. "I've come to say good-bye. I'm going away for a while."

I must have looked puzzled because she hastened to add, "I'm not leaving town or anything like that. I'm just not going to come to church for a while."

Though I waited, she gave no further explanation. Gently I probed. "Has someone done something to offend you?"

"No," she said. "It's nothing like that."

"Would you like to tell me about it?"

She flashed a glance my way, and in her eyes there was a startled look. For a moment I thought she might flee the now suffocating confines of my office, but with an effort she willed herself to stay.

Taking a deep breath she asked, "Are you sure you want to hear this?"

"I'm sure."

"I'm having an affair with my boss," she said, the words rushing out of her. "I know it's wrong. I know I'm a bad person, but I can't seem to help myself. That's why I'm going to stop coming to church."

She looked at me, and I nodded for her to continue.

"God must be sick of me," she said, shame coloring every word. "Every time I pray I confess my sins and promise God I will never do it again. Yet even while I'm praying another part of my mind is planning our next clandestine rendezvous. It's disgusting. I can't even stand myself.

"I've decided that the only honorable thing to do is to stop pretending that I love God. I'm not going to pray anymore until I truly mean it. And I'm not coming back to church until I get my life straightened out. I may be a bad person, but I'm not a hypocrite."

Looking at her intently I said, "Rachel, you can do that if you want to, but I think you are making a terrible mistake. The only hope you have is right here with the people of God."

"What do you mean?" she asked with a puzzled frown.

"Obviously making promises you can't keep isn't working, so why don't you simply try being totally honest with the Lord. Instead of promising Him that you will never commit adultery again, try praying something like this: 'Lord Jesus, I'm terribly ashamed of what I'm doing, but I can't seem to help myself. Or maybe I'm just not willing to stop. I don't know. And as crazy as it may seem in light of my behavior, I do love You and I want to be Your person. I guess what I'm trying to say is, if You can keep loving me just a little longer surely I will become the person You have called me to be.'"

After promising to think about it, Rachel excused herself, and I was left to ponder her dilemma. Having come face-to-face with her sinful self, she could not stomach what she saw. Since her behavior sickened her, disgusted her, she projected her feelings onto God. If she could hardly stand herself, then she was sure that God must be sick to death of her. Most of us can probably identify with her feelings. Who hasn't been tempted to write himself off as a lost cause at one time or another?

Confronting our sins is a necessary but perilous step on the road to recovery. If we get stuck here, however, we will surely die. Neither regret nor self-recrimination can save us now. Our only hope is the regenerative power of God's forgiveness.

To move to the next step we will have to change our focus. It is time to stop looking at what we have done (our sins) and start looking at what He has done for us (our salvation). "God made him [Jesus] who had no sin to be sin for us, so that in him we might become the righteousness of God" (2 Cor. 5:21 NIV).

It is time we stopped looking back at our past failures and started looking up at our glorious future. "Therefore, if anyone is in Christ, he is a new creation; the old has gone, the new has come! All this is from God" (2 Cor. 5:17–18 NIV).

How, you may be wondering, can God forgive you considering the terrible things you have done? A good question, but I have a better one for you.

Why else would He forgive you? If you hadn't done terrible things you would have no need to be forgiven. The very fact that you have failed so miserably, sinned so shamefully, is exactly what qualifies you for His mercy! God does not forgive us because we deserve to be forgiven, but because we so desperately need to be. Remember, He is a forgiving God, and while we are the objects of His mercy, we are not the cause of it.

> It is time we stopped looking back at our past failures and started looking up at our glorious future.

Thankfully Rachel took my advice and continued coming to church. For a while nothing changed, at least nothing we could see. Then little by little we noticed that she was coming to life again. The sparkle returned to her eye, and once more she worshiped with a holy contagion. By focusing on the finished work of Jesus rather than on her sinful past she was able, not only to accept God's forgiveness, but to forgive herself as well.

Step 3: Forgive Yourself

Now we come to the toughest task of all: forgiving ourselves. It was hard to take an honest look at our sins, but we did it. Harder still to believe that God knows the worst about us and still believes the best, but He does. Now the time has come for us to see ourselves as God see us. Sinners, yes, but deserving of forgiveness nonetheless. Failing here we will never be able to forgive ourselves.

> God does not forgive us because we deserve to be forgiven, but because we so desperately need to be.

Like many of us Diane struggled with this very issue. Over and over she asked herself: "How do I forgive myself when I don't feel like I have ever done anything to redeem myself?"

That cuts right to the heart of things doesn't it? The age-old question: How can I atone for my sins?

Not through our own efforts, Diane can tell you that. For years she tried to redeem her past. Somewhere she picked up the idea that if she could succeed where she had failed before, then she could put her sinful mistakes behind her. Unfortunately things never worked out. No matter how hard she tried, she always seemed to fail. Failure piled upon failure until she was trapped in a reoccurring nightmare. The harder she tried, the more hopeless her situation became.

In reality it didn't matter. Present success can never atone for past sins. No matter how exemplary we live, we can never remove our past wrongs. The finished work of Jesus is our only hope.

Few of us truly appreciate the great lengths to which God had to go in order to provide our forgiveness. No matter how much He loved us He could not simply forgive our sins. Being absolutely just, God cannot allow a single sin to go unpunished; nor can He forgive a solitary sinner until His justice is fully satisfied, until every sin—past, present, and future—is punished.

Had God wiped out the entire human race that would have been just, exactly what we deserved, "For the wages of sin is death" (Rom. 6:23). But God could not do that either, for even as He is just He is also merciful. And being a merciful God He could not turn His back on our lost race. Had He done so He would have betrayed that part of His eternal character. Because of who He is, God was compelled to satisfy

> He is a forgiving God, and while we are the objects of His mercy, we are not the cause of it.

both the just demands of His righteous character and the merciful requirements of His loving-kindness.

Therein lay His dilemma: How could He be both just and merciful? How could He forgive our sins without betraying the just demands of His holy nature? Moreover, how could He judge our sins without denying His love and mercy?

The Cross was the only answer, for in the Cross both God's mercy and His justice were fully vindicated. Through His sacrificial death, Jesus manifested the Father's unconditional love even as He suffered the full penalty for our sins, thus satisfying the just demands of God's righteous character.

Therefore the finished work of Christ is God's only basis for forgiving us. He does not forgive us because we deserve to be forgiven, nor because we have suffered enough, or grieved enough, but only because Jesus has already suffered the punishment for our sins. "He himself bore our sins in his body on the tree" (1 Peter 2:24 NIV).

If God, therefore, has forgiven us, who are we to judge ourselves? If the sinless life and sacrificial death of Jesus is sufficient to satisfy the holy demands of a just God, who are we to demand more? Are we holier than God? Hardly. *Therefore we forgive ourselves because in Christ God has already forgiven us.*

I wish I could tell you that Diane grasped this truth in a single moment of spiritual revelation, but I can't. Her shame was too long-standing, her past too painful. Nonetheless, little by little she came to understand the unconditional love of God. In time she was able to put her trust in Jesus' blood and righteousness.

Through the miracle of God's forgiveness she was finally able to forgive herself. She is no longer a tormented woman, haunted by past failures and present fears. She made some mistakes to be sure, did some things she wishes she could undo, but she is no longer living a life of bitter regret. Through His sacrificial death and glorious resurrection Jesus changed all of that. Today Diane is happily married and the mother of four beautiful children. Together with her husband she is celebrating the miracle of forgiveness—both God's gracious gift of forgiveness and the gift she gave herself.

Forgiving yourself does not mean that you will never remember your past failures again. But it does mean that you will no longer allow your past to define who you are. You are a new creation in Christ (2 Cor. 5:17), a child of God and a joint heir with Him (Rom. 8:15–17). You will probably always have some regrets, wish you had done some things differently, but they will no longer paralyze you. Nor will you feel an obsession to punish yourself for past wrongdoing. Although nothing can change the past, not even forgiveness, you are now free to create a new past that will supplant the old. Every spiritual achievement, great or small, becomes material out of which you are writing a new past, line upon line.

That is what Rachel did. After quitting her job to get away from her lover, she began building a new life. It wasn't easy, especially at first, but with God's help she persevered. She found a new job, and after a time God brought a wonderful Christian man into her life. After much prayer and counsel they decided to get married. Recently they celebrated their silver wedding anniversary. With God's help Rachel has truly written a new past!

> Receive His forgiveness, forgive yourself, and get started on creating a new past—a glorious past where Christ is Lord!

As a boy growing up I used to sing, "It is no secret what God can do. What He's done for others He'll do for you. With arms wide open He'll pardon you. It is no secret what God can do." What God has done for Diane and Rachel and tens of thousands of others He will do for you. Receive His forgiveness, forgive yourself, and get started on creating a new past—a glorious past where Christ is Lord!

Chapter 16

MAKING
RESTITUTION

A few weeks ago I was speaking at a men's conference on the subject of personal integrity. In the course of my message I related a painfully embarrassing incident that occurred while I was on a publicity tour promoting my book titled, *How to Be a Man of Character in a World of Compromise*. The guys listened intently as I told them of arriving late at the airport to discover that I had forgotten to refuel the rental car. That really should not have been a problem since the rental company will gladly refuel the car for about $3.00 a gallon.

Nonetheless this is where my story takes its most embarrassing turn. When the agent at the check-in counter asked me if I had refueled the car, I lied, or at least I did not tell the whole truth. Instead of simply answering no, I said, "The fuel gauge is registering full."

Without looking up from her paperwork she asked, "Do you have a receipt for the gasoline?"

Once more I had an opportunity to do the right thing. All I had to do was tell her that I had not refueled the car. Instead I simply said, "No." She must have sensed I was not being completely truthful because she pressed me. "What," she asked, "was the name of the gasoline station where you refueled the car?"

This time I did not even pretend to tell the truth. "I don't remember," I mumbled as I turned away and walked toward the concourse. I could feel her eyes boring into me, but I didn't look back.

The irony of it all was readily apparent. Even as I was flying around the country promoting a book on character I was lying through my teeth. If it hadn't been so tragic it would have been comical. Such duplicity, such deceit. And for what? Five dollars worth of gasoline. To make matters worse, the money wasn't even coming out of my own pocket. The publisher was covering all of my expenses.

Of course God dealt with me ever so severely, and I went on to tell the men how I repented of my sin and received His forgiveness. In addition, I informed them I was now dealing with that particular temptation from a position of strength rather than weakness. Now, whenever I rent a car I take the fuel option, which means I pay for a full tank of gas up front, and I can return it completely empty if I choose.

Having bared my soul and confessed my sinfulness before the entire group, I was feeling more than a little vulnerable. It was a risk I had chosen to take in hopes of inspiring other men to take an honest look at themselves. Instead one man decided to take a closer look at me, or so it seemed at the time. Raising his hand, he asked, "Did you make restitution?"

Stalling for time while I tried to collect my thoughts, I said, "What exactly do you mean by restitution?"

"As I understand restitution," he replied, "it means to right a wrong. I guess what I'm asking is, what did you do to make things right? Did you telephone the attendant at the car rental counter and tell her that you had lied? Did you send a check to the rental company to cover the fuel expense?"

"I wish I could tell you that I did all of that, but the truth is I did nothing at all. I made no restitution."

In retrospect, I don't think the man was trying to embarrass me. In fact, he made it a point to apologize to me after the session. He truly wanted to know what God expects of us when it comes to restitution. What part does it play in overcoming the trouble we have brought upon ourselves?

A Theology of Restitution

Interestingly enough in doing research for this chapter I have discovered that there is very little material written on restitution. The commentaries

I consulted on the various Bible passages dealing with the subject had little or nothing to say. Nor did any of the books on spiritual disciplines include it, though they all mentioned confession. Even Oswald Chambers was strangely silent on the subject.

Be that as it may, my experience tells me that it is an integral part of our spiritual journey. Restitution requires us not only to confront the damage our sinful choices have produced, but to go a step farther. Now we must do everything within our power to right those wrongs, to heal those hurts, and to restore those rela-

> Restitution requires us to do everything within our power to right those wrongs, to heal those hurts, and to restore those relationships.

tionships. In the process, God often allows us to feel the pain of those we have sinned against. This too is part of our restoration.

One husband and father, whose infidelity caused his wife and children unspeakable pain, tells of parking his car in the driveway leading to the dorm where his college-age daughter lived. While waiting for her to join him, he was overwhelmed with a terrible sadness and began sobbing. All at once he saw a mental image of his daughter sitting in her compact car in that very spot. Like him she was weeping piteously. Now he understood his tears. They were not for him, but for her. God, in His mercy, was allowing him to partake of her suffering. He had always known that his sin had wounded her, but now he truly understood her pain.

This kind of sorrow should not be confused with either despair or bitter regret. Having already received the forgiveness of our sins we are free from debilitating remorse. The pain we now experience is a form of godly sorrow, and it produces spiritual fruit.

> See what this godly sorrow has produced in you: what earnestness, what eagerness to clear yourselves, what indignation, what alarm, what longing, what concern, what readiness to see justice done. (2 Cor. 7:11 NIV)

With these thoughts in mind let's turn our attention to the Scriptures.

Generally speaking, the passages regarding restitution address the area of personal property (Ex. 22:1–4; Lev. 6:1–7), but they also mention damage to the tabernacle and its furnishings (Lev. 5:14–16), as well as extortion and false testimony (Lev. 6:4–5).

As a general rule, the law of restitution required full payment plus 20 percent. Leviticus 6:5 says: "He must make restitution in full, add a fifth of the value to it and give it all to the owner on the day he presents his guilt offering" (NIV). In the case of stolen cattle or sheep the measure of restitution went up. If the thief had slaughtered the animals or had sold them he "must pay back five head of cattle for the ox and four sheep for the sheep" (Ex. 22:1 NIV). "If the stolen animal is found alive in his possession . . . he must pay back double" (see Ex. 22:4 NIV). Proverbs 6:31 declared: "If [a thief] is caught, he must pay sevenfold, though it costs him all the wealth of his house" (NIV). "A thief must certainly make restitution, but if he has nothing, he must be sold to pay for his theft" (Ex. 22:3 NIV).

The only reference to restitution found in the New Testament is an example rather than a command. Following his conversion, Zacchaeus, the chief tax collector, declared: "Look, Lord! Here and now I give half of my possessions to the poor, and if I have cheated anybody out of anything, I will pay back four times the amount" (Luke 19:8 NIV). It is important to note that restitution is not a prerequisite to forgiveness, rather it is tangible proof of the redemptive work grace is doing in our heart.

While it is impossible to read these references without concluding that restitution was a serious matter to the ancient people of God, I do not want to make more of it than God does. What we are talking about is a spiritual principle rather than a legalistic requirement. Although we are not required to make restitution in order to receive salvation, our long-term spiritual and emotional wholeness may well depend upon it.

> Although we are not required to make restitution in order to receive salvation, our long-term spiritual and emotional wholeness may well depend upon it.

God only expects us to make restitution for that which is in our power to restore. Since much of the collateral damage caused by our sinful choices is of an emotional or spiritual nature there may be little we can do in the way of restitution. Beyond a heartfelt apology there is not much we can do except pray. In those areas where restitution is possible it should be done humbly, in a way that brings glory to God and not attention to ourselves. In addition we should be especially sensitive to the feelings of the injured party and his family. Restitution should never cause him or those he loves further pain or embarrassment. If necessary the actual act of restitution can be done through an intermediary to spare the feelings of the wronged person and his family.

Making Restitution

Noticing the return address on the envelope, I felt my pulse quicken. Although it had been more than twenty years since I had spoken to the sender, I did not need to read the letter to know what it was about. Nonetheless I extracted the carefully typed pages and began to read. In an instant I was carried back to a distant Sunday evening in 1967.

In my mind I saw it all again. The small sanctuary, furnished with oak pews and deep red carpet. The congregation was sitting attentively, made up mostly of blue-collar people whom I had known a good portion of my young life. Our pastor was standing behind the pulpit, the light reflecting off of his glasses. He was an unassuming man, almost apologetic in nature. His humility and soft-spoken ways were what initially appealed to the congregation. But, as is often the case, those very characteristics now grated on more than a few of the more influential members.

I had heard the complaints: "He's not a dynamic leader." "His preaching doesn't inspire faith." "I feel worse when I leave church than when I came." "Why does he have to be so melancholy?" On and on it went.

Being young and zealous, I felt it was my responsibility to do something. So on that Sunday evening, during testimony time, I stood to my feet and launched into a bombastic testimony about the sufficiency of Christ. I quoted Romans 8:37, "In all these things we are more than conquerors through Him who loved us." The congregation responded with a chorus of hearty amens. Building up steam, I moved to Philippians 4:13, "I can do all things through Christ who strengthens me." More amens, with a hallelujah or two thrown in for good measure. Now I really turned up the heat. "The church of Jesus Christ is not a woebegone raga-muffin," I thundered. "She is as 'terrible as an army with banners' (Song 6:4 KJV). Through faith we can do all things. We can subdue kingdoms, work righteousness, obtain promises, stop the mouths of lions, quench the violence of the fire, escape the edge of the sword, out of weakness be made strong, turn to flight the armies of our enemies and even see the dead raised to life." (See Heb. 11:33–35)

Looking straight at our pastor, I concluded, "We must preach our faith, not our doubts. Nobody wants to hear about our doubts. Everybody has enough doubts of their own."

Having delivered the coup de grace I took my seat. Though I had not mentioned the pastor by name, nor referred to him directly in any way, there was no mistaking what I had done. To anyone who had ears to hear the message was plain enough. I had rebuked the pastor, the presiding elder in our congregation, and I had done it publicly. Had anyone felt inclined to correct me, since the Scriptures clearly forbid what I had done (see 1 Tim. 5:1), I had left myself ample room to protest my innocence. I was merely giving a testimony. Just encouraging the church in the faith.

Meekly I sat with my head bowed humbly as if I were in prayer. Around me I sensed, more than heard, murmurs of approval. After a few seconds I risked a look at our pastor, the man who had given me my start in the ministry. He appeared shell-shocked. His face was a sickly color and filled with hurt. In his eyes I saw what could only be described as a look of betrayal, as if he could not believe what I had done to him.

In a matter of seconds he seemed to pull himself together, and the service went on. Although he did not demand an apology, confrontation not being his style, I knew I owed him one and a public one at that. During his sermon I sensed the Holy Spirit directing me to make amends, publicly, before the service ended, but I resisted. Finally the benediction was given and service dismissed. On the way out more than a few people patted me on the back and thanked me for my "encouraging" words, but I took little comfort in what they said.

For two or three days, perhaps as long as a week, I was deeply troubled in my spirit, but in time I was able to put the whole thing behind me. Life went on, and that incident was pushed to the back of my mind where it joined a number of other "little" things I had chosen to ignore rather than deal with. None of them were very significant, at least from my perspective, but as the years passed their cumulative weight wore on me. From time to time God would deal with me about one or another of them. So painfully poignant were the memories of my sinful failures in those holy moments that I was often moved to tears. Always I found a wonderful release after acknowledging my sin and receiving God's forgiveness. Yet for all of that I never resolved the incident with my pastor. Occasionally the Holy Spirit would encourage me to make restitution, but I always had an excuse. What good would it do after all these years? Surely he had put the incident behind him by now. Nothing good could come from digging it up at this late date.

The letter I now held in my hand was from his youngest son, who was now a pastor himself. He quickly brought me up to date regarding his parents—where they were living, the condition of their health, what they were doing, etc. He then made reference to the size of congregation I served, the number of books I had written, and the "success" I had achieved in ministry. Finally he came to the reason for his letter.

In plain English he described the deep hurt my actions had caused his parents, particularly his father. After reminding me of the investment his father had made in my life and ministry, he asked me if I could find it in my heart to write his father. He made it clear he was not asking me to apologize, just a thank-you, perhaps. He concluded by telling me how much it would mean to his father if he could hear from me.

Sitting at my desk I bowed my head and wept. Guilt flooded my soul and shame. For more than twenty years that good man had lived with the wound I had so thoughtlessly inflicted. He was not bitter, not angry, just hurt.

Would I write him? I would do more than that. I would confess my sin and ask his forgiveness. I would apologize for my reckless words. I would make what restitution I could. Oh, thank You Jesus, for giving me one more chance to right this terrible wrong.

As I put pen to paper I felt the weight I had carried all those years slide off my shoulders. Funny, I had never realized how heavy it was until it was gone. When I finally finished writing the day was nearly done, just a smear of light outside the office window. Kneeling, I asked God to do what I could not do. I asked Him to put His healing hands on the pastor's heart, to heal the deep wounds my careless words had inflicted so many years ago. "Oh, God," I prayed, "may my letter of apology have as profound an impact for good as my hurtful words had for evil."

A few days later I received a gracious reply in which the pastor accepted my apology and tendered his forgiveness. Once more God had used restitution as the instrument through which His healing grace flowed. I could not take back my hurtful words, but with God's help I was able to replace them with fresh words of love and appreciation.

Unfortunately not every attempt at restitution is met with such a favorable response, at least not initially. Gina, a pastor's wife, tells of a broken relationship in her life that spanned several years. It was especially painful because circumstances required her and the estranged friend to interact with each other on a regular basis.

After the initial falling out there were no more outbursts, just an unnatural politeness. They spoke to each other, carefully lest they inflict some new pain, and their guardedness was as painful as anything they might have said. They made small talk, tried to pretend everything was as it should be, but there was a deadness in their voices, a tragic reminder of the terrible thing that had happened, a thing from which their friendship might never recover.

In 1996 a guest minister came to their church and spoke on the ministry of reconciliation. The Lord used his ministry to touch Gina's heart, and she decided to write a letter of apology. Though she felt the broken relationship was at least as much Lisa's fault as her own, she chose only to address her own mistakes. Prayerfully she wrote the letter, specifically identified her wrongdoing, and asked Lisa to forgive her.

Lisa's response was hardly what Gina had hoped. "She didn't run up to me and say 'I forgive you,' or 'You're wonderful,' or anything," Gina confided. "She simply said 'Thank you,' nothing more. Nor did things change much. Conversation was still strained. There seemed to be a wall separating us, always."

Five or six months passed in which Gina battled both anger and wounded pride. Then one day she felt an intense compulsion to pray for Lisa and her husband. Though it was hard she set her hurt feelings aside and entered into intense intercession.

At church the following Sunday evening, Lisa and her husband asked for special prayer. Instantly Gina felt the same sense of urgency that had prompted her to intercede earlier in the week. Quickly she made her way to where Lisa and Greg were standing and began to pray fervently for them. As she prayed there was a nearly overwhelming sense of the Spirit's presence. Both Greg and Lisa were weeping when she finished. As she turned to go, Lisa gave her a hug, something she hadn't done in years.

The next day Gina received a letter from Lisa in which she apologized for her wrongdoing and ask for Gina's forgiveness. "What I had tried to accomplish by myself six months earlier," said Gina, "God healed in a moment."

In no way do I want to minimize what God did through prayer that final Sunday evening, but by the same token I feel it would be unwise not to point out the part restitution played. Had Gina not been willing to seek reconciliation via her letter, it is not likely Lisa would have been open to receive her prayers. And only God knows what preparatory work the Holy Spirit was able to do in Lisa's heart as a result of Gina's letter of restitution. Yes, God healed their relationship in a "moment," but there were months of preparation!

Of course not all restitution involves relationships. Sometimes there are moral and ethical issues to be resolved. For instance, I know of a pastor who inadvertently took church property when he resigned his pastorate. It was not a big thing—two small electrical heaters costing less than seventy-five dollars. Although he had moved to another state, every time he saw those heaters God pricked his conscience. He intended to send a check to the church to pay for them, but somehow he never got around to it.

More than two years went by, and he still had not returned the heaters or sent a check. While he was attending a minister's conference, God convicted him. So forcefully did the Lord deal with him that he felt he had to resolve the issue immediately.

It just so happened that the pastor who had followed him at the church was also attending the conference. After seeking him out, the former pastor explained what he had done. "Here's a check made payable to the church for $120.00. Eighty dollars is to pay for the two heaters. The other forty dollars is restitution."

Although I question his judgment in taking the heaters in the first place, I do have to admire a man like that. It could not have been easy to confess his sin, his theft, to the new pastor. Most of us, I'm afraid, would have conveniently "forgotten" where the heaters came from, or we would have found a way to justify what we had done. The heaters were old, we might have reasoned, or the church wasn't using them anyway.

The ministry of restitution has a number of benefits, both for the person making restitution and the one receiving it. Obviously it restores that which was taken illegally or inappropriately. It rights a wrong, at least insofar as a wrong can be made right. Since restitution is an acknowledgment of wrongdoing, it also provides a basis for the wronged party to offer forgiveness, an act necessary for his recovery.

> Restitution provides a means whereby the wrongdoer may demonstrate the sincerity of his repentance, it also serves as a strong deterrent to future sin.

To forgive is never easy, but it is nearly impossible when the wrongdoer neither acknowledges his guilt nor seeks our forgiveness. The benefit to the one making restitution is at least twofold. First it provides a means whereby the wrongdoer may demonstrate the sincerity of his repentance. On the flip side it also serves as a strong deterrent to future sin.

Beyond Restitution

Maybe you are the injured party, the one who has been sinned against, but no one has ever made restitution to you. What should you do? Demand your rights? Carry a grudge? Find a way to get even? You can if you choose to, but only at a terrible cost to yourself. The acid of bitterness always destroys the container in which it is carried.

Consider Ken's situation. If ever a man had a right to be bitter, he did. While his wife was in a psychiatric hospital receiving treatment for a bipolar disorder, she became involved in an affair with another patient, a man named Larry. Although their relationship was discovered, the counselor decided it would be better if Ken was not informed. Both Belinda (Ken's wife) and Larry agreed to terminate the relationship. Unfortunately once they were released from the hospital they resumed the affair. Once again it came to light, this time during outpatient follow-up sessions.

The counselor decided that Ken should be informed at this point. An appointment was set up for the following day. When Ken and Belinda arrived, Larry was already present. Although Ken had no idea who Larry was or why he was there, he soon found out.

After dumping the whole sordid mess in Ken's lap, the counselor asked if there was anything he wanted to say. For two or three minutes Ken just sat there, too stunned to speak. Then he turned to Larry and said in a voice thick with pain, "When you least expect it, expect it! You are worse than an animal, and I will make you pay. If ever I see you again I will kill you."

By this time Ken was shaking with rage and towering over Larry, who huddled in the far corner of the counselor's office. Though the counselor tried to calm him down, Ken continued to scream. "You are the sorriest excuse for a human being I have ever seen! You are nothing but a predator! You don't deserve to live! I will get you—you can count on that! I will have my revenge!"

Though the affair with Larry ended, Belinda now found herself caught up in emotions she could not control. Over the next several months she had a series of short-term affairs, finally becoming pregnant as a result of one of her trysts. The subsequent guilt was more than she could bear, causing her to become deeply depressed. One day Ken came home and found her dead. She had killed herself.

Ken's grief was nearly unbearable. He blamed himself. For months after Belinda's funeral he lived in a fog, battling depression. Then little by little he began to recover. Finally there was only one thing he could not release—his bitterness toward Larry. To Ken's way of thinking, if Larry hadn't taken advantage of Belinda in her time of depression, none of this would have happened. Belinda would still be alive.

In time Ken managed to lock that bitterness deep inside himself. Sometime later he remarried, but not even the love of his new wife could heal the hate that lay like a time bomb in the very core of his being. To his family and friends Ken appeared to be fully recovered. Only he knew the truth. Inside him the bomb was ticking.

One weekend Ken and his wife drove to Austin to attend a Christian concert. While waiting for the concert to begin, he happened to notice a man sitting a few rows in front of them who bore a striking resemblance to Larry. With an effort he pushed that thought from his mind. It couldn't be Larry. The last he had heard Larry was living in another state. Still the thought persisted, like a stubborn toothache. Then the man turned to wave at a friend.

Suddenly all of the hatred and anger Ken had kept under such tight control boiled up inside of him and he began to shake. His wife turned to him, concern on her face. "Kenny, what's wrong," she asked. "Are you sick?"

He tried to speak but couldn't. Anger was literally choking him. Reaching for a scrap of paper he scribbled a note. "The man with the beard, sitting about three rows in front of us, is the first man Belinda had an affair with."

Now his wife paled. Although she did not know the depth of Ken's hatred, she had a better idea than anyone else. Leaning toward him she said, "Let's leave. Let's just get out of here."

But Ken was not about to leave. He had waited too long for this. When the concert was finally over he pushed his way through the crowd until he was standing directly in front of Larry. "Hello, Larry," he said. "Do you remember me?"

"I don't think so," Larry replied. "Should I?"

"I'm Ken Evans. You may remember me as Belinda Evans's husband."

Larry's jaw dropped. All the color drained out of his face, and he began to hyperventilate. Stepping closer, Ken could smell his fear. As Larry tried to ease away he asked inanely, "How is Belinda these days?"

"She's dead, Larry," Ken said, taking a sadistic pleasure in the man's growing terror. "Thanks to you she killed herself."

Larry began to stammer. "I'm sorry. I . . . er . . . I . . . didn't mean for any of this to happen. I . . . er . . . I . . . remember what you said and . . . er . . ."

Although Ken had expected to derive great satisfaction from the long-awaited confrontation he now discovered that he took no pleasure in either Larry's humiliation or fear. As Larry cowered before him he got a glimpse of what Larry's life had been like. Since that terrible day in the hospital he had lived in fear, tormented by the memory of Ken's angry threats. Though Larry had put his life back together he always knew this day would come—"When you least expect it, expect it!"

Ken remembers thinking, *Surely as I have been tormented by anger and bitterness, Larry has been haunted by fear and shame. We are both prisoners of the past, each of us suffering in his own way.*

Even as Ken blocked Larry's escape, cornering him against a pew, God was speaking to him. In that still, small voice the Spirit seemed to say, "Will destroying Larry undo the past? Will it bring Belinda back? Isn't it time to let it go? Hasn't everyone suffered enough?"

While Ken was thinking on these things, the anger began to drain out of him. For just a moment he tried to resist the Spirit's holy work, but then he gave himself to it. As he did a supernatural peace enveloped him. To his amazement he heard himself speaking with deep compassion. "Larry," he said, "I forgive you. I truly forgive you for everything you did. I release you from the bondage of fear and guilt. I bless you with peace, my brother."

Larry began to weep. Not the bitter tears of regret, but the life-giving tears of release. After all these years he was finally free. Free from the guilt and shame that had haunted him. Free from the fear that his past would one day catch up with him and destroy him.

"And furthermore," Ken continued, "I want to ask you to forgive me for the angry words I screamed at you and for all the fear they have brought into your life."

As Ken was speaking a miracle happened. Not only was Larry released from the bondage of his past, but Ken was freed from his bitterness as well. For the first time since that day in the counselor's office years before, he was free from anger. The time bomb of hatred and bitterness was gone, destroyed by the miracle of forgiveness.

Who can explain the mystery of forgiveness? Sometimes it is a painfully slow process, achieved only after the wounded one has made the most determined efforts. Occasionally it is a gift—freely given, totally unexpected. Suddenly the hurt and anger are gone and in their place are healing words of grace. That's the way it happened for Ken. What he could not do himself, God did for him. God enabled him to forgive Larry, and in the process he discovered his own freedom as well.

It would have been nice had Larry made some effort at restitution, but he didn't. Perhaps he was afraid, or maybe he didn't know what to do. Be that as it may, Ken found something better than restitution—the gift of forgiveness. And with it he found life and freedom, not only for Larry, but for himself as well.

Take a moment as we come to the end of this chapter and ask yourself what God is saying to you. Pay particular attention to your thoughts and feelings, for that is how God usually speaks to us. Is there someone to whom you need to make restitution? Don't delay. Take action right now. Do everything within your power to make things right.

Is there someone you need to forgive? Is the time bomb of bitterness even now ticking toward an explosion? Don't wait for them to apologize or make restitution. Seize the initiative, and forgive them before it is too late. If you delay and that time bomb of bitterness explodes it will hurt no one as much as yourself.

Years ago I saw a cartoon in which one of the characters had taped an explosive device to his chest. Unbuttoning his shirt he showed it to his friend and proudly explained, "When Fred slaps me on the chest today, the way he always does, this bomb will explode and blow his hand off." Of course there was one fatal flaw in his plan. While the bomb was blowing Fred's hand off it would be blowing his own heart out. That's the way it is with anger and unforgiveness. We always end up hurting ourselves more than anyone else.

> Forgiveness does not change the past, but it does unlock the future!

More often than not our release comes as we release others. When Ken forgave Larry he not only set him free, but he also unlocked the door to the cell where he had imprisoned himself. Even as God reversed the captivity of Job (see Job 42:10 KJV) when he prayed for his friends (those who had falsely accused him) so does the Lord deliver us when we forgive those who have sinned against us. As I have said before, forgiveness does not change the past, but it does unlock the future!

.

Chapter 17

AFTER
THE STORM

Few things are more spectacular than a thunderstorm high in the Rockies, especially if you are safely ensconced in a weather-tight cabin. Jagged flashes of lightning pierce the blue-black gloom, causing the towering peaks to momentarily stand in naked relief against the troubled sky. A few seconds later the sharp crack of thunder can be heard as it rolls down the mountainside to be trapped in the deep canyons where it reverberates like the beating of a distant drum. Torrents of rain, whipped by the wind, lash the windows while tattooing the tin roof. Then it is over, for these late afternoon storms are as brief as they are spectacular, leaving the semi-arid terrain both cleansed and refreshed.

So it is with the storms in our lives. Oftentimes they are both violent and spectacular, but in the end they are ever renewing. They roar into our lives, threatening everything that is precious—family, career, even our health. For a time the storm is all we can see. It not only dominates our world, it *is* our world. Everywhere we turn there is fire and ice, wind and wave. When it seems we can bear no more, God speaks to us out of the storm (Job 40:6). Heed His words and we will live. Ignore them and we will surely die, a casualty not of the storm, but of our own willfulness.

Consider your own life. After the storm has passed, haven't you discovered a bright new world? All the filth and debris has been swept away, giving you a chance to begin afresh. "Therefore, if anyone is in Christ, he is a new creation; old things have passed away; behold, all things have become new" (2 Cor. 5:17).

Although there are many examples of life after the storm, none touches my heart more than the example of my brother Bob. When I think of him two pictures come to mind—a before and after. In the first he is twenty-two years old. A good-looking man, he stands two inches under six feet tall, with broad shoulders and a flat belly. His hair is the color of sunburned grass, neither blond nor brown, but somewhere in between. He wears it long, shoulder length, and being as fine as baby hair it blows in the wind. A droopy mustache of indeterminate length completes the picture, making him look like nothing so much as a misplaced hippie.

For all his physical prowess there is a certain vulnerability about him, a neediness. He is like a child on the first day of school—fiercely independent, yet uncertain and frightened on the inside. His need for approval is palpable. He smiles a lot, but not with his eyes. There is sadness there and, just beneath the surface, a haunted look.

He is recently divorced—the first person in our immediate family to fail at marriage—with an eighteen-month-old son who now lives with his mother in a distant state. We do not know it, but Bob is beginning a seventeen-year odyssey that will take him from the pits of despair to the heights of personal achievement. Along the way he will divorce a second time and remarry for the third time. He will also be elected the national president of Phi Theta Kappa, earn both a M.S. and a Ph.D.; yet for all of that he will remain strangely unfulfilled.

In the second picture Bob is a middle-aged man. The mustache is gone, as is much of his hair. So is the neediness, replaced by a certain contentment. He is seated at his dining room table, enjoying the early morning stillness, his Bible open before him. Carefully he allows the worn pages to flip past his fingers, enjoying both the feel of the pages and the soft sound they make. This holy Book that he ignored for so many years has now become a faithful friend and companion. Of this moment Bob wrote:

> It's around 6:00 A.M. on a Sunday morning and our home is at rest while I complete my preparations to teach our adult Bible Study class.

Imagine that, me, the prodigal, the run-away, the desolate one, now teaching a Bible Study class.

Anita has not yet risen. Will and Heather are both curled up in their beds with the covers pulled to their chins, at least they were a few minutes ago when I peeked in on them. I am overwhelmed with a sense of peace that I rarely knew as a young man. If I tried, I think that I could almost make out Jesus sitting at the table with me. My time of devotion and prayer seems so comforting and natural I wonder how I could have ever not desired to serve Him.

I wonder how did this take place? How can I now feel so at peace when for so long I lived with such angst on a daily basis? The simple answer is that I finally let Jesus become Lord of my life. Although the answer is simple, allowing it to happen was not. For me, not forgiving myself was the single greatest barrier I had to overcome.

By his own admission, most of the storms Bob faced were of his own making—thus his need to forgive himself. Through immaturity and willfulness he made a number of bad choices, many of which carried lifelong consequences. As a result his life was one continuous storm. By sheer determination he managed to find success in spite of the storms, but the thing he wanted most—peace with God—continued to elude him. Only after experiencing the unconditional love of Jesus in a truly supernatural way was he finally able to forgive himself and move into the safe harbor of God's peace.

As much as we might wish it did, life doesn't stop after the storm. Though we may experience a time of rest, you can be sure there will be more challenges to be faced and more storms to be braved. Therefore let us consider what to do now that the immediate storm is over.

Celebrate God's Grace

In Acts 27, Luke gives us a graphic description of a violent storm that struck the ship on which he and Paul were passengers. Hardly had they set sail for Phoenix, a harbor of Crete, before the wind shifted. Soon it turned into a full-blown northeaster, what the sailors of that day called a Euroclydon. By morning the wind had reached typhoon strength. The waves were mountainous, and the ship was taking a fearful beating, threatening to break up at any moment. In desperation the crew used cables to undergird it, drawing them tight in hopes of holding the vessel together.

For fourteen days the storm raged without a break. Night and day the wind screamed with a frightful fury, driving the ship before it. When it seemed they would surely capsize the crew began throwing the cargo overboard, then the ship's tackle—anything to give it more buoyancy. Finally, Luke told us, all hope was lost.

To make matters worse, if such a thing were possible, he pointed out that Paul had warned them not to sail. "'Men, I perceive that this voyage will end with disaster and much loss, not only of the cargo and ship, but also our lives.' Nevertheless the centurion was more persuaded by the helmsman and the owner of the ship than by the things spoken by Paul" (Acts 27:10–11).

What a metaphorical picture of the storms we encounter in our lives. In spite of the clear warnings of Scripture and the counsel of others, we set sail on a life-course of our own choosing. Soon we find ourselves battling life-threatening storms. Drawing upon the resources of a lifetime, we do everything within our power to survive. But it is too little, too late. Our best efforts are no match for the fury of the storm; there is nothing we can do to save ourselves, and soon all hope is lost.

Think back on the storms we have just come through. Whether we are talking about King David, Bob, Maria, Diane and Denise, or Ken, they all have at least one thing in common: they cannot save themselves. The storm is greater than they are. See them as they hurl the hurtful cargo of their past overboard in a desperate attempt to save themselves. David dumps his adultery, promises never to take another man's wife. But he cannot undo what he has already done. Bob hurls his willfulness overboard, but try as he might, he cannot reverse the mistakes of the past. Diane puts all thoughts of taking her own life behind her, vows she will never attempt suicide again; still, the evidence of her sin lays like a stain on her daughter's fair cheek. There is absolutely nothing she can do to atone for her past. In spite of their most determined efforts they cannot rewrite a single line of their painful past. Nor can they escape the storm that rages on, threatening to destroy them for time and eternity.

Yet they were not destroyed! They not only survived, but triumphed. Why? Because when they had exhausted all human resources they cast themselves on the mercies of God. Like those shipwrecked sailors of Acts 27 they clung to boards or pieces of the ship until they were washed up on an island of grace.

By all rights they should have perished in the storm, they should have drowned at sea, but they didn't. God had a better plan. "For He made Him who knew no sin to be sin for us, that we might become the righteousness of God in Him" (2 Cor. 5:21).

Think on this Scripture, for it is marvelous beyond imagining. It is the gospel in a single verse. Grasp this, and you will comprehend the mystery of godliness.

How, I ask you, was the sinless Son of God made to be sin for us? By sinning? God forbid! He "was in all points tempted as we are, yet without sin" (Heb. 4:15).

The Son was not made to be sin by His own doing, but by an act of God. Father God reached down and took all the sins of the world—among them King David's adultery and murder, Bob's willfulness, Maria's anger, Diane's utter despair, Ken's hatred and bitterness, my jealousy and envy—and laid them all upon His Son. By an act of God Jesus was made to be sin for us!

How then do we "become the righteousness of God" in Him? (2 Cor. 5:21). By living a sinless life? Hardly. "For all have sinned and fall short of the glory of God" (Rom. 3:23). "If we say that we have no sin, we deceive ourselves, and the truth is not in us . . . We make Him a liar, and His word is not in us" (1 John 1:8, 10).

How then do we "become the righteousness of God" in Him? (2 Cor. 5:21). By performing righteous deeds? Not a chance! "There is none righteous, no not one" (Rom. 3:10). "We are all like an unclean thing, / And all our righteousnesses are like filthy rags" (Isa. 64:6).

We become the righteousness of God in Him *by an act of God*. It is His doing, completely apart from anything we can do. Father God reaches down and takes the sinlessness of His Son and His perfect righteousness

Father God reaches down and takes the sinlessness of His Son and His perfect righteousness and imputes them to us.

and imputes them to us. Therefore, "by one Man's [Jesus] obedience many will be made righteous" (Rom. 5:19). In other words, we are saved from the storm not by our efforts, but by His. All of this is God's doing! So it is only fitting, when the storm is over, to celebrate the grace of God.

Remember the Lessons Learned

Having survived a treacherous storm it is natural to want to put the whole thing behind you and move on. The experience was likely not only painful, but embarrassing as well. I can certainly identify with those feelings, having experienced them myself. Still, no matter how difficult it may be, wisdom requires us to examine our past. It is the only way we can learn from our mistakes.

While each life experience has lessons unique unto itself, there are some universal principles that apply to us all. I suppose it is possible to learn these truths without having to live them, but I've never met anyone who has. Human nature seems to require all of us to make our own mistakes. After living more than half a century, and having made more than my share of blunders, here are some of the lessons I've learned.

1. *Every action has a consequence—some good, some bad.* Some poor decisions lead to painful but temporary embarrassments, while others have permanent, life-altering consequences. Although God always stands ready to forgive our sinful mistakes, not even forgiveness can change the past.

2. *Every experience—good or bad—can be redeemed.* God has a long history of redeeming our failures, turning our worst blunders into opportunities for personal growth and spiritual development. Whatever your failures, you need not despair. With God's help you can overcome them.

3. *Every mistake can become a lesson learned.* What a thought! I can learn from this tragic experience. It need not destroy me. This pain, this awful, unrelenting pain, can be made an ally. Yes, failure is a harsh teacher, but her very harshness sensitizes us to lessons we might otherwise never learn.

4. *God always forgives, but life doesn't.* Don't waste time on either bitterness or regret. Accept your situation and move on.

5. *God's grace is always greater than our sin.* The roll call of the redeemed is filled with scoundrels and con men, philanderers and prostitutes, drunks and derelicts, not to mention ordinary sinners like you and me. For as James S. Stewart, the Scottish preacher, said, "There is nothing in heaven or earth so dogged and determined and stubborn and persistent as the grace [of God] that wills to save!"[1]

There are other, more personal lessons to be sure. Things that only you are privy to. Write them down in a journal or on the flyleaf of your Bible. Refer to them regularly during your devotional times. Review them before making any major decisions. In this way you can minimize the risk of making the same mistakes again.

Focus on the Future

Make up your mind right now that you are not going to live in the past. Determine that you will learn from your mistakes, that you will do your best not to make the same mistakes again, but don't give in to the temptation to continually berate yourself. Regret is simply a luxury you cannot afford.

> So it is only fitting, when the storm is over, to celebrate the grace of God.

I once heard a noted psychologist say that the two saddest words in the human vocabulary are "if only." He went on to explain that many people feel trapped in their failures and spend a lifetime saying "if only": If only I had tried harder. If only I had been a better parent. If only I hadn't been unfaithful. If only . . .

To avoid this kind of self-imposed bondage, he suggested that we substitute the words "next time": Next time I will use better judgment. Next time I will try harder. Next time I will be a better parent, a better spouse. Next time . . .

"If only" focuses on past failures and sentences us to a lifetime of regret. "Next time" turns our attention to the future and inspires us to try again.

As one survivor put it: We have to recognize the difference between acknowledging what is truly our fault versus reliving past failures over and over. The first is an act of faith, while the other is an act of unending self-recrimination. The difference can be seen in the fruit of the action. Whenever we relive past failures it is always in the form of "woulda, shoulda, coulda." In other words, we end up thinking of what I could have done, or what I should have done, or what I would have done, had things been different. This often leads into a vortex of despair where the only pathway to survival is to engage in rituals of meaningless remorse. In a sense, reliving past failures turns one's life into a broken record that echoes the old country song, "I'm sorry, so sorry."

In contrast, acknowledging our genuine role in past failures allows us to see where we made a choice that resulted in a painful life-road. Having recognized our sinful choice and the direction it is leading, we can then repent (change direction) and allow God to put us back on the right road.

Reliving past failures over and over is like driving down a highway with your windshield completely blacked out. Your only view of the road is in the rearview mirror. You can sure see where you've been, but you have no ability to see where you are going. Acknowledging true responsibility in past failures is more like appropriate glances in the rearview mirror to be sure we remain aware of how God is leading us into the future.

Face the Next Storm Unafraid

I wish I could tell you that having survived this storm you will have smooth sailing from here on out, but I can't. Honesty forces me to admit that storms are an inevitable part of life. Jesus said, "In the world you will have tribulation [storms]; but be of good cheer, I have overcome the world" (John 16:33).

Some have suggested that if we stay in the center of God's perfect will we will be protected from the storms of life. That hardly seems likely given the record of Scripture. Consider the twelve disciples who found themselves doing battle with high winds and rough seas (see Mark 6:45–53). They were exactly where Jesus told them to be, doing exactly what He had told them to do, yet they were facing one of the worst storms of their lives.

> The miracle of Christianity is not that it delivers us from every storm, for it doesn't, but that in Christ we have resources to live victoriously in the midst of the storm!

The same thing could be said for Paul and his missionary team when they arrived in Macedonia. Although the Spirit's direction could not have been clearer (see Acts 16:9–10), they had nothing but trouble: "For when we came into Macedonia, this body of ours had no rest, but we were harassed at every turn—conflicts on the outside, fears within" (2 Cor. 7:5 NIV).

The miracle of Christianity is not that it delivers us from every storm, for it doesn't, but that in Christ we have resources to live victoriously in the midst of the storm! Let the rains come, let the winds blow, let the waters rise. In Jesus we are more than conquerors.

Who shall separate us from the love of Christ? Shall trouble or hardship or persecution or famine or nakedness or danger or sword? As it is written:

"For your sake we face death all day long;
    we are considered as sheep to be slaughtered."

No, in all these things we are more than conquerors through him who loved us. For I am convinced that neither death nor life, neither angels nor demons, neither the present nor the future, nor any powers, neither height nor depth, nor anything else in all creation, will be able to separate us from the love of God that is in Christ Jesus our Lord. (Rom. 8:35–39 NIV)

If we are properly prepared the storm becomes a challenge, an adventure, an opportunity for testing ourselves against the elements. Unprepared, however, the storm can be a terrifying, even life-threatening, experience. Consider the storm Weldon and I braved in the Gulf of Alaska. Our lives were at risk, not because the storm was so terribly severe, but because we were totally unprepared. Had we had the right equipment—all-weather gear, a compass, a map, a radio, flares, and a survival pack—it would have simply given us a chance to test our skills. As it was, it took a divine "coincidence" to save us from a night at sea or worse.

When I am in the midst of a life storm I find myself yearning for a safe harbor, for a calm, trouble-free existence. Yet as I review my life I discover that the stormy times have an aliveness, a vividness, that the calmer, safer present lacks. Almost everything I know about life and godliness I have learned in the storm. Faced with circumstances that were beyond me, I was forced to trust the faithfulness of God and to draw upon His strength. Having survived the storm, I discover that in standing against the gale I have grown stronger in my faith. Indeed, I can hardly remember anything I have learned during the trouble-free periods of my life, but I have gleaned a wealth of knowledge while standing shoulder to shoulder with God, battling the vicissitudes of life.

I am not suggesting that we court the storms of life, like those daredevil weathermen who chase tornadoes or fly into the eye of a hurricane, but only that we can face them unafraid when they come, as inevitably they will. And you can be sure that you do not stand alone. The angel of the Lord who stood by Paul in the midst of the storm (see Acts 27:23) will stand beside you. As Paul said, "I urge you to keep up your courage, because not one of you will be lost; . . . Last night an angel of the God whose I am and whom I serve stood beside me and said, 'Do not be afraid'" (Acts 27:22–23 NIV).

What, you may be wondering, can you do to prepare for the coming storm? First, review the promises of God. Hide them in your heart. Meditate upon them. They are the soul's compass, enabling us to chart our course even when the smothering fog of despair tempts us to doubt the goodness of God. Next, remember the storms you have already come through. He who saw you safely through those troubled waters will not forsake you now. Then, consider the example of others. God is no respecter of

> The promises of God are the soul's compass, enabling us to chart our course even when the smothering fog of despair tempts us to doubt the goodness of the Father.

persons, and He who brought them through will do the same for you. Finally, look to Jesus who is the author and finisher of our faith (see Heb. 12:2).

Robert Louis Stevenson, in one of his beautiful stories, relates how a ship was being buffeted by a terrible storm. One sailor disobeyed the captain's order and made his way across the deck to the foredeck and up to the pilot's wheel. There the pilot had been tied to the mast lest the fury of the storm sweep him overboard. Lashed to the mast behind him, and with a confident grasp on the wheel in front of him, the pilot turned for a moment and smiled at the frightened sailor. The sailor returned to the fearful crew and assured them that everything was all right. "I have seen the pilot's face," he said, "and he was smiling."

No matter how terrible the storm, our Savior and pilot is always smiling. He said, "I have told you these things, so that in me you may have peace. In this world you will have trouble [storms]. But take heart! I have overcome the world" (John 16:33 NIV). And so He has!

Notes

Section I: Strength for the Storms Life Brings

Chapter 1
1. Joni Eareckson with Joe Musser, *Joni* (Grand Rapids: Zondervan, 1976).

Chapter 2
1. *Encyclopedia Americana*: Franklin Pierce (Grolier Interactive Inc., 1996).
2. Max Lucado, *In the Grip of Grace* (Dallas: Word, 1996), front cover of book jacket.

Chapter 3
1. John Killinger, *For God's Sake, Be Human* (Waco, Tex.: Word), 149.
2. Maxie Dunnam, *The Communicator's Commentary Volume 8: Galations, Ephesians, Philippians, Colossians, Philemon* (Waco, Tex.: Word, 1982), 321.

Chapter 4
1. H. Norman Wright, *Crisis Counseling* (San Bernardino, Calif.: Here's Life Publishers, Inc., 1985), 127.

Chapter 5

1. These stories are adapted from a message preached by Helen Roseveare entitled "The Spirit's Enablement" and are included in John
   W. Alexander, ed. *Confessing Christ as Lord: The Urbana 81 Com-
   pendium* (Downer's Grove, Ill.: InterVarsity, 1982), 170–172.

Section 2: Strength for the Storms that Others Bring

Chapter 6

1. C. S. Lewis, *A Grief Observed* (New York: Seabury Press, 1961), 9.
2. Elaine St. Johns, quoted in *Dawnings: Finding God's Light in the
   Darkness*, ed. Phyllis Hobe (Waco, Tex.: Word, 1981), 36–37.
3. Ibid., 37.

Chapter 8

1. Hannah Arendt quoted in Lewis B. Smedes, *Forgive and Forget*
   (New York: Harper and Row, 1984), xi.

Chapter 9

1. David Jackman, *The Communicator's Commentary, Volume 7,
   Judges, Ruth* (Dallas: Word, 1991), 343.
2. Paul Tournier, *Reflections on Life's Most Crucial Questions* (New
   York: Harper and Row, 1976), 123–124.

Chapter 10

1. Roseveare, "The Spirit's Enablement," in *Confessing Christ as Lord*,
   168.

Section 3: Strength for the Storms
We Bring on Ourselves

Chapter 14.

1. Lucado, *Grip of Grace*, x.

2. Madeleine L'Engle, reprint from *Walking on Water: Reflections on Faith and Art* (Wheaton, Ill.: Harold Shaw Publishers, copyright Crosswicks 1980).

Chapter 15

1. Quoted in R. Earl Allen, *Strength from Shadows* (Nashville: Broadman Press, 1967), 27.
2. Quoted in Charles Hembree, *Pocket of Pebbles* (Grand Rapids: Baker), 118.

Chapter 16

1. James S. Stewart, *The Wind of the Spirit* (Nashville: Abingdon Press, 1968), 143.